TIME FOR A BOOK

A BOOK ABOUT TIME

GONZALO GILI

Self published by the author

ISBN 978-956-401-335-0 (paperback)

ISBN 978-956-401-334-3 (ebook)

Front cover: "Starling Murmuration", designed by Pedro Palma Casanova. Phenomenon where starlings fly together in coordinated, synchronized patterns created only by the relationship between each individual bird.

Book finished in Santiago de Chile, December 2019.

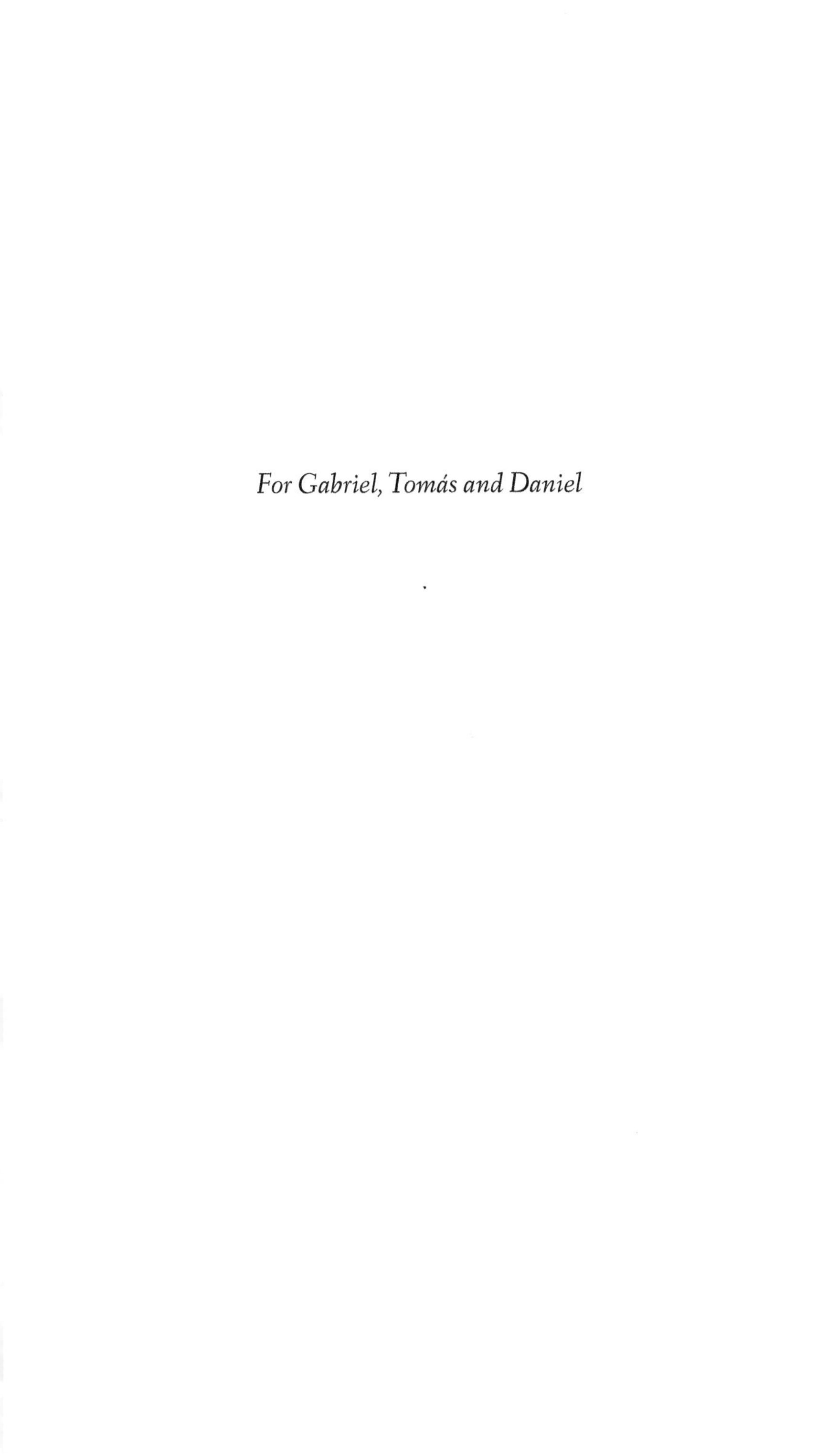

For Gabriel, Tomás and Daniel

CONTENTS

"El tiempo es decidido,
no suena su campana,
se acrecienta, camina,
por dentro de nosotros,
aparece
como un agua profunda
en la mirada"

"Time is decisive,
It does not ring its bell,

It grows, walks,
Inside ourselves,
It appears
Like deep water
In our eyes"

FROM "ODA AL TIEMPO" BY PABLO NERUDA. CHILEAN POET, NOBEL PRIZE WINNER 1971

This thing all things devours,
Birds, beasts, trees, flowers.
Gnaws iron, bites steel,
Grinds hard stones to meal.
Slays king, ruins town,
And beats high mountain down.

ONE OF GOLLUM'S RIDDLES FOR BILBO BAGGINS. THE HOBBIT, J.R.R. TOLKIEN

INTRODUCTION

A book about time is, in essence, a book about everything; time is such a ubiquitous concept that it permeates into all aspects of our lives, sometimes in an obvious manner, such as when we are late for an appointment, and at other times more subtly like when we quietly listen to a piece of music. But this mundane contact we have with time makes it a difficult subject to grasp and to understand transforming it into a fascinating subject to study.

In this book, I have attempted to investigate the widest aspects of what we call time. Trying first to get something close to a definition of what we mean by the concept of time and then delving into a free exploration of how this concept is present in every single aspect of our essence and our lives. I have tried to discuss the different and varied ways in which we experience time every day, as well as its presence in the universe as a whole. But the book is not a scholarly book so it will probably be (most certainly) full of inaccuracies and personal interpretations. The aim of the book is to try and generate some space for you to create insights and a new way of looking at this infinite subject we call time.

Whilst writing the book I learned a variety of things about many subjects such as history, science, other cultures, biology, the arts and music, just to name a few. One of my hopes is that the reader will also learn new things and that this new knowledge will wake the desire to learn even more about our own world, our history, what we know about the way the universe works and maybe with this knowledge be more prepared to make a better future for ourselves and our species.

I wrote this book to share ideas and concepts, things that have been born out of my own experience and thought, both being activities that need time to develop and that we sometimes forget to exercise in our everyday lives. I have tried not to be technical in my writing, and indeed, this is not a textbook or a book about physics or mathematics, nevertheless, you will have to forgive if in some chapters a few numbers have crept in to try and explain some principles or rarities. If I had to put a label on the contents of this book I would feel comfortable saying that it is "Fiction" since it does not pretend to propose any certain truths. The book is about experiences both personal and general and it also contains several stories, all of them fictional, but most of them based on real events.

It is a very personal book and I make no excuses for that, everything I have written is based on my personal thoughts and I make myself fully responsible for them. I have tried to be truthful in all I have written, investigating the facts and even citing the sources where that seemed relevant, but as we all know most things are true until proven otherwise and so I can not make myself liable for any changes that lie outside the realms of this book. If there is anything that I have written that deviates from the truth, I apologise and stand corrected since there was no intention of deceiving the reader.

As my writing progressed I started to understand that on an intimate level this book was a way to understand how time was passing for me, how we start to get old (which in fact happens at all ages!), how we start to think about the end of our journey on this planet and maybe, of what I wanted to leave behind for my children and grandchildren to read. You could say that this book has been a necessary instrument for me to learn about myself and accept that time is an inexorable part of life.

It took me over five years to finish this book, finding time from my "normal" work, my family, my friends and also finding time to read, investigate and think, in fact the whole process in itself revolved around the concept of "finding time": first in order to achieve the goal of writing a book and also "finding time" in our everyday situations, relationships and experiences, even in mundane things such as crossing the road, reading a book, opening a door or even waiting for a bus. Through this journey, I experienced several changing states and moods, at times it was elation at having been able to write down things that were so important and dear to me, especially since I am not a writer and this whole process was a challenge! At other times it was a feeling of disdain, thinking that it was really a waste of time, especially when I saw, along the time I spent researching and writing, new books on the subject of Time being published by what I consider to be "real" authors. In the end I believe that although millions of books may be published on this subject, the book that you are about to read is unique since it is my book, with my thoughts and my ideas and the hope is that you will find it interesting enough to spend your time reading it and sharing these ideas. So in the same way as I would not be able to write Einstein's books, or Professor Hawking's books or Rovelli's book on the subject of Time, not one of them would be able to write this book, my book.

This book also made me come to terms with something that I had been told but had failed to take seriously: My tendency to try to be a perfectionist, believe me, that this is no narcissist compliment since one of the downsides of perfectionism is that it makes you **not do** things if you think that they will not be made to the standards that you impose on yourself. In other words, and turning this into my book project, if my words, paragraphs, pages and chapters were not perfect (in my own eyes!), if the conditions for writing were not perfect, if I didn't feel perfect, etc. were all "good" excuses for me not to write! The result: nothing got written and so there was the frustration of something not being achieved, the imperfect perfectionist! My conclusion: perfectionism can be a bad thing so use it with care!

Realizing this I adopted the following resolution: I wrote whenever I could, and I wrote as it "came out", reading, re-reading and re-writing came later in the hope that some of the things I wrote would be saved from the editing floor (Oops that's perfectionist-me talking again!).

Is there any lesson about time to be learned from all this? Yes. I understood that I was too worried about using my time in the best possible way as I was, unconsciously, realizing that time is scarce, precious and irreversible. So I tried to use it perfectly but in this attempt at perfection I tied myself down and put barriers that barred me from doing certain things that I wanted to do, creating frustration and, by the way, using up the precious time that I was trying to treasure in the most inefficient way possible: worrying and thinking that what I was doing was not good enough.

~

As this is an ideas-book I will be very happy to hear your thoughts about what you will read, the good, the bad and even the ugly. If there is enough feedback it might even prompt me to publish a Creative Commons supplement of this book or open a blog to exchange the ideas. All thoughts can be addressed to abouttimebook@gmail.com.

In the same sense of this being a collaborative and investigative work I have put many references for further reading or inspiration throughout the text. All of them you will also find listed in the back of this book. The references are not necessarily academic sources, but I have tried to filter out the most reliable sources unless otherwise stated.

Some Definitions

Throughout the text, I have used the nomenclature of the Common Era (CE) to denote dates before or after the birth of Jesus Christ, which in western civilization is the common point of reference. So BCE (Before Common Era) is the equivalent of BC (Before Christ) and CE is the equivalent of AD (Anno Domini, "in the year of the Lord").

I have used the term "we" throughout the book to denote the "we" we share as a species, so, for example, the phrase "when we invented the wheel" describes the fact that we –as a species- invented the wheel and is equivalent to having written "when the homo sapiens invented the wheel".

Time for my Thanks

Although this section is at the beginning of the book it is one of the last sections that I wrote, I left it to the end because the journey of writing these pages has been accompanied by many people, some unwittingly, as are the people and events observed from a distance throughout my life and others more actively as the many people that were involved in conversations about the topics covered in this book or the ones that read and made comments on some of these pages. I will mention a few as a sign of gratitude and in no way as responsible for any of the babble contained in these chapters, which, alas, is entirely mine. A long list of "thank yous" tends to be very tedious and a "*skippable*" part of any book, suffice it to say that there is a general and sincere gratitude to all my family, my teachers of all subjects, my friends, colleagues and students who have given me many wonderful challenges, insights and stimulations that have made thinking and writing possible. A deserved acknowledgement and thanks also belongs to the group of co-students of Chikung and Tai Chi Chuan, which I practise regularly, and who have given me hours of the most stimulating discussions on the subjects of life, the universe and everything! Thank you.

A most special thanks go to my wife Mariella for her unlimited love and support and for being the victim of the very first read of the crude early manuscript and who in spite of that, made the most careful and detailed comments that helped me to move forwards towards the final drafts. Thanks to my friend Jim, for his invaluable comments on the book's structure and potentially misleading or incomplete sections. To my friend and artist Pedro who worked to create the wonderful book cover based on one of his original art designs.

Also, as quiet and inviting companions, my thanks to the many cafés around Las Condes and Providencia in Santiago, Chile where I spent many hours thinking, writing and re-writing as well as drinking some fine coffee. Finally, thanks to my partner and friend Juan Pedro for never asking why I was so late arriving at the office some mornings!

Time for the Chapters

One of my generous, respected and kind reviewers suggested that I revised the original order of the chapters, and I did. I also arranged the chapters into two parts, the first part dealing with the more scientific themes and the second part with the issues associated with life and some philosophical matters. So the final order of chapters is:

Part I: Time for Science

Chapter 1, What is Time, delves into the way time is measured and I give a first-hand account of what it is like to live through a large earthquake and how, in those circumstances, the passing of time is perceived in special ways.

In Chapter 2, Time in the Beginning, we go back to what it is thought to be the very beginning of time, the Big Bang, and from there I take a look at evolution and also my light-hearted, non-relationship with the great Professor Stephen Hawking.

In Chapter 3, Frozen in Time, I explore the different ways in which time can be captured.

Chapter 4, Time to Travel, looks at the ways we can travel in time and also how travelling around the world has some intriguing consequences.

Chapter 5, Time to Escape, I look at time rhythms, patterns and the special state of mind we call sleep, in which we spend about a third of our existence.

Chapter 6, Time for a Story, shows the power of language and the written word for creating stories that describe time for future generations.

Chapter 7, Time to Listen, takes a special look at hearing and describes how through different time-related effects, we experience sounds and music.

Part II: Time for Life

In Chapter 8, Time to be Born, I discuss the beginning of our life and also the time when our lives end, our death; there is also a personal story about the birth of my own children with a twist at the end.

Chapter 9, Time is Now, introduces the concepts of *Before, After* and the special singularity we call *Now*, the only point in time when our senses jump into action.

Chapter 10, Tomorrow-me, investigates who we are and how that identity changes throughout our lives.

Chapter 11, Time for Choices, explores the way all our life-decisions combine together to make up our lives, there is a small tale of how the right or wrong, choices led a young man to an assassination which is part of the start of the First World War.

Chapter 12, Time for Beliefs, explores faiths, religions and the things we believe in order to make sense of who we are.

Chapter 13, Time for More Time, looks at how we have been waging an increasing battle to do more within our day with the effect of overcrowding our lives.

Finally in Chapter 14, Time vs. Time, I compare the way biology and technology are able to learn and how this is starting to change the way we are evolving. In this last chapter, I share with you some of my predictions about the not so distant future.

And now it is time to read.

I

PART I: TIME FOR SCIENCE

1

WHAT IS TIME?

SINCE WE ARE NOT REALLY sure what time is, we may have several different points of view that try to explain the phenomenon. This confusion is not helped with our vocabulary and our semantic definitions of the word "time". We seem to use this word in multiple and different ways, in fact, if you look up the formal definition in the Oxford Standard Dictionary you will find three definitions of the word as a verb and six definitions as a noun.

The concept of time is different for each being that experiences it. For example, the way we have chosen to divide time makes sense only to us humans in our particular time perception. So, our definition of "second" will probably not make much sense to a Patagonian cypress tree (Fitzroya Cupressoides) whose known lifespan is over 3,000 years[1]; it would be too short a time frame to be useful. In the same way, it might be much too long to a Mayfly whose life span "only" lasts about 24 hours![2]

What is it like to live in other timeframes? Probably not all that different from what we experience. As mentioned, the sensation of the passing of time is relative and particular to each being that experiences it. If you could ask each of these different species whether their lives felt short or long, what would they say? One way to try to answer that question would be to follow the normal biological maturation and decay of organic matter, so we could expect that a 23 hour old Mayfly might be feeling very tired and experiencing difficulties in flying and hunting for food, after all, 23 hours would be equivalent to a human over the age of 78 years of age. In the same way, an 800-year-old Cypress tree might feel at its prime, full of life and invincible, his 800 years being roughly equivalent to an 18-year-old human being.

Measuring Time

The measurement of time is just like any other metric we have invented to describe the world around us. It uses units we have defined and that make sense of our observations. In the case of time we have two well-known and observed phenomena that we have used to kick-start our definitions:

1. The time it takes our planet to rotate one full circle around its own axis: the "day"
2. The time it takes our planet to circle around our star, the Sun: approximately 365 days or a "year"

Those are real observations and, as it turns out, not too accurate definitions of time. The rest of it, hours, minutes and seconds are just figments of our imagination!

. . .

The hour system is generally attributed to the Egyptians who were fond of grouping their numbers in 12s to do their counting[3], this is believed to be based on the fact that there are 12 lunar cycles in one year. Their earliest time-telling machines were simply sundials, that is: a stick in the ground with the shadow of the stick acting as a reference to the position of the sun in the sky which in turn is a measure of the time of day. The shadow draws (roughly) a circle as it moves around the stick and that trajectory was divided into 12, so bingo we have a 24-hour day! Just in case you are wondering, the other 12 hours come from the night period, which is, as it turned out by measuring the stars in the sky, of roughly the same length. This all happened in around 1,500 BCE, roughly 3,500 years ago!

From this point on we must travel forward in time some 1,300 years to around 200 BCE in Greece to explain our definition of 'seconds'. Greeks were fond of the Babylonian sexagesimal number system, that is, grouping things in 60s, no one is really sure why the sexagesimal system was chosen by the Babylonians, some say it is because it is the smallest number divisible by the first six counting numbers (1,2,3,4,5,6). So naturally, for them, they divided each hour into 60 parts and, in the same way, each one of those hours into another 60 parts, thus we get the divisions defined as: *partes minutae primae* or 'minutes' and *parte minutae secundae* or 'seconds'.

The story continues in the modern era, in the 18th century, with the invention and general usage of the metric system of measurements, from this point on all measurements smaller than 1 second were given the metric nomenclature, that is based in groupings of 10, thus we get the millisecond (0.001 seconds), the nanosecond (0.000000001 seconds) and so on. In the same period of time and for the big numbers, the most relevant concept defined was the light-year, used principally in astronomy; a light-year denotes the *distance* that light travels in the period of one year. It is interesting to note the association that was already being made between time and space: a light-year denotes a *distance* and it uses the passing of *time* as the reference unit. Although in a different way, the light-year, already started to mix space and time together some 50 years before Einstein's publication of his Special Theory of Relativity in 1905, where he described in detail the relationship between those two concepts.

And just as a final proof of how artificial and man-made the concepts of how we measure time really are, we note that the current official definition of a second is the duration of 9,192,631,770 energy transitions of the caesium atom. Now you can't get more contrived than that number to define such a fundamental measurement! One has to wonder then if there might be another way to define this precious commodity: Time.

Another way to measure time?

Let us try a couple of thought experiments:

Let's say we had invented the concept of minutes and seconds in the 18th century, this is the time when we started using the metric system of measurement, grouping things in tens[4]. That would have probably meant that our day would have been divided into 10 periods of day-hours and 10 periods of night-hours giving us a 20-hour day. In the same way, we could have chosen to divide each of those hours into 100 minutes (or *decinets* ?) and each of those minutes into 100 seconds (or *centons* ?).

That being the case we would have found that our

watches and times of day would have looked a little bit like the images below. As you can see it is also a perfectly feasible way of measuring time, it's just a matter of how we decide to do it.

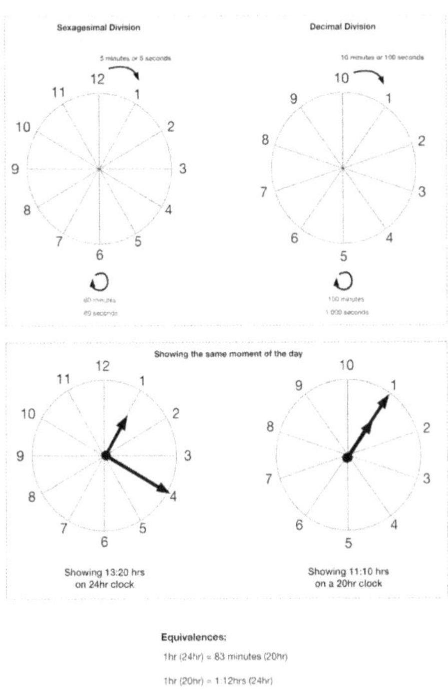

Comparison of the 24 hour system with a system based on 20 hour days

As an alternative, if we had invented minutes and seconds in the 20th century, we might have chosen the definition of a second to coincide with exactly 10,000,000,000 energy transitions of the caesium atom? Thus avoiding the cumbersome number used today of 9,192,631,770 energy transitions.

. . .

For our second thought experiment consider the differences between the lives of the long-lived Patagonian cypress, the Mayfly mentioned earlier and our own life expectancy. If we take the human life expectancy to be 80 years old (current world average is a little below this but first world average is even higher than 80 years!) then we can make some (fun) perception comparisons: A human 10-year-old child, full of energy and want for learning about the world would be equivalent to a cypress tree living well into its 4th century at 375 years of age, while in the Mayfly world it would "just" be 3 hours into his life.

At 21, humans are usually considered young adults and able to have an independent life with all the responsibilities and benefits of our modern societies, the cypress would reach this stage in its year 788 and the Mayfly 6.3 hours into its life.

At 35, it is relatively common for a human to have established a family with children, an important human state in its life cycle, the cypress will reach this stage of its life at the mature age of 1,313 years, having already lived for over 10 centuries, while the fleeting Mayfly would be just celebrating 10.5 hours of life.

At the end of human life, say 79 years old, most of what each individual human will accomplish during life would be done and we enter a stage of relative fragility and decline, for the cypress this would be expected 2,963 years into its life, while for the Mayfly this seniority would appear at the grand old age of 23.7 hours!

Time made to measure

As I have stated, measuring time has been defined within our human context and dimensions, it could not be in any other way. But it is important to realize this fact to understand that the way we experience time is very particular to the way we are built and the senses that we have at our disposal. The next time you see one of those tiny, leapy and harmless jumping-spiders in your kitchen floor, take a good look at it and notice the way it moves. You will realise that it seems to move in tiny "instantaneous" jumps being in one position at one time and at another the next! There is no magic there, it is just the fact that it can move at a rate that our vision sensors (eyes!) cannot detect. It would take a high-speed camera to be able to catch all of those tiny moves[5], but since our eyes are not made to be able to detect such fast movements, it appears to us as if the spider is moving instantaneously from one place to another. We use the same effect to make movies work, we trick our eyes and brains by showing a series of still images in rapid succession in order to have the illusion of movement. Our eyes-brain cannot identify this rapid succession as independent events and so they assume that they are part of a sequence in time that is unfolding before our eyes and thus we see it as a smooth movement.

So, our sense of time probably only makes "sense" to us in our everyday life and is not an absolute measure of how time really behaves. Another example of this is the way we need to measure time when we talk about very large or very small quantities. If we wanted to talk about our closest galaxy neighbour, we would need to wrap these numbers around our brain:

The closest know galaxy is called the Large Magellanic Cloud (LMC)[6] and it is 1,693,433,080,000,000,000 km away from us. If we travelled this distance at "rocket speed" (7.9 km/s) it would take us around 6,700,000,000 years to reach LMC! That's quite a large number of zeros to get around our brains.

At the other end of the spectrum, there is what we might call the world of "tiny" time. In my youth as one of the first digital engineers working in a still mostly analogue workplace, it was a great discovery for me when I realised that my designs and circuitry only made sense when I changed the time scale of the way I was thinking. Circuit switching processes happen in nanoseconds (tiny) or picoseconds (incredibly tiny) slices of time. Just as a reference one picosecond is the equivalent of 0.000000000001 seconds![7], I suddenly realised that the "second" was not a small unit of measure after all, quite the contrary, within that second thousands or millions of things could happen! That became my entry to a whole new world of time perception.

With all these complexities and limitations around us and the fact that we live immersed in this perpetually unfolding concept of time, there are moments when extraordinary, that is: out-of-the-ordinary, events make our normal perceptions behave in an out-of-the-normal fashion, when our senses start to pick up conflicting signals they are not accustomed to sensing in our normal day-to-day lives. At those moments, although absolute and unstoppable time still carries on at its normal rate, we perceive it's unfolding more irregularly: sometimes running fast and at other times very slowly, almost as if we were living in a slow-motion world. Such events usually cause great emotional stress or anxiety as our bodies and minds try to make sense of the erratic perceptions happening around us. An example of such an experience is living through a magnitude 8.8 earthquake.

Earthquake

04:16:00 Sitting in my car in the darkness, the car is parked outside my house in the same spot as it is parked every night. No street lights are lit so everything is darkness; a clear sky lets an almost full moon shed some light into the extra-ordinary night. My car keys are in my hand; I sit in the driver's seat, take a deep breath and listen. The murky night is filled with sounds: dogs barking, car alarms blasting, voices, people rushing, pots and pans clacking. I put the keys in the ignition, and after a while turn it watching the dashboard light up, I don't start the engine, I just leave the car on. The radio fades-in, the car clock shows "04:18, February 27, 2010" and all that can be heard coming from the radio is a sharp hiss. I try to tune to a news station, hiss, hiss, try another station only to hear more hiss, finally, I press the 'search' button to find any radio station that is transmitting tonight and after a few flashes of the frequency dial a voice comes on,

"...power cuts all over the country have been reported. In fact, our station has just re-started transmissions, not more than ten minutes ago. Mobile networks are down and all the communications we have are landline telephone calls that sporadically manage to get through. Once again remember: We have just had a major earthquake, probably over 8º in the Richter scale. We have no confirmation of its magnitude but we understand that the epicentre is situated in the Maule region. If you are in a safe place, stay there. Large power cuts affect most of the country....."

Over 8º Richter, "that's big" – I thought.

. . .

Summer evenings tend to stretch out into the night especially on a Saturday. The weather is still warm and the summer holiday mood still hangs in the air. Schools have not yet started after the summer break although there are only a few days before the beginning of term. This particular Saturday was the last one of the month of February and that's still summer in the southern hemisphere. Chile is a seismic country, it's a fact that Chileans and anybody who has lived there for some time know and accept. It is something that is carried in the blood, not one person who has spent any time there can say that they do not know what it is like to feel the earth tremble beneath their feet.

Earthquakes are very impartial; they do not distinguish between the rich, living in spacious houses or condominiums in the posh neighbourhoods or the more modest city dwellers in their apartments or even those in social housing in the poorest areas of cities and town. When an earthquake strikes, it strikes everyone and everyone feels it. This same familiarity with one of nature's most powerful expressions tends to make Chileans slightly nonchalant about these events since they are very common and you can get one or two tremors every month, the most common practise is to just ignore them and get on with life. This is possible, in a way, because construction and basic infrastructure throughout the country is of a very high standard in terms of its seismic qualities, on a par with more developed seismic nations such as Japan. This is one of several strange oddities about this country in that admittedly there are a lot of things that are still very much of the Third World such as: income distribution, public transport, gender-equality and others, but when it comes to anti-seismic construction Chile is one of the top 3 nations in the world.

Most of Chile lies in what is known as the Pacific "ring

of fire", a roughly circular area whose circumference runs along all of the western coast of the continent of America, crosses the Arctic, passes along the Pacific coast of Russia, China, Indonesia, Japan, Australia and New Zealand. This contour is where different tectonic plates join and are in constant movement due to the action of the heat that is generated at the Earth's core. This movement causes tensions between the plates and those tensions give rise to earth movements on the surface: earthquakes. In the case of Chile the Nazca tectonic plate, which is where most of the Pacific Ocean is contained, is moving eastwards and pushes into the South American plate. At the junction, the Nazca plate slowly creeps under the South American plate, this creeping (or subduction to use the technical term) does not happen smoothly, it happens in bursts. Subduction creates tension between the plates until that tension energy is finally released in a burst, causing the earth to tear and rupture as the plates give way to each other. That is what Chileans feel as tremors or earthquakes.

00:16:00 Movement of the bed, one of the drawbacks of inviting my eight-year-old son, Dany, to sleep downstairs in the main bedroom with me. He is a restless sleeper, "You are like a spinning top!" I used to say to him, he had been spinning this way in his sleep since he was a baby so it was not a surprise to feel movements and even kicks and punches as he made himself comfortable on his side of the bed. His bedroom was upstairs but that night I had invited him to come downstairs with me since both his older brothers, who also slept upstairs, were out with friends and would arrive in the early hours. My wife was assisting a conference abroad so it was just the two of us at home and it made sense to keep each other company.

01:46:00 I turned the television off after watching an episode of the series Prison Break and picked up my book to read myself to sleep.

01:48:00 I switched off the light and turned to sleep on my side.

02:13:00 Movement of the bed, my son changes position once again.

03:34:14 That's the exact time, most experts agree, when the rupture of the plate started at a depth of 30.1 km below the sea bed and approximately 6 km from the coast. This is where the earthquake was created; scientifically it is called the epicentre and it was situated over 300 km from my house. In this story, I will show times at the epicentre in italics.

03:34:41 The first, but still not perceptible, ground shock wave from the rupture arrives at our house some 330 km from the epicentre. My son and I are fast asleep.Energy released from the epicentre travels through the Earth at various speeds depending on the depth and the type of soil, as a reference we can say that a seismic wave can propagate at anything between about 5 to 15 km/s. Like any other phenomenon, it is not instantaneous in time but has a build-up, a peak or peaks and a decline in time. The earthquake in Chile in 2010 had the following energy profile in time:

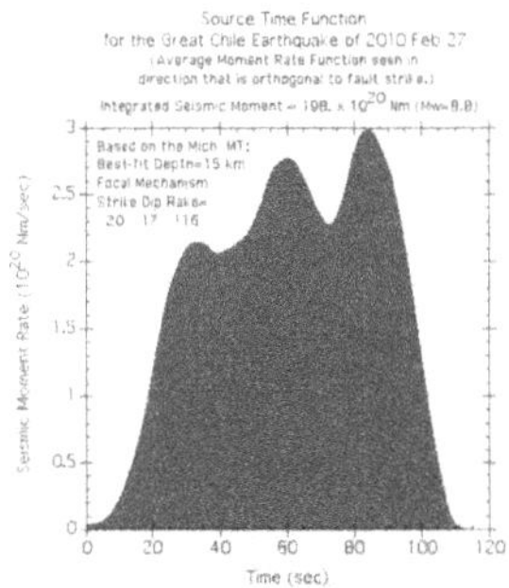

Graph from: "INFORME TECNICO ACTUALIZADO 27 MAYO 2010 TERREMOTO CAUQUENES 27 FEBRERO 2010", SERVICIO SISMOLOGICO, Sergio Barrientos, UNIVERSIDAD DE CHILE, Santiago, May 27th 2010

03:34:44 *The first peak of energy is released from the epicentre.*

03:35:02 Movement of the bed, another turn from my son wakes me. I wait for him to settle down and listen to the rhythm of his breathing, the best way to tell whether he is sleeping or not is to listen to his breathing. His breathing is deep, slow and rhythmic, he is fast asleep and has stopped shifting in the bed, yet the movement of the bed continues. " Maybe it's a tremor," I think, "it will soon pass" and I carry on listening.

03:35:06 The movement continues and gently grows. I listen and hear the creaking sounds a house makes when it is being slightly shaken by a tremor. The sound is very similar to the sound wood makes when it starts to heat up under the Sun, it's like the sound of wooden rafters when they are either cooling down after a hot day or warming up in the mornings as the sun rises and heats them, it's a very distinctive sound. "It's a tremor and it will soon pass, its good that I asked Dany to be here downstairs with me in case he wakes and feels scared," I thought.

03:35:12 I listen and the creaking sounds start to be accompanied by deeper and louder noises. It was going to be a big one.

03:35:14 *The second peak of energy is released from the epicentre.*

Listening is an extremely important part of knowing what to do under stressful circumstances. Normally we tend to take for granted the sounds our ears pick up, but when there is a perceived danger, our ears are one of the most important senses, more so if you are in darkness.

03:35:39 *The third peak of energy is released from the epicentre.*

03:35:43 The movement and noise do not stop, in fact, they seem to increase in volume. I sit up on the bed and turn to put my feet on the ground.

03:35:51 This is the time the first peak of energy coming from the ruptured earth, at the epicentre, is perceived by us over 300 km away. As the Earth split it caused the release of the pressure as the Nazca plate inserted itself a little further under the South American plate. The tear of the Earth took 110 seconds to complete and the cleft produced by it was 450 km long.

03:36:02 I try to get up off the bed but it's not easy to keep balance. I listen and the house continues creaking with a loud and deep rumble accompanying it in the background. It sounds as if a parade of heavily ladened lorries were passing right outside our front door.

03:36:04 *The rupture ceases and the plates start to settle in their new positions, the new arrangement of the plates have now left most geographical places displaced between 12 to 14 meters to the east and some coastal areas have risen a further 2 meters above sea level.*

03:36:13 I walk slowly towards the bedroom door and onwards to the hall and front door of the house, my son is still asleep in bed. As I walk I am conscious of the way my bare feet feel on the ceramic surface of our floor, it was as if the floor was made of a totally malleable substance that undulated under me.

03:36:16 I stand in the corridor and listen and hear how the sound of clinking glasses has joined the creaking and rumbling noises. The rumbling gets louder the movement goes on.

03:36:19 One of the worst things about being in the middle of an earthquake is that you do not know how long it will last. You have no idea or control as to when the movement will stop. In fact, as the movement and force is not uniform, you sometimes feel as if it's subsiding only to find yourself suddenly jolted once again by another burst of energy.

03:36:21 The second peak is felt in our house.

03:36:22 I turn back and decide to get my son off the bed so that we can stand under one of the lintels of the house, supposedly the safest place, according to the emergency recommendations you hear sometimes on TV or radio.

03:36:26 I gently shake my son, who is still sleeping through all this, and say “Wake up” and after a little while repeat “Wake up”, he opens one eye and complains: “Noooo, I am sleeping, it’s too early. Leave it out dad, I want to sleep”. He thought it was morning and I was waking him up to go somewhere. I gently grabbed him in my arms and walked out of the bedroom. My son half asleep in my arms, me walking feeling the uneasy sensation of a floor that did not feel solid under each cautions step I took.

03:36:32 “What’s happening?” my son asks half asleep. "It's an earthquake son, but it's OK, it will soon pass," I say. "Ah, OK," he says and goes back to sleep in my arms with such a casual and relaxed attitude that it brings a smile to my face.

03:36:37 We stand in our safe place, under a lintel. I listen and the rumbling, creaking and clinking get louder and louder. I listen with great attention in case some new, unexpected or dangerous noise appears mixed within the cacophony of sounds.

03:36:42 The rumbling gets louder and seems to come from the back garden. As our house is built on a small hill, the house behind is about two meters higher than ours, although it has a very thick and high contention wall, listening to the rumble coming from the back garden all I could think about was “What would I do if the contention wall gives way and our neighbour's garden and swimming pool crash into our garden and house?!

03:36:46 The third most powerful and last peak of energy released is felt by us.

03:36:52 I peep out towards the back windows from where I stand but see only darkness. I peep towards the front of the house and see that all the streetlights and the neighbour's house lights have gone out. Power cut. As the Moon was out and almost full, some of the road and our car parked outside were still visible.

03:36:59 I listen to the sounds and they do not seem to subside. "It will stop soon", "It will stop soon" I keep repeating in my head as I hold my son tightly in my arms.

03:37:11 The time when the propagation of the end of the rupture finally arrives at our house.

03:37:15 I listen to the sounds and try to keep my balance as I stand with my son in my arms. I am barefoot so I feel the floor of the house directly beneath my feet. I feel how the wooden floor in the hall under the lintel seems to undulate beneath my feet. It feels as if a gigantic earthworm was passing right under my feet.

03:37:32 The noise starts to subside. It's very difficult to say when an earthquake finishes, as your legs and your balance do not recover instantaneously and you still feel as if the ground was moving for a long time afterwards. So you listen. All the noises start to diminish and I look around and see that nothing seems to be out of place, I walk back with my son in my arms, take a good look at him and see that in fact he is not asleep but has remained very quiet grabbing firmly the front of my pyjama tops. "Is it over?" he asks, "Yes" I say "and we are all right, nothing has happened". I put him down on the bed again and sit next to him. "Is it over?" he asks again, "Yes, but there might be some more tremors but they will not be as strong as this one" I say, "OK" he replies.

I leave him lying on the bed half-asleep and run upstairs to check that everything is ok. From the upstairs window, we have a wide view of the city below us, normally at night you would see the myriad of street lights covering the north-eastern part of the city but tonight it was not a normal night and all that could be seen was darkness, the power cuts were widespread.

03:39:12 As I looked out of the second-floor window I felt a shock hit my bare feet and climb up my legs. It was an after-shock tremor, this is very common after an earthquake, the Earth has not yet settled into its new arrangement and generally smaller movements are to be expected. When you are inside a building, especially off the ground floor, an earthquake can feel as if a large vehicle has crashed into the structure you are in. It can feel like something has applied great pressure to the structure and you feel the effects of it through your body almost like a great and explosive push on the base of your feet. It is quite different from when you are on the ground where the earth movement that you feel can take many forms: it can move horizontally under your feet, it can feel as if you are lifted momentarily by a vertical movement or, as it was the case in this earthquake, as if the ground was undulating beneath your feet.

03:39:42 I quickly went down the stairs taking care not to slip as the floor continued moving. By the time I got to stand next to my bed where my son was, the aftershock was almost over. “Are you OK?” I asked, “I’m OK” he replied, not very worried about the whole thing.

03:41:03 It’s dark, “Where are the torches?” I wondered. I went to the kitchen and got the LED torch that we keep for emergencies, switched it on....it worked! Back to the bedroom and checked the landline telephone for a tone, it was dead. No communications. I knew my older sons were in a friend's house sharing a few drinks, it was some relief knowing that they were not in a public place or a club somewhere where it might be more dangerous. At least in a friend's house, the situation is more controlled, I thought. There was no immediate way to communicate with anyone, family or friends. I picked up my mobile phone “No Network” it declared, nevertheless I typed in some text messages to my sons and wife in case the network re-established at some point.

03:43:24 I considered taking the car and going over to where my sons were and bringing them home but then I thought it might be too risky to drive around the city in the dark and with a lot of panic-stricken people on the roads. There was also no way to contact my wife who was abroad. With any luck, she might hear about the earthquake tomorrow when communication was back up again.

03:44:00 This is the time when the first tsunami wave hit the coasts of Chile. As the warning systems failed that night due to technical and human errors, the tsunamis following the earthquake took the lives of 156 people leaving 25 missing.[8] The earthquake itself killed approximately 341 people[9].

03:46:32 The landline telephone rings: “Hi Dad we are OK. We are here at Coto’s house” I hear one of my sons say on the other side of the line. “We are fine too!” I replied. “Take care and stay there till it is light, I will go and pick you up then”, “OK” he replies and the line goes dead again.

03:48:12 "Let's look for a battery radio," I told my son who was now quite awake and following me everywhere I went with the LED torch in his hands. We looked in drawers, boxes, baskets, shelves, everywhere we could think of but there were no portable radios anywhere we looked.

04:02:23 I suddenly remembered an old shortwave portable radio I used to have and went into the walk-in closet to look for it. Sure enough there it was in a box with some of my old “techie” things. I opened the battery compartment and there were 4 AA batteries in place but they were leaking and so the whole space was a gooey, messy thing. "Shit," I said and then glanced over at my son who was staring at me with big surprised eyes.

04:08:43 "Let's use the radio in the car," I thought and told my son to stay by the front door where I could see him while I went into the car to see if I picked a signal from the radio and got to know the extent of what had happened.

04:16:00 Sitting in my car in the darkness, the car is parked outside my house in the same spot as it is parked every night. I watch my son standing by the front door with the

LED torch in his hand and think how much he has grown in these past 6 months. Life goes on.

A large earthquake such as the one experienced that night lasting for just 110 seconds and causing a rupture 450 km long, not only had the power to cause fear, devastation, death and a secondary natural disaster in the form of a tsunami,[10] it also had enough energy to leave us with a permanent reminder of its power. As other large earthquakes have done in the past and will do in the future, the energy released had the effect of modifying the Earth's spin, in this case shortening our days by 1.26 microseconds.[11,12,13].

The event lasting only 110 seconds released the equivalent to 20 billion tons of TNT[14] (approximately 182 million tons every second!) and was perceived as a myriad of different sensations as far as time is concerned. In general, as you live through it, it seems infinitely long, this is probably the effect of not knowing when it will end, similar to when you drive for the first time somewhere you have never been before, the way back is always quicker! Once the earthquake is over if you asked yourself how long it actually was, one is often caught short perceiving that it was actually shorter than it's real length. Time perception is disrupted by high-stress situations, as we will explore further in other chapters of this book.

2

TIME IN THE BEGINNING

The Story So Far

IT'S NOT easy to look at the complete extension of time from its very beginning from our own time-restricted perspective. We only spend between 70 to 80 years on this Earth as conscious beings, so imagining the vastness of time is no easy matter. Comparing hundreds, thousands and millions of years is alien to our own daily experiences that do not stretch that far in time, nevertheless, we will try and do just that in this chapter.

Let's begin. As far as we understand, this is more or less the story of how we have got to where we are today:

- Our "Big" starting point is the Big Bang, which happened some 13.8 billion years ago, that's 13,800 million years ago or 13,800,000,000 years ago, written out in full just to try and get the right dimensions and perspective.
- From that point in time, it took our planet 9,200,000 million years to form as the original

mass of hot gas turned to solid and liquid. That's a very long time indeed, in fact, it took over two-thirds of the entire known time just to form our planet Earth. The date of its formation is believed to be 4,600 million years ago.

- After the formation of our planet, the simplest unicellular form of life is believed to have taken a further 320 million years to appear.
- From that point evolution and gene propagation took over and in a myriad of variations, mutations and millions upon millions of cell generations, a period of 4,278 million years had to pass for the first *homo* species to appear and a further 1.8 million years till our present anatomically modern man, *homo sapiens*, appeared in Africa. And that would be approximately 250,000 years ago.
- Keep in mind that written language appeared only 3,500 years ago.

In summary: After the beginning of known time, our planet took 9,200 million years (MY) to form, a further 320 MY was required for the simplest life to appear, the first homo species took an additional 4,300 MY to evolve and finally our species, homo sapiens, needed a further 1.8 MY to emerge in our current form, all of this after a process of evolution and natural selection that filtered the best abilities and traits for survival in the environment of our planet. On this evolutionary road, many species have been created and have disappeared, as an example, at one point in time there were other related homo species in existence, one of them, the Neanderthal, only managed to survive for a mere 0.3 MY.

The following figure illustrates the time spans described above in the form of a diagram that shows, through the relative size of each sphere, the different magnitudes of the time periods just described.

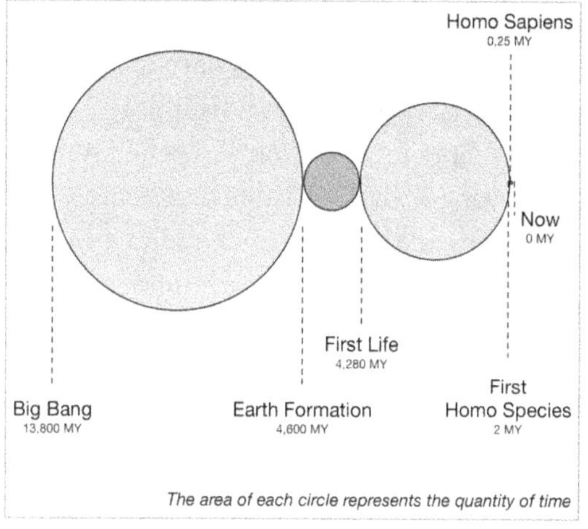

Representation of time from the Big Bang to Today

Even though we try to understand and relate to these numbers, it is very difficult to actually grasp the dimensions that they describe. In our own small life-time we have no references to help us, suffice it to say that we are talking about hugely large expanses of time to create the necessary conditions for our appearance on this planet and this contrasts greatly to the extremely small time of our existence as a species. We have only been around for a mere 0.25 MY (250,000 years) and even more striking is our own diminutive personal lifetime which spans for about 0.000075 MY (75 years).

Yet another way to try and grasp the time extensions is presented in the following table:

MILLION YEARS AGO	TIME ELAPSED FROM PREVIOUS EVENT IN MILLIONS OF YEARS	EVENT
13,800	-	Big Bang
4,600	9,200	Formation of Earth
4,280	320	Point of First Life
2.0	4,300	First Homo species
0.25	1.8	Homo Sapiens

Time span between key evolution milestones

With this in mind we can try to answer the following common question in a different way: How old am I? An alternative possible answer would be: "*The material I am made out of is approximately 13,800 million years old, this material has been on this planet for about 4,600 million years, the form I take is just over 250,000 years old and my individual self is 55 years old*".

Evolution

From the point of First Life, that is, the moment when the very first living organisms appeared on this planet some 4,280 million years ago, a sustained chain of biological change was triggered and it has given rise to many life forms and species, each one with a different set of strategies and capabilities to cope with their surroundings. This biological chain of events we have called evolution and we have discovered that it uses a process of natural selection in order to refine and adjust each living form with the objective of improving their survival and reproduction probabilities.

All observable evidence overwhelmingly shows us that biological life is in permanent evolution, from the smallest biological creature that can be identified, for example, a single cell bacteria, to the large and complex biological structures such as ourselves, human beings. From the publication of the book *On The Origin of the Species*, by Charles Darwin, we have slowly come to understand the evolutionary process and although there are still some detractors, based mostly on religious beliefs, the theory is widely accepted as an explanation of how we have come to exist and evolve.

Evolutionary theory is firmly based on the understanding of the essential component part of living species: genes. Genes define the way in which a life-form develops and reproduces, genes also provide the tools to help every living organism have the best possible chance of survival. One of the main concepts to grasp when trying to understand evolutionary theory is that there is no pre-established plan behind the work of genes, there is no strategy for engineering a better solution for a grasping device, such as a hand, or a development program for a better viewing device such as an eye. Quite the contrary, evolutionary development is a very wasteful and brutal method of continual improvement, it relies on the fact that if something does not work, it simply ceases to exist or dies and something else takes over. This method is not very efficient within the timeframe of a single life-span because the results are seen through many generations, but over a long period of time, it is a very effective method of adaptation to the environment for a large population of living organisms. From our perspective it is slow and inefficient, we have just seen that it has taken over 4,300 MILLION years for the process to create our own species, which corresponds to millions upon millions of generations, trials and errors, failures and successes, to finally arrive at a species with our characteristics. Of course, this argument is exactly the same for every single species alive today, we are just an example of many other evolutionary chains.

Since there is no master-plan in evolution and natural selection, evolutionary refinements within species are achieved by the adoption of small changes that may appear in each generation. These changes emerge due to the variability given by the reproduction process, especially by sexual reproduction where two different gene pools mix and the strongest traits prevail. Also, the randomness of some gene mutations can spontaneously generate useful abilities, making the species more prepared for survival or reproduction. As described, the process of natural selection is just a merciless process of trial and error, but when coupled with the advantage of extremely long time frames (millions of years) this low-efficiency system has given rise to the life forms that now populate Earth.

Breeds

But we do not have to wait for millions of years to see evolution at work, since the time we started domesticating animals we have manipulated their genetic material by choosing their mating partners in order to modify particular species for our own purposes. The most remarkable example of how we have interfered in the development of a species is the case of the dog. Dogs have been around humans for over 14,000 years, they evolved from the wolf (Canis Lupus) into the domesticated dog (Canis Lupus

Familiaris) some 27,000 years ago[1], and became the first animals to be domesticated by humans. It is believed that the first dog species followed humans to take advantage of all the food remains that they left behind and that slowly humans saw the benefits of having these semi-wild creatures around to guard off other predators. From these small beginnings, a long relationship started to develop.

Although there are not many documented facts about actual dates, we know that once we domesticated the dog we started to selectively breed the species in order to enhance certain traits over others. That's how we bred dogs that helped us to hunt, dogs that helped us defend against other predators, dogs that were useful at sniffing out food or danger and also, once we domesticated other animals, dogs to help with the task of herding livestock.

This process that we can call "assisted" selection, as opposed to "natural" selection which I have discussed earlier, acts very quickly and its effects can be seen in just a matter of a few generations, that means that in just one hundred years or so, we have been able to observe marked changes in some dog breeds that have gone through the process of "assisted" selection by man[2]. The bull terrier, for example, has been transformed from quite a fit-looking dog at the beginning of the 20th century to what it is now, a much rounded and squat bodied canine. The German shepherd, a dog usually associated with policing or guarding, has been bred to be a larger dog incrementing its weight by about 50% in just a century of breeding. The English bulldog has also been made to increase its weight and the general thickness of its body with its skin becoming looser in the process. Nowadays there are over 400 different types of dog breeds in the world, all of them have had some sort of manipulation by man and demonstrate, at first hand, evolution at work, albeit artificially manipulated by man. This same manipulation, however, has brought about huge problems to some of the breeds since changes, forced in such small timeframes, have generated innumerable health issues on the dog population such as breathing problems, heat control problems, hip and elbow problems, mobility issues amongst other malaises. Finally, breeding and domestication generate cross-species dependencies where the domesticator is in control of the domesticated species providing for most of its basic needs such as shelter and food and hence eliminating the need for the domesticated animal to fend for itself thus relying fully on the dominant species for its survival, a kind of parasitic life if you like.

Assisted evolution has not only been practised on dogs, all domesticated animals have been specifically bred for their function related to the service of humans: cows (some for milk, others for meat, their hide, etc.), sheep, horses, cats, pigs, chickens, mules, amongst others. We might even say that the definition of a "domesticated" animal is an animal that has been assisted in its evolution to provide a service! The same has happened with other living organisms such as vegetables, trees and plants, each one tailored to the needs of the dominant species on the planet, homo sapiens.

Genetic engineering

Evolution by natural selection takes millions of years to develop environmentally-adapted species in a process mostly based on sexual reproduction to provide the necessary gene mixing and random events that can generate unexpected evolutionary advantages. All of these ingredients work in a process of trial and error where the good mixes survive and the rest die and disappear. Assisted or guided selection, where one species breeds another for specific purposes, can be developed in much shorter time frames of even a few hundred years. But now that we have started to unravel the genetic code which defines each species, we are at the threshold of immense new possibilities to manipulate evolution, some of them with positive effects, as in the case where certain diseases might be eradicated from the population by genetic editing, while others with less certain outcomes, like the possibility of engineering, enhanced capabilities (mental or physical) onto some individuals by modifying their DNA and hence make them superior to others.

Homo sapiens

Evolution as we know it is a non-stop process, that means that at this very moment, as I sit here writing and you sit there reading, we are part of the continuous evolution of humankind. The time frames are so slow that we are not really aware of the changes we, or even our offspring, endure, nevertheless, evolution is present and in permanent flux.

With this in mind, we might ask ourselves the question: What are we evolving into?

If we look at the past 10,000 years of history in 1,000-year steps we see the amazing development of our capabilities as a species. Keep in mind that 10,000 years might seem like a very long time but it is only 0.0002% of the span of existence of our planet. In the following table, I have chosen six areas with which to measure these 1,000-year steps and have described the most relevant advances in that millennia. This is not an easy task in some cases and you might disagree with the selection:

YEAR	HEALTH	EDUCATION	TRANSPORT	RELIGION	SCIENCE AND TECHNOLOGY	COMMUNICATIONS
8,000 BCE	Herbal/Magic	By Imitation	Primitive Boats/Feet	Worship		
7,000 BCE	Herbal/Magic	By Imitation	Primitive Boats/Feet	Shrines		
6,000 BCE	Herbal/Magic	By Imitation	Sailing Boats		Handmade Bricks	
5,000 BCE	Herbal/Magic	By Imitation	Domestication of Donkey	Sacrificial Ideology		
4,000 BCE	Herbal/Magic	Schools in Greece			Plough / Iron & Steel	
3,000 BCE	Herbal/Magic	Writing	Wheel / Domestication of the Horse			Papyrus / Drums / Horns
2,000 BCE	Diseases Identified		Spoked Wheel	Widespread religious practices	Irrigation devices	Couriers
1,000 BCE	Surgery in Europe			Earliest monotheistic religion (Egypt)		
0	Arabic Encyclopaedia of Medicine	First Libraries and Universities	Horseshoe / Wheelbarrow	Jesus Christ / Buddha / Confucius / Muhammad	Sundials / Clocks / Watches	Paper / Postal Services
1,000 CE	Germ theory of disease	Invention of Press	Engines / Flight / Submarines	Christianity / Islam / Hinduism / Buddhism	Mechanics / Electronics	Telecommunications / Computers / Networks
2,000 CE	Human Genome Described	Remote Learning	Electric Power / Autonomous Vehicles		Internet / Mobile	Online / Mobile
3,000 CE	?	?	?	?	?	?

Human Evolution in 1,000 year steps

Just a small digression at this point since, as I was researching this topic, I came across an interesting website www.histography.io that graphically portrays the most significant events in human history. Apart from being a lot of fun it demonstrates the power of collaborative, digital and graphical communication: *collaborative* since all the data is taken from Wikipedia, a collaboratively constructed encyclopaedia, *digital* because that is the current enabling technology and *graphical* because it uses the image as a means to extract the real power and information behind all this data. We can easily imagine how the same data shown as a page of endless text would be much more tedious and less able to give us any useful insights. I recommend you take a quick look at this website.

Even taking 1,000-year leaps in time we see that the last millennium has been one of much-accelerated advance on all fronts. What will it be like in 3,016 CE? It is clearly impossible to predict. Nobody alive 1,000 years ago, in

1,016 CE say, could have predicted any of the advancements to be experienced 1,000 years into the future. For instance, it would have been beyond the imagination of people in 1,016 CE that in 2,016 CE, people would carry in their pockets a device that would enable them to speak and even write to anyone they chose in the world - the mobile phone. If we take this long term view, and realize that there are no "1,000 year plans" of development in our world cultures, then just like we saw when discussing evolution, the way things actually turn out seem to depend on the accumulation of small events, gathered through time, rather than grand, planned changes. This is generally true except for some random natural events, such as meteorites striking the Earth, as seems to have happened before the extinction of the dinosaurs. Such events can make devastating and sudden changes in the habitability of our planet which in turn can trigger multiple and permanent modifications to the whole ecosystem. These events are the equivalent of the random mutations to be discussed in the section of this book on evolution, as we will see, those mutations also introduce sudden changes to the evolutionary chain. We will also start to appreciate a strong similarity in the way the universe, species and cultures evolve and that is, as a series of small, unplanned, incremental steps over very long time periods.

In this organic, adaptive and dynamic system of life, there is no way of knowing what destiny or even the next stop will be in this journey of thousands of years! Changes take millennia to manifest themselves and are produced by the interaction of the millions of cells present in living organisms, with the millions of atoms and molecules present in the planet as a whole. As a species, we have advanced a great deal in technology and the understanding of our most immediate surroundings but looking ahead for more than a hundred years or so, is something beyond our nature or our apparent needs.

Intelligence

Without any doubt, the most striking and powerful characteristic of homo sapiens is what we call intelligence. This is our "superpower", as it were, and what sets us apart from other animals, we are not as strong as a gorilla, or as fast as a cheetah, nor can we fly like an eagle but we have a brain capable of doing some very amazing things.

As far as we know the capabilities and potential of our brain and minds at birth have not changed much since we became the species that we are, over 250,000 years ago. That being said, our cognition capacity and the way we have defined intelligence have evolved throughout history. This has been measured with the results of IQ (Intelligence Quotient) tests taken in the last centuries[3]. In general, these results show that we have become more "conceptual" in how we view our environment and we have developed and accepted the idea of hypothesizing in order to discuss or solve problems. That means, for example, that we have gone from thinking of our problems as mere tangible matter-of-fact problems like how to hunt, how to fight off enemies etc., and have developed skills that let us solve more intangible problems such as how to build an algorithm for the recognition of human faces. This change is thought to arise from external effects such as culture and education that have shaped us, through learning, to perform the tasks that our society needs from us.

Nevertheless, it seems like our brain intelligence capacity has remained constant and if somehow we were able to bring back to life a human from, say, Ancient Egypt, then given the right re-education and training, that person could manage to lead a normal life in the twenty-first century. The opposite would also be true, a citizen of the twenty-first century could be transported back, retrained and live quite a happy life in the times of the Pharaohs, albeit with only the comforts that that age could give him or her.

Time for a Bang

And so once again, back to the beginning of this chapter, that is, let's rewind to 13.8 billion years ago. Not being a theoretical physicist I still find it difficult to accept The Big Bang Theory. I am not talking about the comedy TV show of the early 2010s, I mean the big "this-is-where-it-all-started" theory that to me, seems difficult to visualise and comprehend from my limited human perspective.

As I say, I am not a physicist and maybe the cause of my disbelief is pure ignorance. I haven't read all the literature, and the higher mathematics of the proofs are well beyond my patience, I can only claim to be an engineer-turned-communicator which might be like saying that I am a square peg in a round hole.

But the idea that all the matter that we know exists today was, at some instant in time, gathered together in a single infinitesimal point seems to me rather far-fetched. I love mathematics, after all, mathematics is the tool that has enabled us to evolve into the technological era we currently enjoy. Without mathematics, life as we know it would not be possible, we would have no computers, no cars, no telephones, no modern medicine, no science and certainly no engineering. Therefore as much as I respect mathematics and understand the concepts of singularities and infinity, I also know that all of these constructs are just models of the real world that we experience, and a model is an approximation but not a direct reflection of the real world, they are the best descriptions that we can manage for what we observe around us.

The whole of the cosmic history of how we came to being, all those 13.8 billion years of it, takes some stretch of the imagination to envisage and understand if indeed we ever can! But the fact that the whole universe, all of it, all the matter, atoms in existence in the known universe, at one point in time were concentrated on a singularity, a single point of space-time, well, to me, seems amazingly difficult to believe or understand and leads me to think that we still have some work to do on this matter.

As humans, we understand our surroundings as stories and stories have the classical three-phase structure: a beginning, a middle and an end. So to fulfil our need for a tale we must find a beginning for our grand universal story and a lot of research has been, and still is, focused on this subject. When did it all begin? Where? And under what circumstances did it all start? A fine search for a fine story but we are not going to delve on that aspect of the search, after all, at least for now, we are mostly convinced that it all started at this Big Bang instant. What concerns me here is the fact that once we start the search for the beginning of the story, our infinitely inquisitive mind will force us to ask the following related question, and so, much like a four-year-old child, who will ask "Why?" after the answer to any previous question, we will repeatedly say: Well if that is the beginning, What came before that?

If we define that there was a beginning, then we are stuck with the nagging notion that there must have been a time before the beginning and that if time did start at this point, then we will ask, what was happening before? The definition of time starting at some definable instant will always make us think of the time before that instant. Was there no "time" concept present before? And if that were so, did it mean that there existed a kind of frozen, immovable universe? Or, did another type of "time" concept exist? A time that maybe transcurred more slowly or maybe, faster. Another possibility is that the concept of time present before "time" as we know it, cannot be understood in the way we currently understand it, that is, a time concept associated with the movement of objects, or associated with a sequence of events. Maybe this "other" time concept was expressed or manifested in some other dimension such as the changes in energy conditions like light or temperature. Yet another conceptual explanation we can describe is that time did not really start at that point, but that the Big Bang only defines a change in phase or era, much like it is described by the Mesoamerican Long Count calendar (part of the Mayan calendar) and that sometimes is misunderstood as foretelling the end of the world when it merely describes changes in epochs. If we accept that there was a Big Bang event in the distant past, my personal view is closer to the latter one, one of continuity, of ever-presence, where time closes a cycle only to open a brand new one.

So in my role as an inexpert, that is a non-expert, and with all these doubts in mind, I dare to propose a theory of my own, and why not? Another model with an as-yet-unknown margin of error. Out of my infinite respect for all the research and work carried out by the physics community I will maintain the idea that there was a singularity at this Big Bang point, but it makes more sense to me that all the matter that was supposed to be contained in the singularity-point, in fact, seeped through a point or fissure in space-time that, momentarily, connected our void to another universe, thus creating this universe with exactly the amount of matter that the neighbouring universe lost at that precise moment. So my theory replaces the singularity-point with an infinitesimally small fissure-point and since we have embarked in this not-too-serious hypotheses I shall call this theory the Singular Fissure Theory. I have no mathematics to prove it, and indeed I shall never have such mathematics to prove it, but to me, this "explanation" makes more sense than the previous explanation: a single connecting hole (Fissure) linking two universes and spilling matter from one to the other to create our own universe.

Time to consult the experts

With my brand new theory just described, and with the conviction of having a whole person convinced of its veracity, that is: me, it was time to call on the experts to see if I could find some scientific grounds in order for my theory to be validated.

Our whole western history has been littered with brilliant minds that have helped humanity to advance in the knowledge about the universe, scientific minds such as Plato, da Vinci, Newton, Darwin, Einstein, Hawking, and in the art fields minds like Shakespeare, Beethoven, Mozart, Michelangelo amongst many others, have all given us insights into who we are and have helped explain a little bit more about why we might be here and all the other essential questions we constantly pose ourselves.

Sharing the same timespan of life with one of these minds is just a random occurrence that may or may not happen to any of us, in my case I was fortunate to share about 55 years on this planet with Stephen Hawking (1942-2018) one of the great physicists of modern time.

Although we never actually met or had any sort of relationship (that's my immediate disclaimer!) we shared several important milestones in each other's life spans just by the mere coincidence of existing simultaneously. Our non-relationship in time started on the year that I was born which happened to be the same year that he was diagnosed with the motor neurone disease, which accompanied him for the rest of his life. A few years later we not-shared eighteen wonderful years of living in the same country, the UK, where we cruised through the Thatcher years, the Falklands or Malvinas war, enjoyed bands like The Police and Queen, saw the birth of the personal computer, the Walkman (the first portable music player), amongst many other things. In between the madness of the 80's, he published –totally unknown to me as I was starting the first year of my engineering career at that moment- a paper with what is known as the Hartle-Hawking State Model which proposed that the universe had no boundaries before the Big Bang and that hence the concept of time before that point has no meaning (the reasons and derivation of this model are well beyond this book!). Time progressed and the year his father died was the year I had just started my Master's degree at Imperial College where, many years later, he would be awarded an Honorary Doctorate from the same institution. When he published his extraordinary book "A Brief History Of Time" I was just starting my first job at Philips Research Laboratories, near Reading in Berkshire, England. The next chapter of this non-relationship takes us both to Chile where I had already been living for several years and where he decided to visit and give a few lectures in the country's capital and also travel to Antarctica where Chile is one of the countries that holds sovereignty. Later, in an interview in The Guardian newspaper, he described the experience of visiting the frozen continent as one of the best moments of his life. The year he published his book "The Universe in a Nutshell" my third son was born and some years later, on his second trip to Chile where I still lived, I had just started lecturing at a university in Santiago. The final chapter of our common passage on this planet was in the year 2018 when the disease he carried for most of his life finally extinguished him and when, on that same year, I finished the first draft of this book and wrote this paragraph.

As we already had a precious non-relationship and thinking that my new theory was worthy of a first-look by such a great mind I found the time in-between our busy schedules of never meeting or knowing each other and on May 3rd 2014, the same year that he declared himself to be an atheist and that the film "The Theory of Everything" based on his biographical story hit the screens, I summoned the courage to write the following letter to Professor Hawking and share with him my personal Singular Fissure Theory:

Dear Professor Hawking,

I write to you with a great deal of nervousness and a little embarrassment since I am not a physicist (this might be advantageous since I have no fear of peer "bullying" after I express, what may be, unsound ideas in this letter).

I just don't buy The Big Bang Theory, not all of it at least!

I have to admit that I have not read all the literature regarding this theory, and that the higher mathematics of the proofs are...well...beyond my knowledge or patience, I am only an engineer....

But the idea that all matter that we know today was, at some instant, gathered together in a single point seems to me rather hard to believe. I love mathematics, after all, mathematics is the tool that has enabled us to evolve into the technological state we currently enjoy. Without mathematics, our lives would be a lot harder and certainly more boring. We would have no computers, no cars, no telephones, no modern medicine, no science and certainly no engineering. Therefore as much as I respect mathematics and understand the concepts of singularities and infinity, I also know that all of these constructs are models of the real world that we live in. Therefore not all that mathematics produces has a direct reflection in the real world, they are sometimes the best approximation that we can make with the models that we have.

In general, the whole of the cosmic history, of how we came into being, all 13.82 billion years of it, takes some stretch of the imagination to envisage and understand, if indeed we can! But the fact that the whole universe, all of it, all the matter, atoms in existence in the known universe, at one point in time were concentrated on a singularity, a point of spacetime, well, to me, seems that we still have some work to do to properly describe what went on...it is amazingly difficult to believe or understand.

Again, not being an expert, I dare to propose another view. Why not? Another model: maintaining that there was a singularity at this big bang point, it makes more sense to me that all the matter that was supposed to be contained in the singularity-point, in fact, "seeped" through a point or fissure in spacetime that, momentarily, connected our void-universe to another universe. Thus, our universe was created with exactly the amount of matter that this neighbour universe lost at that precise time. Something like a "Singular Fissure Theory". I have no mathematics to prove this, and indeed I shall never have such mathematics to prove it, but to me, this "explanation" makes more practical sense than the previous explanation.

I hope that I haven't wasted your time with these thoughts. I have probably over-simplified years of research and have committed grave assumptions. But nevertheless, I think that it is a good thing to be able to express ones ideas.

I much admire your work and have read some of your books. I hope you are well and send you warm greetings.

Regards,

Gonzalo Gili
BSc(Eng), DIC, MSc(Eng)

I searched on the Internet and found an email address to send this letter in a Cambridge University website, it sounded quite legitimate so I used it. Once sent, the email did not bounce, so I guessed it must have got through to its destination. Now it was just a matter of, well, time!

I have always found "waiting" a very exciting and even

thrilling time. I am talking here about "good" waiting, not the sort of waiting you do at a doctor's office, hospital or in a bank queue, but the kind where something illuminating or pleasant might happen. I have even come to realize that this is one of the things I enjoy the most when I do online shopping. Let me explain, I live in a country that is not on the normal delivery routes of any online business, in fact, you may think that this country is almost literally, at the end of the Earth. Not only that, although it is not an island it is not easy to get to it in a hurry. On one side it has the Andean range of mountains and on the other, the Pacific Ocean; as I have mentioned before I live in Chile. All this means that buying online from international businesses is quite an expensive and time-stretched business. At the moment, normal delivery times from Europe are running at 3 to 4 weeks. From the US it can be a bit faster. All of this waiting for a product you have bought creates great expectation and a great adrenalin flow once the item finally arrives at your door.

My email to Professor Hawking would not have this sort of delivery issues since electronic communication is almost instantaneous. Delay would be due to several other things like his busy schedule, the filtering process that sorts out his emails –I assumed he had a Personal Assistant that would help him- and finally the filter that touched on my ego: the worthiness of the communication received.

So I waited.

Waiting leads to expectation and more waiting.

No reply.

Maybe he was very busy at that moment, I thought.

No reply.

Time passed and days turned to weeks and months and no reply, till I finally lost the interest for a reply, understanding that such a great mind would not have the time to waste on such an amateur proposal.

A year later, reviewing the chapters for this book, I found this unfinished chapter and with renewed hope, I looked for the emails I had sent and searched again for email addresses for the professor. As they say: Hope is the last thing you lose!

I found a couple more email addresses, which were different from the ones I had used before and with rekindled excitement decided to write to him once again. After sending the same letter to the new email addresses, one of them "bounced" with the fatal message that it did not exist. I had tried three different ones and from one of them came a reply! Wow, I looked at the reply in my inbox for a long time, at last, real contact with the great mind itself, whatever was in the reply email almost did not matter at that point next to the fact of having received and answer from Professor Hawking, at last, our paths had crossed and not in a virtual, imagined sense but in a real interaction between two living beings.

Total emotion.

After several minutes of imagining several outcomes for what was about to happen, I gathered my feelings and double-clicked on the email to open it and read its content. And this is what it said:

Thank you for your email to Professor Hawking.

As you can imagine, Prof. Hawking receives many such every day. He very much regrets that due to the severe limitations he works under, and the enormous number of requests he receives, he is unable to compose a reply to every message, and we do not have the resources to deal with many of the specific scientific enquiries and theories we receive.

Please see the website http://www.hawking.org.uk for more

information about Professor Hawking, his life and his work.

http://www.hawking.org.uk

Well it was not what I had expected, I had just read a standard, pre-written response, but nevertheless and in contrast with the previous experience, somehow it left me with the sense of a real contact, the real crossing of two life paths, I had got much further than I might have expected and much, much further than any possible communication I could ever have imagined with other past great minds such as Einstein, da Vinci or any other, just because of the time coincidence, the time harmony if you like, of being present in the universe at the same time.

Sadly Professor Hawking ceased to exist on 14th March 2018, coincidently on the same date as the 139th anniversary of the birth of Albert Einstein.

As a final epitaph to this story I can say that the closest our paths really did cross was in February 2019 when, on a trip to London, I visited Westminster Abbey and stood right next to his mortal remains which lie a few meters away from the tombs of Sir Isaac Newton and Charles Darwin. As I stood in awe and realization that finally, our material paths had really crossed I read the words on his memorial stone:

"Here lies what was mortal of Stephen Hawking 1942-2018"

As the declared atheist that he was, the words form a beautiful balance between what is known about the nature of our mortal existence and the immortality he achieved through the legacy of his work. These words surround a small mathematical equation known as Hawking's equation, which he specifically asked to be written on his grave once he passed away. The formula reads:

$$T = \frac{hc^3}{8\pi GMk}$$

Hawking's Equation

The equation describes the energy that a black hole releases, expressing the temperature (T) as a function of the mass (M) of the black hole and it basically states that the bigger the black hole the less energy it will emit[4], in other words, this is the scientific explanation of the commonly stated fact that within a black hole nothing, not even time, can escape.

3

FROZEN IN TIME

Still Images

EXPOSURE AND APERTURE are technical terms in photography but they are also tools to capture time. Photography has given us an incredible way to explore the invisibility of time, what we cannot capture with our sensory visual organs, our eyes, we can sense using photographic technology. Time in the form of still images, still images capturing the form of time.

Take for example an everyday experience: How many times have we looked at a picture and had ourselves transported to that moment in time? Instantly. That frozen slice of time shown on paper or a screen manages to visually capture what was happening at that particular moment in time. The slice of time was probably just $1/250^{th}$ or $1/60^{th}$ of a second, that is the time it takes to record an image in a camera. The moment when you look at a picture taken in the past and your mind time-travels to that instant, is one of the instances where we perceive the passing of time, sometimes it seems as if that moment happened just yesterday, while at other times it appears as if it was at some distant time in the past and yet sometimes there is no recollection of that moment at all.

According to the famous artist, writer and filmmaker Susan Sontag[1]:

> *"All photographs are memento mori. To take a photograph is to participate in another person's (or thing's) mortality, vulnerability, mutability. Precisely by slicing out this moment and freezing it, all photographs testify to time's relentless melt."*
>
> SUSAN SONTAG

Although this quote may seem like a rather sombre view of photography, in fact, it describes the power of this technique to dissect time and, in some ways, to look within and see its relentless motion. The melt that Sontag mentions is very akin to our unawareness of the way our own bodies change, or melt, in time. Since we are ever-present observers of our bodies, time seems to move in very small steps, so small in fact that we do not seem to notice. This sedate pace allows us to adapt naturally to its passing but surprises us when we look back and observe the marked differences time has imprinted on us. The same effect can be seen in the way we do not realize how our children have grown or changed because we are in permanent contact with them, it only takes a photograph taken more than a couple of months ago to see the effects of the time melt.

It is sometimes said that some of the native people of the Americas believed that taking their picture stole a portion of their soul. There is no real evidence to show that this was a real belief or just some invention of the dominating Europeans at the time. What is interesting to think about is just how vulnerable our bodies become once a picture is taken. Just think of the many ways our image can be handled or manipulated and shared using various technologies and you will understand what I mean. Your image can appear in a publication without your permission, it could appear in an image search on the Internet without your consent, it may even be an unwitting part of a film or TV news report as you leisurely stroll in the background not knowing that you were being recorded. From that point of view those Native Americans, if they did believe in soul-stealing were indeed onto something, an image of ourselves that appears in any place that we cannot directly control might be misused and harm us. This concept has been expanded and taken to many depths when we start to call it "copyright", indeed, there are whole industries that move millions of dollars based on such ideas.

But photography can be pushed even further with some creativity and art. Several artists have explored time using the camera in different ways[2]: Pelle Cass is a photographer from Brookline in Massachusetts who uses his camera to superimpose hundreds of images taken of the same space but at different times. For example, there is an image of a basketball court that looks overcrowded with players, each one frozen in a different time during a match, there is also an abundance of basketballs hanging in the air just as they were pictured at that particular moment in time. Another image shows a scene taken at a boating lake with an impossible to imagine number of canoes, sailboats, surfboards and kayaks in a seemingly rush hour traffic jam that is almost hypnotic to watch[3]. In both of these cases, we glimpse at a strange world where events accumulate in time rather than pass by ephemerally.

Another artist, Fong Qi Wei[4], has explored time through photography in a similar way to Cass superimposing different times over one single space. In this case, Wei is interested in showing how the different times of day are seen at one particular place. In a sequence of photographs, he calls "Time Painting" we see a whole day, from dawn to dusk, on a single photograph displayed as brush-stroke layers that convey the passing of time very effectively.

The work of photographer Bobby Neel Adams explores, in a series of photographs called Age Maps[5], how time affects our bodies and, most dramatically, our faces. What we see in his images is the juxtaposition of a photograph of a person taken as a child with another taken as an adult, the images are carefully matched so that the final image looks like a complete face, care is taken to leave half the face as the child and half as the adult. It is very interesting, although a bit spooky, work worth investigating.

But photography is not the first technology that enabled us to freeze time. The very first attempts to freeze time were created, literally, by our own hands using very primitive technology: colour pigmentation. This type of recording of the past can be found in caves and the oldest found date from over 39,000 years ago[6]. What we see in these early paintings are various everyday scenes like hunting, or tending to animals but the most striking images and the ones repeated the world over, are images of hands, more precisely, the prints of hands or handprints. Our ancestors have left us with an impression of themselves in one of the most simple and reproducible ways possible, we can even recreate exactly what we can see in those caves by putting our hand on a wall, spreading out our fingers and spraying our hand and its surroundings with paint or some other pigment, when your hand is lifted you will see the shape of your hand looking exactly like those early paintings. Although we can only speculate around the reasons for making these images, what our ancestors achieved is the freezing of a moment in time. We can perfectly imagine how the scene might have developed: we can speculate that the artist was not alone, maybe someone else helped spraying the pigment on him or her, we can even imagine the atmosphere within the dark cave, maybe lit by a torch or a fire where some meat was being cooked for the night's supper. We have no way of being certain of the veracity of the scene that we can imagine in our minds just by looking at the handprints, but without any doubt, the prints do conjure up a moment in time, in this case, a long way in our past.

Since pre-historic times we have used what we now call Art to capture moments and freeze time in order to transmit or express a form or an idea. Art is not just the simple functional representation of the world we observe. In art, as in any type of communication, there is an emitter: the artist, a medium: his/her art and a receptor: the audience, both the emitter and receptor are involved in this form of communication process and both will add their own context and interpretation. In other words, what we see in a painting need not be the same as what is seen by everyone else.

Indeed it might not even be the same as the original author intended us to "see". Image interpretation, whether it is in art, photography or even a scene in the street, will evoke several resources from our own brain and consciousness, such as, context, knowledge, culture, experience, etc. and from all of these factors, a personal interpretation for what is being perceived will be attempted. Since all the components mentioned are different in each individual, there will exist a wide margin for interpretation.

As an example, we will examine two paintings: the first one, "La Gioconda" by Leonardo da Vinci, painted in 1505 and the second one, "Netherlandish Proverbs" by Pieter Brueghel, painted in 1559.

Most people will recognize the "Gioconda" or "Mona Lisa", one of the most famous paintings in the world by the artist and genius Leonardo di ser Piero da Vinci, or just "Leonardo", painted around the year 1505. What is interesting when looking at this painting is that although the artist embodied the famous mysterious and ambiguous expression on the subject's face, it is still easy for us to relate to the mood and overall feeling it projects: the posture, the gaze, the smile and the whole "humanness" of La Gioconda still conveys feelings we recognize today, indeed a child with no knowledge of 16th century Italian art history but with some learned emotional and social concepts, would have no difficulty in trying to interpret whether the subject was "happy", "sad" or "worried", even though they might arrive at different answers, the emotional signals that we learn to interpret from a young age have changed little in time. Nevertheless, we should not be surprised if different children conjured up different interpretations of what the picture is portraying, who the subject was and what sort of place she lived in, the accounts would vary according to each child's particular experience and context.

It is more difficult to truly interpret the message of a picture: the clothes, the social position, the scenery, and even the time of day. All these depend on the context and culture, something that the passage of time does indeed change. These observations start to hint at a very interesting fact that, although time passes and we evolve in the social, cultural and technological aspects, our raw humanness tends to remain relatively stable throughout the ages, with our emotional selves able to withstand time in a more consistent way than our cultural and environmental realities.

Another way that art can manipulate time is by showing different moments simultaneously to evoke a sequence of events rather than a moment in time. This technique was often used by the Dutch painter Pieter Brueghel to narrate whole stories or even several different stories in one canvas as can be seen in his painting "Netherlandish Proverbs" painted in 1559. This painting is a compendium of a large number of Dutch proverbs and is believed to depicts no less than 112 of them such as "Never believe someone who carries fire in one hand and water in the other": warning about two-faced people, "To bang one's head against a brick wall": To try to achieve the impossible. There is also the more obscure "To stick out the broom": To have fun while the master is away. If you find a copy of the painting, see if you can spot these and identify the others[7].

So, through freezing different moments of time and harmoniously displaying them together, artists can achieve scenes that go beyond a single moment but also depict complete stories, rather like a book or a recording in a film or movie.

An interesting way of looking at the relationship between a painting and the observer, particularly an old painting, is described by the author and critic John Berger when he talks about the connection of an image in a painting with the observer as a sort of tunnel in time, a time tunnel that binds the image to the viewer conveying visual clues and information that enable the viewer to take a glimpse at another time or universe.[8]

Nature Freeze

Not only do humans freeze time in the way I have just described, nature also achieves the same through various interventions, some of them taking us back thousands while others billions of years into the past and delivering to us another slice of frozen time.

Midday of August 24th, 79 CE: According to eyewitness accounts[9] the first plume of smoke and ash was seen over the Vesuvius, a volcano that is some 10 km from the city of Naples in southern Italy and about 8 km away from what was the town of Pompeii[10]. The eruption of Vesuvius left an estimated 2,000 dead out of a population of approximately 11,000 people, that is, almost 20% of the town met their death as a consequence of this eruption. The visible plumes of smoke came accompanied by violent earth tremors, extreme rises in temperature, toxic gas emanations, falling rocks and stones and a massive blanket of volcanic ash that eventually fell over the town, covering the whole area in 25 meters of a perfectly designed time capsule. Current studies show that most people did not die from inhaling the poisonous gases that emanated from the volcano but met a more violent and instant death through the immense heat that was experienced, with estimated temperatures of up to 300° C. This fact is easily observed in the detailed plaster cast models made of the people found in the area, their expressions are mostly of pain, despair and in the act of protection rather than struggling for their last breath. The same is true of the animals we see, again suffering from what looks like extreme bodily contractions consistent with the effects of great, sudden pain.

Apart from bone remains, which have been of extreme usefulness in proving the rapid rise in temperature theory, there were no bodies found as such. What was found buried in the ash were the spaces or voids where the bodies lay at the time of death. With great vision and ingenuity, the Italian archaeologist Giuseppe Fiorelli used a technique of injecting plaster into the voids in order to get casts of the bodies that once had occupied those spaces and hence he reconstructed, from the ashes, the last moments of the people of Pompeii of the first century CE.

Aside from the natural tragedy that was involved, Pompeii's fame arises from the frozen image of time that the volcanic catastrophe left for us. The tonnes of volcanic rock and ash managed to make a time capsule strong enough to withstand the passage of almost 2,000 years to enable us to take a glimpse at the way our ancestors lived and behaved. It is not difficult to find ruins of passed civilizations indeed, all continents have saved glimpses of the past and we can see objects that were made such as houses, tools, jewellery, etc. But looking back in time at ourselves has been something more elusive unless it was done through artists interpretations. In Pompeii, we can have a first-hand look at bodies, expressions and even everyday situations of the people who lived in that town just as they were, with no interpretation, a direct connection in time.

Through investigation some interesting facts have been discovered, for example, most people found in Pompeii were quite healthy, rich people and slaves alike, this was discovered in particular through analysis of their teeth and bone structures which showed that most people had well-balanced and abundant food consumption. Another fact that has come through in time is that there was an immense [11]quantity of wealth in this town, some family coffers found held what was equivalent to the amount of money an army official could earn in 10 years. On the more human, emotional side, we find families huddled together, people crouching, dogs eating, people lying on their backs, children with their mothers and even couples embracing. Every single pose we see in those figures is of a human situation we can immediately relate to, even though these people lived almost 2,000 years ago we can connect directly with their feelings, at some primal level time does not seem to have affected our basic human core.

One mystery that we can also reflect upon is the reason why so many people died, after all, it may seem at first hand that a volcanic event is quite a slow process from which it would be relatively easy to escape. In the case of Pompeii, some 9,000 people did in fact escape, but there is evidence that the eruption was accompanied by many earth movements that caused buildings to collapse, crushing people in the process. The eruption also brought with it toxic gas emanations, propelled and caused rocks to fall from the sky and, as mentioned before, what is now believed to be the most important cause of most deaths, it brought temperature waves that reached over 300° C, this temperature is high enough to instantly kill human life. The bodies that at some point were thought to show signs of asphyxiation have now been determined to have perished due to extreme heat. If this is the case then the agonizing frozen-in-time facial expressions that we observe in the body plasters of Pompeii were in fact caused by the very last seconds of life of bodies suffering from extreme heat shock as the heat waves surged across the town[12].

We can turn back the clock even further and look at time slices that nature has left for us that are thousands or millions of years old, again we turn to natural processes and this time focus our attention on fossilized remains. Presently, the oldest fossil that has been found, corresponds to microbes some 3.7 billion years old[13]. If we want to refer to some fossils that are somewhat more evolved and classified as animals we can look at some primitive sponge-like creatures that lived in ocean reefs[14], that would make us look back some 650 million into the past.

Lyuba means "love" in Russian and it is also the name given to one of the oldest and best-preserved mammal fossil found in recent history. Lyuba was a 30-35 day old baby mammoth that, while out on a stroll with its mother, broke through the frozen surface of a lake and landed head first in the lake floor swallowing mud from the lake bottom which made it choke and die from asphyxiation. This tragic story happened over 40,000 years ago and through painstaking research and expert analysis, scientists have pieced together this sequence of events and so have a fairly certain idea of the last moments that lead to Lyuba's death[15]. This is another example of how we have learned to read the clues left to us by time in order to piece together the stories that made those clues in the first place.

If we turn our minds to the oldest preserved human remains, we may think of Egyptian mummies which date from around 3,000 BCE, but in fact, there are older, less famous mummies which are dated at around 7,000 BCE that have been found in the Atacama Desert in northern Chile. Known as the Chinchorro mummies after the Chinchorro culture to which they belonged, a culture that used mummification techniques to keep the remains of their dead[16]. Mummification gives us many valuable glimpses of past people such as, their feeding habits, health, beliefs, hierarchies and other aspects of their culture, nevertheless, the process itself is very invasive and alters many vital clues that might be of interest in discovering some aspects of the past. That's the reason why scientists get so excited when they find "natural mummies" such as Ötzi or the "Iceman" found in 1991 in the Alps at the frontier between Germany and Italy. Ötzi lived between 3,400 and 3,100 BCE, studies have shown that he was a 45-year-old man, 1.65 metres in height and weighing around 61 kilograms, who froze rapidly after death and was thus preserved almost intact to the present day. Such finds in "natural" circumstances give scientists the best possible scenarios to use the many techniques available today to investigate and rebuild a fairly complete picture of the individual's health, habits, origins and general lifestyle, turning and inanimate, frozen slice of time (literary and figuratively in this case) into a complete description of a bygone age almost as if a book or a film had been found and were used to unravel previously hidden secrets.

Moving Images

Such is the complexity of time and the way we perceive it that the same freezing effect achieved with still images in photography is used to give the illusion of movement in time, freezing becomes movement and this makes a moving record of time, using film or video technology. Moving pictures are a series of still images displayed at a continuous, uniform rate, the rate is chosen to trick our eyes and brains into thinking that what we are seeing is a continuous stream or flow of time so that we interpret it as a moving image. The trick we play on our eyes is based on the fact that there is a small delay in the capacity of our eyes and brains to distinguish between one image and the next. This delay is in the range of 0.1 seconds, so if we flash images at a higher rate than this, the eye-brain combination is not able to tell them apart and interprets them as a single, moving image. Film, television and video normally use anything from 24 to 30 images (also called "frames") per second. In this case, the images change every 0.04 to 0.03 seconds, meaning that the images are changing at a rate over twice the speed at which we can visually distinguish them as separate, and hence the moving image trick is achieved.

Film or video can record for us not only an instant but also a continuous stream of moments, which together with sound, stimulate our senses and intensify the way we perceive this archived moment of time. The result is to give us a more immersive and powerful experience of past events. From this freezing of time, we obtain apparent movement when and where we want it.

Movement and time are invariably linked together. There

cannot be movement if time is not involved, the passing of time enables movement to happen. We can think of movement as the change in the way an object occupies space as time unfolds. Think of a ballet performance, as the dancers perform their various pieces, we can feel how time is flowing to enable the movements to occur. If time was frozen, as we can will it to happen in our minds or by pausing a video recording, then there is no ballet, no dancing is present, just figures taking up different poses or positions. If we let time flow again, the postures, movements and jumps melt into the flow of the dance and become, once again, a performance in time.

Through this example, we also appreciate how technology such as video o film has enabled us to better understand the flow of time. With suitable apparatus or computer programs we can have full control of how time passes, we can slow time or make it faster, we can even, under these special circumstances, make time flow backwards and have the experience of what it would be like if that were to happen in the real world.

When we want to slow down a movie to observe the details of passing time, we have two options:

1. We take a normal film (shot at the standard rate of 24 or 25 frames per second or fps) and display those frames at a slower rate. This achieves a slowing down of the sequence but the image starts to feel "jumpy" or blurred since there are no more frames of information to display other than those 24 or 25.
2. We shoot the movie at a much faster rate than normal (say 1,000 frames per second) and then display those frames at the normal rate of 24 or

> 25 frames per second. Using this method we can observe the details contained in time. For example if a sequence is shot at 1,000 fps and shown back at 25 fps it creates a time expansion of 40, that is, we can watch a sequence 40 times as slow as it really happened without losing details, so following the example, 10 seconds captured this way would be shown in 40 seconds at a normal rate.

Femtophotography is an extreme technique for capturing and recording time at extreme speeds in order to show the greatest amount of time detail and it has enabled us to see time advancing in a way that we have not been able to see before[17]. This type of time photography can take millions of images or frames every second. The fastest femtocamera can take over 4.4 trillion (4.4 million million) frames per second that is the same as saying that the time captured by each one of those frames is equivalent to the time it takes light to travel 0.07 millimetres. Indeed, such a speed enables us to see light travelling through space. You can see this in a video called "Laser pulse shooting through a bottle and visualized at a trillion frames per second"[18] (several version of this video can be found online) where a pulse of laser light has been captured as it crosses, from the bottom to the top, of a plastic bottle filled with water, quite amazing!

Nature also provides us with a way to piece together moving accounts of times gone by. To unlock these treasures that our universe has provided, we have needed to train ourselves for thousands of years in order to have the correct tools and knowledge to decipher the clues that we have encountered. Several disciplines allow us to achieve this:

- **Astronomy** has made possible the piecing together of the very beginnings of our universe, with these studies we can go back and recreate what happened 13.8 billion years ago at the time of the Big Bang and the creation of our universe.
- **Geology** can take us back 4.5 billion years to the time of the creation of our planet and can describe how a mass of hot matter eventually turned into the mixture of solids, liquids and gases that we call Earth.
- **Archaeology** takes up the story from about 3.3 million years ago when our species started to appear on this planet and started to leave remnants of their cultures and habits for us to piece together.
- **Historians** have chronicled and unlocked stories of our past events since the invention of written records. This is the most direct way to access past events though we must account for the particular interpretations of the recording reporter.
- **Forensic Science** is also worth a mention since with very little clues, forensic scientists, can piece together events as they might have happened in the near or distant past. This science is often related to crime investigation but in fact, forensic scientists also work in conjunction with archaeologists, for example, to determine aspects of the nutrition, habits or diseases of past civilizations.

Each one of these branches of knowledge allow us to construct a part of the moving story of time as we currently know it, from the very beginnings to the present day. The tools that each discipline has at its disposal are varied and range from measuring the radioactive decay of carbon, counting layers of rock, the rings on tree trunks or shifts in the electromagnetic spectrum, amongst many other methods[19].

Slicing Time

If we think of capturing a slice of time as freezing, such as when we take a photograph with a camera, we can ask ourselves how thin can we make these slices and if there is a limit to how thinly we can cut-up time. Modern physics sheds some light into the minimum possible slice of time, for this we need to mention Max Planck a German physicist. Without going into the detailed maths, we can say that Mr Planck defined a whole set of measurements that govern the world of the very tiny, this is part of a branch of physics called "quantum mechanics".

As we might know or remember from school, quantum mechanics is the study of our world at the smallest scale of particles and energies. In this world, there is a small unit of measure called "Planck time"[20] which by definition is the smallest measurable amount of time. Its definition goes something like this:

To start with we must define the term "Planck length": this is the smallest measurable distance that can be defined with classical physics (Newtonian Physics). This is the distance where space and time cease to exist in the way we are accustomed to experience it and we enter the world of quantum mechanic. Thus any distance smaller than this cannot be determined and can only be defined in the realm of quantum mechanics where, by definition, we cannot be certain of the position and distance of quantum elements. The actual numerical value for this distance is derived from a formula, which combines the speed of light and two constants: the gravitational constant and the Planck constant. Just to visualize the tiny size of this length, if we said that a small grain of sand was the same size as the known observable universe, then within this grain of sand, the Planck length would be represented by the width of a speck of dust. That's small.

Having defined the smallest possible distance, we can define Plank time as the time that a photon of light (with its known and fixed speed) takes to travel one Planck length, in other words: Planck time is the time that light takes to travel a Planck distance. So what is "Planck time" in seconds? Well, it is the infinitesimal number of 3.3×10^{-44} seconds! Or
0.00000000000000000000000000000000000000000000033 seconds, that's 43 zeroes before those "3s"!

This definition, however, works within the realm of our current state-of-the-art knowledge of physics, within our current model of how we see and interpret our world. But, is this the only way of understanding the basic unit of time? Modern science is based on the principles of dissection, that is, when we want to understand something we start "cutting it up" into smaller and smaller pieces. This is the way we approach science in the west, we have all been raised in this manner (author included). If we want to understand how something works, we first take it apart, then we do the same with the resulting pieces, and we repeat this operation until we either lose interest or somehow cannot continue. With this method of taking things apart in order to investigate, it is not surprising that our model of the world eventually ends up in discrete, isolated pieces! Is there another way to investigate? Can we handle in our minds the idea of continuous, analogue elements? Or do we always need to end up with discrete, "digital" models? Is the speed of light such an absolute, as we believe it to be or is there another universal defining constant we have not discovered as yet? On the other hand if what we know has been able to explain the story this far, well indeed, that may be a sign that the model is correct after all!

4

TIME TO TRAVEL

I AM a firm believer that we can picture our lives as a journey through time. In that sense, we are all time travellers and life is a one-way trip through time. Furthermore, if we do think of our lives as a journey then we can explore whether we can control the speed at which we do this travelling or if that speed is fixed and cannot be manipulated, at least in terms of our perception.

Relative Perceptions

We experience the difference in how time is perceived every day and at every moment, let's put this into perspective and think about different animals and how they might perceive their surroundings. Take a common house fly, Have you ever tried to catch one? Think of how the fly might see or sense you, to us the fly seems to have lightning speed reflexes, always being one step ahead of us and always managing to get away. To the fly, we may seem like giant, slow, clumsy animals so slow that the fly, without any risk, can predict any movement we make. On the other side of the spectrum, if we play for speed with an elephant we will be at an advantage in that we can cruise through time, at least as far as perceptions go, much faster than the pachyderm, to the elephant we may look as fast and nifty as the fly looks to us. If we go beyond the animal kingdom and think of plants and trees, the same time perceptions apply. A tree is in constant self-generated motion (that's not counting external effects like the wind). If you looked at a tree's life span and you compressed it into a timeframe more familiar to us (say with some sort of time-lapse photographic technique) you would be able to see this constant movement in action and realize how busy the tree has really being all its life pushing itself out of the ground, growing according to the nutrients it finds, stretching its branches and leaves to catch the best possible sun in the position it finds itself, maybe even competing with other trees that it finds in its surroundings, going through the permanent cycle of growing new leaves and discarding them with the seasons, battling as best it can with the heat of summer and the cold of winter, altogether having a very busy tree-life[1].

So time seems to pass, or at least is perceived as passing, at a different speed to different creatures even though we all share the same general frame of reference defined by the planet we inhabit, that is, we all share the same day length and yearly cycles. How can that be? Or a better question: Why is that so? This kind of observation seems to point to the idea that time perception depends very much on the *needs* of the being doing the perception. In other words, we travel through time at the speed that suits our needs. We slice through the time continuum in the most suitable steps that accommodate our size, structure and mental processing capacity.

. . .

There are things that all living creatures share by the mere fact of living on this particular planet: day, night and the timespan between one and the other, these are common and shared constants for all creatures, the seasons and the climate change that is associated with it, the way that all these conditions change depending on which latitude we live at, etc. We can do little about our size and structure, these have evolved after millions of years and the external influences are also beyond our control, but we can manipulate our processing capacity, our mind and our thinking processes. This gives us a few clues as to how we can regulate the speed at which we travel through time. Maybe if we learn to be aware of the processes that affect the speed of travel through the use of our mind, we might learn to control it and slow it down when we need to or even speed it up if we require it.

To our everyday experience, time travels in only one direction, forwards, or at least what we perceive as forwards. We can remember the past, but we cannot "remember" the future. The future is a state that is yet unknown, undetermined, but one that we are approaching and moving towards with total certainty. The certainty is that it will happen, and we have different ways of thinking about this. For example, we say that,

The future will "arrive", but we have no way of predicting what this future will "bring".

In this case, we personify the future as someone or something that will arrive and that may bring things. But there are alternative ways of preparing for the uncertainty of the future, we can think of re-wording the same phrase but from the point of view of the travel analogy and we might say something like,

We will continue this "journey" through time and we will arrive at some point in the future but have little way of predicting what we will "find" once we get there.

Both statements convey the same ideas and concepts but take two very different approaches. In the first case, we are passive observers and have little or no control of what will happen to us, an unknown external entity will arrive and bring us the future, what is brought may be good or bad, we don't know and have no control over it. In the second approach, and the way I propose we should choose to approach life, the passing of time is taken as a journey in which you are an active player, you accept that you are on a journey that will have unknowns (good or bad) on the way, uncertainties, but this view gives you the power of choice that the former approach denies you, you can choose which way to go on this journey, you can choose your companions, you can even choose where to stop and where to spend more time.

Obviously, this is just an analogy and I do not propose it as the absolute truth or a religion, the point I want to make is that at this conceptual level, we can choose how we perceive the way time affects our lives.

Future Prediction

Although we have stated that the future is uncertain, the statement is only a generalization and to most intents, a lie.

We predict the future all the time, an important part of what has given human beings an advantage in this world is our capacity to make predictions of the future. We are not alone in this, most animals make some prediction of the future all the time, this ability is extremely important to their survival. To exemplify this let us think of a gazelle in the plains of Africa, a gazelle is pray to many predators and must always be on the lookout in order to survive. As part of its survival instinct it knows, or can predict, that if it finds a leopard in close proximity its future can be in jeopardy and so it must take some evasive action like, run away. These reactions are built-in and we call them instincts, other reactions might be learned through time or by copying others especially our own parents. So a danger reflex set off by a less beneficial future can trigger responses for survival. The same happens with other stimuli that animals encounter in order to procreate, feed, find shelter and other activities. Going back to our example, although we cannot describe the detailed complexity of the processes within the brain of a gazelle, some form of future prediction is definitely happening in order to take the correct remedial or pre-determined action.

With humans, the future prediction process is more complex, more developed and multidimensional. Let's visualise first something relatively "ordered" and think about the way we play a board game like chess. Chess is a future-prediction game. As we play we are constantly monitoring our opponent's and our own moves and from this information, we make up future-scenario predictions which will help us decide on our next move. As you become a better player, by playing many games, your previous matches and moves will accumulate to form your experience and help you make faster and more accurate predictions and hence better moves. Chess has been so well documented and studied that we have been able to "teach" computers to play it at the highest levels and even beat world champions or masters.

It is generally agreed that a tournament player needs to predict the effect of a move at least 5 steps ahead. As there are around 30 possible legal moves per board position, a computer would need to perform (30*10)! calculations (remember that the symbol "!" in mathematics means "factorial", that is, the multiplication of each number in a sequence, for example: "5!" is the result of the multiplication 1*2*3*4*5), "10" because 5 moves ahead implies 10 complete opponent/opponent moves, so that is 300! calculations or $3x10^{614}$, a very large number indeed, to be performed in the 3 minutes allowed between moves. Not surprisingly various strategies and algorithms that enable faster calculation times are used for chess-playing computers, which have enabled them to predict the future moves and beat grandmasters.

More everyday examples of future prediction in humans make us realize that we do this all the time. We are constantly working out what will happen next, predicting and choosing the future that best suits us. For example, given the choice of eating an apple or a piece of glass, you would choose the fruit, predicting that the glass would do serious damage to your body. Now, this may seem like an easy example but our daily life is based and constructed upon these choices, which are in fact future predictions. Given the choice of going to work or taking a day off, most people would choose the day off predicting a day of leisure or rest, if we are offered exactly the same product at different prices, most people would choose the cheaper price, predicting that the money saved can be put to future use. If we analyse these examples we might not be too impressed since they are so common. These sorts of predictions we could categorize as consequence predictions, that is, if A happens then there is a probability that B will follow. If you see someone standing in a corner waiting for a traffic light to turn from red to green, surely what will follow in some near future is that the person will cross the road, the probabilities are high.

In the end, future prediction is based upon probabilities. Some events are more likely to happen than others, and we can use our instincts and learned experience to predict the outcome or, in other words, the future. The least likely events are the ones that surprise us the most, just like in the field of information theory, the least likely event is the one that carries the most information. Who could have predicted that on the morning of September 11, 2001 two aeroplanes would crash into the World Trade Centre Towers in New York City? No one without some privileged information and yet they did and it was the biggest news item at the start of the twenty-first century.

Past Records

In a previous chapter of this book I mentioned the concept of how technology such as film or video gives us full control of how time flows, all be it, in an artificial and non-real space. We can watch and perceive scenes played forwards in time and also in reverse, we can even alter the speeds at which we watch time flow, faster or slower than "normal".

All recordings, by definition, are made in the past,

moving images are no exception and they allow us, in a limited way, to travel in time. Through sight and sound, they can evoke, in a very accurate way, "the way it was" in some near or distant past. But can we call this time travelling? Well, it depends. In a way it is, since it has been shown in several studies, especially ones dealing with violence, that the mere act of watching a moving recording (film or video) evokes in your brain the same neural patterns and chemical reactions that would be present if you were observing the same scene in real life. In these study cases, most of the researchers were trying to observe whether violence on TV had any influence in making people more violent, but for our purposes, it shows how recordings can evoke the same feelings you would have if you were present in that past event. Away from the violence example, we can also think of examples that describe how watching different movie genres (comedy, romance, horror, etc.) evoke the feelings and responses you would have if you were living the same situation, indeed this is exactly what the movie director is trying to achieve through his or her work. A pioneer in the research of this phenomenon is Dr Marco Iacoboni from UCLA[2] with his work on "mirror neurons". These neurons in our brain enable us to mimic behaviours we observe and in that way make us learn and empathize with others. So in this sense yes, moving images recorded in the past can make you travel in time since they evoke not just images in your retinas but also feelings and emotions that were present in the past or in the setting presented to us in a movie. Looking into the future, and making fanciful predictions, we might even think of a time when technology will allow us not only to look with our eyes but to be connected directly to all the relevant brain areas and have these "movies" directly fed into all our sensorial areas to produce an even more realistic stimulus with a new type of recording yet to be invented.

Nevertheless, you might feel cheated with the last few paragraphs since you might argue that this is not what we mean when we say "time travel". When we speak of "time travelling" we generally mean that we want to take our physical body and transport it in time, that is, actually move our matter either forwards or backwards in time and to experience that new "Now". The answer to this question is more complex since, as far as we understand, what we generally perceive as the "arrow of time" moves in only one direction: forwards, implying that experiencing past or future "Nows" with our whole bodies is not possible. Who knows, we might have to wait a few centuries for this paradigm to be broken with new scientific discoveries.

Travel to the Past

If you still feel like having a *journey-in-time-experience* there is a relatively easy way to achieve it, all you need is a clear sky at night and some wonderful things can happen. As far as we know, light is the element that is able to travel at the greatest speed in the universe. But, although this speed is extremely fast, it is not infinite. In our every day experiences this speed is so fast that it is almost instantaneous, as an example, say you are talking to someone who is one meter away from you, if you are observing his or her face as you speak, the light from it will take just 0.0000000033 seconds to reach you, which for our purposes is instantaneous. But when we combine the finite speed of light and the enormous distances separating planets and stars some interesting effects start to take place.

Take our natural satellite, the Moon, the closest permanent companion of Earth and, to us, seemingly very far away but in celestial distance terms, extremely close. Light from the surface of the Moon takes about 1.3 seconds to arrive at an observer on Earth, that means that what you are "seeing" of the Moon happened 1.3 seconds in the past, still not too impressive as far as time travel goes but we can go further, Mars is about 400 million kilometres away from Earth, so light from its surface takes 22 minutes to get to us, so if we look at Mars from Earth we are seeing the planet as it was 22 minutes in the past, that is a little more like it! With Jupiter, the time taken by light to reach us is 33 minutes. Going further still we need to use the concept of light-years, that is, the distance that light can travel in the period of a year, it is a very large number at over 9.4 billion kilometres. Alpha Centauri, the closest known star to Earth, apart from the Sun, is 4.5 light-years away, so the light from its surface takes 4.5 years to reach us, in other words, what we see of Alpha Centauri really happened 4.5 years ago. Deneb in the Cygnus constellation is 1,550 light-years away so if we were sitting on its surface looking at the Earth we would see Earth as it was 1,550 years ago somewhere around the year 500 CE. The Andromeda Galaxy is 2.5 million light-years away and standing on one of its stars looking onto Earth we would witness the evolution of the Genus Homo[3] just getting started. Now that's time travel!

Travel to the Future

We have already stated that travelling forwards in time is impossible but a little mind experiment can leave us thinking of what it could be like. Imagine having an apartment in New York City and sitting in the kitchen after a day's work, it is evening and you are having your supper, it's 9 PM. You switch on the television to catch up on the latest news and select the BBC News Service channel that happens to be showing a live news programme transmitted directly from Singapore. Because Singapore is on the other side of the world and several time zones away, it is 12 hours ahead of your time so the local time there is 9 AM of the following day. You might sit there thinking: "Well, here I am it is 9 PM and I am looking through this electronic window (the television) into tomorrow!" Because the presenter is standing in front of a live scene of the city of Singapore, taken from a relatively tall building, you can see a bright morning, the modern buildings of the city sharply defined against the skyline, traffic moving on the roads on a busy day and even, in the distance, part of the Singapore shoreline and the sea stretching beyond. You glance out of your "real" window and see the New York night, with the buildings, the lights and the constant murmur of distant traffic. You may even think that if the world were to end at that precise moment a Singaporean would have lived for an extra half a day more than you!

Well, all this reasoning, of course, is not quite accurate since the simultaneous nature of time is not the same as the manner in which we have chosen to divide our days and months, which for practical reasons follow the locally perceived position of the Sun and not the absolute instants of time. Furthermore, when you look into that television screen you are looking into the past and not the future since the image that finally arrives at your eyes has already occurred and has travelled a great distance to get to its destination. In the case in point, a signal from Singapore could take over a second to reach you if it was travelling through a satellite link, television studios and cable networks.

Time Zones

Knowing the correct time accurately anywhere in the world has always been a challenge. By convention, we have arranged our measurement of time according to the position of Earth with respect to the Sun. To be able to accurately recognize this position at any time of the day and in any part of the world we have divided Earth into Time Zones. This arrangement lets us experience sunrises and sunsets at roughly similar moments of the day wherever on Earth we happen to be. I say roughly since the closer you go to the poles the division between day and night is less symmetrical.

Nominally speaking, we have tried to arrange for "noon", strictly speaking, "solar noon" or, the moment in the day when the Sun is at its highest point in the sky, to coincide with 12 o'clock. For most parts this is true but due to different latitudes, the actual time when this happens will vary from place to place. Interestingly the word "noon", which has its roots in Latin, means the "ninth hour from sunrise" or roughly 3 PM. This measurement of time comes from old monasteries where the working day started at 6:00 AM and the main service of the day was at the "ninth hour" from the start of the day, that is, 03:00 PM. This started to change during the 12th century, shifting to the sixth hour, that is 12:00 PM and coinciding with "solar noon", hence the term noon became associated with this particular time of day.

Having accounted for this midday point we have also

divided the Earth into 24 equal vertical slices, pole-to-pole, much like you might do to an orange in order to peel it easily. Each one of these slices turns out to cover 15° of the circumference of Earth and they represent 1 hour of time, hence the whole circumference adds up to 24 hours which is the defined length of time for the Earth to go around the Sun once, what we call *a day*. This means that if we travel along a parallel, that is, perpendicular to the axis along the poles, and cover a distance of 15° (roughly 1,700 km) we will need to adjust our watches by either adding an hour or subtracting an hour, depending on the direction of our travel (east or west respectively). One further definition is necessary to complete the model we have created and that is to define a reference point from where all this is measured and so count the time differences from that point, this reference point is Greenwich in London and measured time either increases by an hour if you are travelling eastwards or decreases by an hour if you travel westwards from this point.

Most of this model of measurement of clock time was designed in the 19th century, Greenwich was given its "Mean Time" status in 1884, this was a necessity since before this model was used each town or community set its own time according to the sunrise and sunset that each one experienced, this was fine when there was little travel between towns, cities or countries but as travel became more important, particularly sea-travel, a more precise form of time standardization was necessary[4].

This arrangement and the definition of Greenwich Mean Time, or GMT, allows us to experience, roughly, a "standard" day all over the world with known and predictable day segments, morning when the Sun rises, midday when the Sun is at its highest point in the sky and finally evening when the Sun sets, each one of these segments happening at roughly similar instances during the day. The term GMT is now in disuse and has been replaced by the term UTC which, to all effects, are interchangeable. UTC is "Coordinated Universal Time" (the original name is in French hence the order of the letters in the acronym) which was agreed upon in the 1970s and is now used to mark all time references, Greenwich is still the reference marking the 0° reference meridian.

Each one of the areas described as being 15° from Greenwich is termed a Time Zone and we can say, for example, that if a city is 3 Time Zones to the east of Greenwich (say Nairobi in Kenya), it is at UTC+3, its time at any moment during the day will be 3 hours ahead of the time in London. Conversely, a city that is in UTC-3 (say Buenos Aires in Argentina) will be 3 hours behind the time in London. All these examples do not take into account daylight savings time which some countries adopt in order to save on electricity or other forms of energy and that account for other differences in time during different parts of the year.

Now, and this is where it all starts to get rather strange if we follow this model through and travel UTC+12 in one direction and UTC-12 in the other direction and because the Earth is round, we will end up at the same place! But what will the time be at this destination point?

As an example, let's say it is 3 PM in London, then we can also say:

London	15:00 hrs, UTC+0	day A
Place 1	03:00 hrs, UTC-12	day A
Place 1	03:00 hrs, UTC+12	day A + 1 (nest day)

This example is telling us that this same point in our planet ("Place 1") is simultaneously at 3 AM of day A and 3 AM of day A+1, that is, the next day. How can this be?

The answer, of course, is that it is not possible and it is only showing us the limitations brought about by the system we created to standardize the way we measure time, something that is continuous and that is not easily modelled by such rigid standards. To cope with this problem, in 1884, the same year London was defined to be the time reference point, the International Date Line was defined that demarcates the beginning and the end of a particular day. This line is located directly on the opposite side of the Greenwich 0° meridian and runs through the middle of the Pacific Ocean without falling on any land mass. So, going back to our example, the actual time at "Place 1" will depend on which side of the International Date Line it happens to be, in one case it will be 12 hours ahead of London while in the other case it will be 12 hours behind.

As we see, in the end, we have quite a complex system in place just to be able to agree on a meaningful answer to the question "What time is it?" Still, some might say that it is a small price to pay in order to know the exact time of your next flight to Singapore!

Time Zone Travel

More strange things arise from this model of timekeeping, let's explore some of them, for example, it is possible to celebrate New Years's Eve in Kiritimati (Christmas Island) in the Pacific Ocean, then take a flight to Hawaii the next day and fly the 2,013 km that separates them and celebrate New Year's Eve all over again, this is possible since Hawaii is 24 hrs behind Kiritimati. Another possibility for this double celebration would be to take a ferry from Samoa (UTC+13) to American Samoa (UTC-11) these islands are only 70 km apart! Notice how a UTC+13 has appeared, there is also a UTC+14 and even half-hour UTCs steps, this is mainly due to local definitions taken by each country and usually arises in areas that lie between time zones and a half hour or whole hour step makes it more convenient for their particular relationship to their surroundings or neighbouring towns or cities.

Now, it is not necessary to travel that far to have similar strange effects.

"Alabama State Line" reads the road sign roughly 92 kilometres west of Atlanta, Georgia, USA when you travel on Interstate-20. You might easily miss this sign on this straight stretch of highway, lined with trees on either side of the double carriageway. The sign is one of those standard green signs written in white letters. The traffic flows smoothly into Alabama and back into Georgia on the other side of the highway. Nothing alerts you to the strange moment that you will be living at the precise instant when you cross that state line.

Some background: The United States of America spans over 6 different time zones, from its Eastern Time Zone, on the east coast, to Hawaiian Time Zone in the west, each one of these time zones being one hour away from its neighbour:

- Eastern Time Zone (EST), UTC-5
- Central Time Zone (CST), UTC-6
- Mountain Time Zone (MST), UTC-7
- Pacific Time Zone (PST), UTC-8
- Alaskan Time Zone (AKST), UTC-9
- Hawaiian Time Zone (HST), UTC-10

Starting from Atlanta on a particular morning at 10:00 AM EST, you get into your car and head down to join the I-20 en route to Birmingham, Alabama. If the traffic is good and the conditions are favourable you will be able to get to the Alabama state line in about 53 minutes, passing through small towns such as Douglasville, Villa Rica and Waco on the way. Fifty-three minutes after leaving Atlanta you will come across the "Alabama State Line" sign and at this point, a couple of things will happen. Firstly, as you are crossing a state line, you will be under the jurisdiction of the state of Alabama the state with the highest per capita death penalty rate in the United States, so beware! In the second place the state boundary is also a Time Zone boundary with an imaginary line marking the separation between US "Eastern Time" and US "Central Time" which happens to be 1 hour behind, so as you cross this line 53 minutes from Atlanta, you will have to set your watch back one hour, that is, setting it to 09:53 AM CST. All of a sudden not only have you gone back in time one hour, you now happen to be seven minutes BEFORE you departed Atlanta that morning!

This can get even stranger with other examples: The city of Columbus in Georgia sits on the Chattahoochee River, the river also happens to be the border between the states of Georgia and Alabama. Right on the other side of the river, on the Alabama side, sits Phenix City. As we have seen Alabama and Georgia are on different time zones so these two cities are "one hour apart" in Time Zone terms although they are a mere 5 minutes walk in real terms. This means that if you happened to live in Phenix City and work in Columbus you could get back home from a long day at work before you even left your desk! in Time Zone terms of course. Fortunately, because of this proximity, Phenix City observes Eastern Time just like its sister town Columbus which saves on a lot of missed work meetings!

Finally, in the same Georgia / Alabama border we can have several ways of celebrating New Year twice in a day. For example, say we are in Rome, Georgia celebrating with some friends the start of a new year, after a few minutes of well-wishing, we could get in our car and travel the 44 kilometres that separate this town from Cedar Bluff in Alabama on the GA-20 road, this will take us approximately 37 minutes, arriving at our destination we have the chance to celebrate and welcome the New Year all over again this time in the Central Time Zone. You might even have time for a stop at the "State Line Tavern" located just a few meters before you cross into Alabama.

The New Year effect can be found in many other places

around the world[5]. An example is between the Iberian neighbours, Spain and Portugal, they share a long border but each country sits on a different Time Zone, Portugal on UTC+0 and Spain on UTC+1. Again you could start your celebration at the Spanish town of Badajoz get in your car and drive for approximately half an hour and arrive swiftly at Elvas in Portugal for another New Year's Eve celebration!

I am now writing these lines on Jan 1st 2018, we have just experienced another instance of the process of continuous, unstoppable time moving, like a wave, inexorably forwards. As we waited yesterday, on New Year's Eve, for the new year to arrive we were able to feel this time-wave covering our planet, a wave that started at the International Time Line as the new year took over from the old one, first covering Asia, with Japan and China, following onto the Indian subcontinent, the Middle East, onto Africa and Europe, crossing the Atlantic Ocean to finally arrive on the east coast of the American continent, expanding it's cover from east to west and finally onto the Pacific Ocean and return to the International Time Line, where it had started. Of course this process repeats itself every single day of the year, but on New Year's Eve, as most of the world is expectant of the calendar change and the media covers each midnight in turn, the event is more evident, we see pictures of fireworks in Sydney, Hong Kong, Mumbai, Paris, New York, Los Angeles with every passing hour. It is one of those days where you can easily imagine the way other parts of the world seem to be, somehow, ahead of you and are already living the year following the one you are presently living!

Aside from the fact that it might be a good way to party,

changing Time Zones can be a challenge to your body's internal timekeepers as I will mention in another chapter when I discuss circadian rhythms.

5

TIME TO ESCAPE

Internal Clocks

WE CAN THINK about the passing of time as something external to our bodies, as something that happens to us or is inflicted upon us from the outside. But we can also turn our attention inwards, within our bodies and minds, and investigate whether we possess any kind of internal timekeeper or clock that allows us to track time or whether we are just simply "free-running" and adapt our way of living to the outside world and external time.

Early evidence supporting the case for the existence of an internal clock was based on experiments with animal and humans under sensory deprivation. Michele Siffre, a research geologist who was himself fascinated by time and the strange effects astronauts and people locked up in bunkers experience, led one example of this type of work. He carried out some extensive studies on the subject of time deprivation and was very lucky that, since he lived in the prime of the Cold War, his research was deemed of great importance and he received funding to carry out his experiments, something that nowadays might be difficult to accomplish for this type of study where humans are put under duress.

Siffre's first study delved into how humans responded when isolated and deprived of any external time cues[1]. In 1962, when he was just 23 years old, he locked himself deep in a cave for two months without any time-keeping references. The method he used for recording his experiment was through a team of researchers placed outside the cave where he was incarcerated, his sole method of communication with this team was using a fixed-line telephone that he would use to indicate to them whenever he: woke up, ate and before going to sleep. Inside the cave he passed the time, reading and carrying out experiments. One of those experiments was that once a day he would count to the team outside from 1 to 120, trying to count out one number each second. Using this simple method, and after some time in the cave, he found that counting to 120, which should have taken him 2 minutes, took him 5 minutes showing that his own internal clock was working at a much slower time rate.

He went further on his research some 10 years later when he locked himself in another cave, this time for a period of six months, and again, without any time referencing clues. There were some interesting conclusions that he shared after his new sets of experiments, the most important was that with no external clues to the passing of time, our body finds its own cycle and it is longer than the 24 hour period we are accustomed to, this is coherent with what he had found in his first confinement. Furthermore, as his isolation time got longer, his body cycle tended to settle itself on a 48-hour period, seemingly working twice as slow as external clocks. The other interesting aspect he concluded from his results was that the mind, presumably in sympathy with the body, also slowed down and believed that time was passing at a slower rate. In the case of the first study, the two month-real-time confinement seemed to Siffre to have occurred in just one month, when they opened the cave at the pre-agreed date, September 14th, by his calculations it was only August 20th.

Later studies undertaken by other scientists such as Charles Czeisler in 1999 have shown that most of the earlier experiments on this matter were flawed in that they did not take in consideration some subtle details in the experimental method, for example it has been shown that even small disturbances in the lighting conditions used in the experiments, such as the presence or absence of artificial light, can have a great impact on the results. It is now more commonly accepted that when our body is left "free-running", that is with no external time references, it will settle in a cycle period of around 24 hours (one day), more precisely, within a range between 23.5 and 24.5 hours. More detailed results show that 25% of people have a cycle below 24 hours and 75% have a cycle above 24 hours, so it seems that even though people like Siffre were flawed in their general experimental methodology, the results still support that our body will tend to "slow-down" when left to its own devices.

Circadian rhythms

At a biological level the natural cycle that our bodies exhibit is called the circadian rhythm. It is a cycle that is shared between humans and most animals, plants and even microbes, it helps the organisms keep track of time so that, for example, the time to rest and sleep is differentiated from the time to be active. The word circadian comes from the Latin and means "about-a-day" (Circa being "about" and diem meaning "day"). It is no surprise that this rhythm is shared by most species on Earth since it is driven principally by the cycle of day and night that we all share due to the Earth's rotation about its axis and our relationship with our closest star, the Sun.

By an amazing degree of coincidence, as I write these paragraphs in 2017 three scientists are been awarded the Nobel Prize in Physiology or Medicine for their work on understanding the circadian cycle. Jeffrey C. Hall, Michael Rosbash and Michael W. Young worked on understanding the mechanism, at the molecular level, involved in the control of the circadian rhythm. They discovered how a gene, called the period gene, controls the build-up of a certain protein during the night which then degrades during the day effectively creating a 24-hour timer that keeps track of the day-night cycle. This cycle is synchronized with the outside world by light falling on the eyes which is then perceived by the suprachiasmatic nucleus (SCN) located in the hypothalamus in the middle of the brain. This complex system effectively controls our wake-sleep periods releasing melatonin to make us sleepy and also, amongst other things, controlling our body temperature, heart rate, reaction times and the functioning of our internal organs.

This delicate system can be disturbed when we have non-conventional sleep patterns like those of people who have to be awake during the night due to their job or other activity and also when travelling through different time zones where, in a very short space of time, we change the external light and activity conditions that we need to keep our bodies in-sync and so suffer the so-called "jet-lag" effect.

The circadian rhythm is not the only model that has been used to describe the way our body clock works during the day. For example, Traditional Chinese Medicine (TCM) describes the most favourable times of the day to perform different types of activities, defining the most appropriate times for the optimal performance of the most important internal organs such as the liver or kidneys. It is interesting to note that although TCM is more of an observational science that has been developed and refined through thousands of years as opposed to the more experimental science of the west, where analysis and internal exploration are the norm, there are still some similarities between both approaches. Apart from the obvious coincidences of wake and sleep times it is interesting to note the correspondence of other events during the day, for example the period between 9 AM and 11 AM where according to the circadian model we are at a moment of high hormonal generation and alertness, TCM coincides with this view in that it is a period of clear thinking and energy generation. Both also coincide that between 3 PM and 5 PM there are high amounts of energy flowing, or available, in our bodies and that it is a time which is apt for focused thinking and work.

There are other types of biological cycles and the study of chronobiology, the science of understanding the body's biological cycles, is permanently advancing in understanding their importance[2]. There are Infradian Rhythms, with periods that cycle at a rate longer than a day, an example of such a rhythm is the human menstrual cycle. There are also Ultradian Rhythms which have cycles with periods smaller than 24 hours, in general, and as we shall discuss in the next section, the term Ultradian is used to describe the cycles that occur within our sleep.

Sleeping

Although we might live to a grand old age and think that we can control how we use the time we spend on this life-journey, a third of that time has been reserved by evolution for a specific purpose and that is, sleeping. Just to put this in perspective, say you live for a total of 80 years then you will be asleep for almost 27 of those years! If we have evolved to invest so much time in this state, we can assume that it must be a very important part of our lives. And indeed it seems to be so, there are many, many studies and investigations that tell us about the importance of sleep. Sleep has a direct influence on our health and every single aspect of our lives, physical and mental, affecting even our own longevity.

Sleep is a very curious state in which we are present but not conscious and although externally it may seem as if we have entered a "standby" state, there is a whole universe of processes going on within us, so much so that if we measure the number of calories that we burn when we are asleep we find that it varies very little to the amount we would spend when awake and in a restful state, the difference being only about 100 fewer calories in favour of the sleep state. So if we are not in "standby" what is going on?

In fact sleep-scientists are still investigating the details of what happens during this state but there is some consensus revolving around three basic activities that are present: Restoration, Energy Conservation and Brain Function. The first two involve the replenishment of the wear and tear we suffer during our awake state, this includes both at the brain level where hormones and neuronal activity is replenished and also in our body, were tissue is repaired and rested. The third activity includes our information processing, memory consolidation and learning, it all takes place during sleep and is vital to the *Before-Now-After* model that I will describe in later chapters.

When we are in our sleep state our perception of time is altered and we are witness to the apparent separation in the way our mind and body feel the passing of time. In many ways, the body seems to have a more rigorous and constant timekeeper than does our mind, but the mind can play various tricks, some researchers have even said that sleeping is the only state where we are allowed to travel freely through time whether it is backwards of forwards. In sleep we generally lose sense of time, for instance, think of the experience when we are watching a film, perhaps late at night after a long day, we don't want to go to sleep because we have waited for some time to watch this film and we don't want to miss any of it. This is a common enough scenario and, sure enough, what follows is a "quick" fall into that precious sleep we are lacking. When we eventually wake up from that "quick" sleep, the film is not over yet, and we are now in a state in which we have no idea how long we were "out" for. We don't know whether we missed 30 seconds or 30 minutes of the film, we got out of sync with the world. Something similar happens in the morning when we wake up without the use of an alarm clock, we have no idea what time it is until we look at a clock or have some reference of the light or other time clues happening around us. Without a doubt, we lose track of time in sleep. Or do we?

. . .

Have you ever wanted to wake up at a precise time in the morning? Maybe because you have to catch a flight or not to miss an important meeting, and somehow, almost magically you wake up, unaided, at precisely the correct time? There is some inconclusive evidence that has been documented[3] that suggests that we can somehow set our internal alarm clocks to trigger at precisely certain times. Some of this research has been carried out in Germany where some of the subjects taking part were told that they would be awakened at a certain time in the morning and others were independently told that they would be awakened two hours later, in other words, that they would be asleep for longer. Eventually, all the subjects taking part in the experiment were awakened at the same time (the earlier time). After waking, the levels of the hormone *adrenocorticotropin* were measured in all the test subjects. This hormone is responsible for helping us deal with our day-to-day stress situations. In the case of the group that was to be awakened earlier, the level of the hormone was found to be much higher at the wake-up time than in the other group. In fact, this hormone started rising about one and a half hours before the stipulated wake up time. The conclusion was that the body, of its own accord, was getting itself ready to wake up at the pre-established hour. No mention was made as to how the body gets perfectly synced up with the external clock-time. I guess that is the subject of another experiment.

Clearly what we are observing here seems to be contradicting itself. On the one hand, we are saying that when we wake up, we are somehow, "lost in time" and we need a firm reference to bring us back in sync with clock-time. This is a clear observation that we all have in our everyday lives, even on a regular wake-up schedule, say a regular wake-up time for getting up for work, we are not quite sure the time until we look at a clock. My personal view of our capacity to self-awake is that in situations were you have a particular need to be awake at a certain moment, your mind and body make a conscious effort to wake up at a certain time by not going into deep sleep, we remain in the lighter stages of sleep in contact with external environment references such as an alarm clock on our bedside table or the lighting conditions we might sense through a window, and this allows us to keep track of external-real time.

Human sleeping patterns have not always been what we are accustomed to in today's world. Once electric lighting gave us the ability to change night for day, our sleep patterns suffered a change to what we now consider to be the norm, that is, the "normal" eight hours of continuous sleep every night. Before industrialization and electricity, it was more common to follow a pattern of "segmented" sleep, where sleep was broken into two or more parts with intervals of wakefulness in between. For example, you could start your "first-sleep" (as it used to be called) at 8 PM and wake up at midnight staying awake for a couple of hours and then return for your "second-sleep" from 2 AM to 6 AM just in time to wake up and tend to your animals or other daily chores. You would still have eight hours of total sleep but they would be segmented into two separate periods. The time between periods of sleep was normally reserved for reflective and intimate activities such as reading, writing, praying or sex, it was even believed that conception was more likely during this period of time. Going to sleep at 8 PM was more likely than it is nowadays since we tended to follow the natural daylight cycle more closely than we do today, we had fewer distractions from electrically powered artefacts and we certainly could not count on the ease with which we now have artificial lighting just at the flick of a switch.

This different use of the time we destine to sleep has been subject to experiments much like the experiments carried out to see how our body's circadian rhythm behaves with no external time references that I discussed earlier in this chapter. This time the subjects of the experiments were left in darkness for fourteen hours every day for a month[4] in order to see how they would naturally use their rest time. What they found was that the subjects, after a while, settled into a four-hour sleep, two-hour awake, four-hour sleep cycle. This has been further documented by Roger Ekirch in his book "At Day's Close: Night in Times Past" where he shows hundreds of references from literature, court records and medical books that mention and describe this segmented sleep pattern.

Dreams

One of the most important brain processes that occur during our sleep phase are dreams. There are many explanations and theories about why and how we dream[5], most agree that it is a necessary part of sleep and that all of us do it, though not everyone remembers the dreams they've had. Dreaming seems to be important in the communication of the unconscious mind with the conscious mind. Before these concepts were established in modern science, this communication was explained as visions from the Gods or other supernatural powers. Dreaming was also believed to be a mechanism to foresee the future or to help deal with important decisions that a community or tribe had to make and there were special "seers" within the community that interpreted these visions in order to guide the group.

Through dreams, our mind allows us to transcend all the physical laws that bind us in the real world and explore it in different ways. We can be transported through time in any direction and have very vivid experiences that otherwise would be impossible to have in the constraints of physical space. But these experiences are possible not through magic or external supernatural powers but are created by our own mind in its normal process of making sense of the world and consolidating the knowledge and information that we collect every day. Individual dreams have been the source of many inspirations for inventions and insights that have advanced the history of our species as a whole. There are stories recounted by many scientists, engineers and artists that recall how their creative moment was evoked through a vision in a dream, the Russian chemist Mendeleev who invented the current arrangement of the Periodic Table of Elements, allegedly saw in a dream the order of the elements fall into place like playing cards. Friedrich Kekulé, another chemist who inspired by a dream of snakes biting their tails to form circles, proposed that the structure of the Benzene molecule was a ring. James Watson, the molecular biologist, with his proposal for the structure of the double helix DNA molecule, which he proposed after dreaming of a spiral staircase. In the arts, the author Mary Shelley and her novel Frankenstein, based on a dream of a man-created monster, Paul McCartney and the songs "Let It Be" and "Yesterday", the first inspired by a dream he had about his mother while the second on a tune that came "into my head" while asleep. Pure art can also be the product of a dream as with the work of Salvador Dalí and the painting "The Persistence of Memory" where he introduces the concept of the melting clocks that dramatically symbolise the effect of dreaming on something, presumably, as solid and inflexible as time itself.

Some people have or have developed the capacity to take control of their dreams, they are called lucid dreamers, they are a precious resource in the study of sleep and dreams since they can give us clues as to what is happening in the dream space. Lucid dreamers have trained and are able to communicate to an external observer through controlled eye movements, this has enabled experiments to be devised that investigate the dream state. In such experiments, several things have been studied, in particular, and related to time perception, Daniel Erlacher from the Institute for Sport Science, University of Bern[6] has documented a study of how time is perceived to pass in our dream state. He has found that when there are motor activities present in the dream, that is, when we see ourselves moving our bodies, as when we are walking or running, the time for the activity takes as much as 40% longer in the sleep domain than in the wake state. He explains his findings by the fact that as we do not have physical feedback available in the sleep mode the actions seem to take longer. In other words, at least under some conditions, time is perceived to pass a great deal slower in the dream state than in wakefulness.

Here we will just mention a still mysterious and little researched brief period of time just before our wakeful state enters sleep. It is called the hypnagogic state (from the Greek: hupnos "sleep" and agogos "leading to"), the observations that are currently being made on this subject are expected to give us a few more clues into the profound differences between sleep and non-sleep. This period is where both states begin to merge and we experience small hallucinations where the reality of the external world, meets our inner processes as we transit from wakefulness into sleep. Although not much has been concluded up to this point, research is going on to try and understand our conscious and our unconscious and also some other related rare conditions such as narcolepsy in which the brain is unable to separate waking life from dreams creating some terrifying hallucinations[7].

All this evidence does seem to point to the fact that although two-thirds of our lives are controlled by the rigours of time's constant pace, we have a natural space where this can be suspended and we can escape from the normal perception of time.

Stress

Escaping the normal pace of time can seem to happen in other ways too, even when we are wide awake. Experiencing a traumatic episode in life sometimes makes us feel as if things are happening at a different speed, usually in slow motion, much like in a movie. Research has been carried out on the subject of stress and time perception in order to assess whether this observation has any physical cause. One of the studies[8] involved dropping the volunteer test subjects from a height of 30 metres and letting them feel "free-fall" to cause in them a feeling of stress. During this rapid descent, two things were measured, first whether the subjects could recognize a rapidly-flickering pattern of numbers shown on a wrist device they wore and secondly, once they were back on the ground, they were asked about their appreciation of the time they took to fall.

What the researchers found was that in terms of the

perception of the length of the fall, the participants declared an average increase of about 36% in the time they thought it took to complete the fall compared to the actual time, they stretched time in their minds by a considerable amount, perceiving that the experience lasted longer than it actually did. The purpose of having the subjects try to recognize the flickering numbers on their wrist devices was to assess the hypothesis that when people are under stress the perception mechanisms "speed-up". To that effect, the flickering rate of the numbers was set just above the speed that would make those numbers recognizable under normal circumstances. If the numbers were recognized then it might be plausible evidence to explain the idea of a time-stretching mechanism going on in our minds, in other words, that our mind processes somehow speeded up to cope with the stressful situation, the effect would be much like the way a slow-motion camera works, that is, shooting at an increased speed and then shown at normal speed thus achieving the slow-motion effect. In fact they found that this was not the case, the numbers were not recognized and so the increase in the speed of perception was not present, our senses worked in the same way and at the same speed as they always do and hence, the stretching of time could not be explained by this particular mechanism. The explanation that the scientists proposed was that the time stretching effect is achieved at the moment of recall, that is, when we remember the event, at that point we tend to extend it's length, almost as if creating our own slow-motion effect, and so it seems longer in time. It is believed that this happens because one of the ways our minds keep track of the passing of time is by measuring the amount of information that was processed at the time an experience takes place, the more information there is to recall, the more time it is assumed that took place when the event occurred[9].

The exact mechanisms through which our brains keep track of time are still under debate, it seems very likely that the area of our brain called the hippocampus is involved in a similar way as it is involved in the modelling of space and distances. Some experiments have found evidence of certain types of neurons that can be trained to fire patterns that last for precise amounts of time, hence allowing us to be aware of how long an event has lasted[10] or when it is time to carry out a certain action or activity. The timekeeping function is implicit in many aspects of the brain's behaviour, take for example the way we store memories: there are at least two time aspects involved, the first is the order in which memories are stored, that is, you remember the sequence of how you got dressed *before* going out of the house and how you drove into work *before* sitting in your office, etc. The other time aspect that we intrinsically store is how long ago that memory occurred, in general we know whether an event happened recently or some time in the past.

Meditation

The knowledge that our bodies seem to have one or more internal clocks and, as we have seen, that these clocks tend to favour a slower time beat than external clock-time, becomes a resource that we can tap into if we are looking for a way to slow down or escape time, at least as far as our perception is concerned. We need to cultivate an inward view or a way to search inside ourselves for these time signals and allow them to regulate our bodies and minds. A technique we have at hand to do this is to experience and practise meditation.

Meditation can take many forms, some involve just the mind while others also involve the body. The roots of all types of meditation stem back to India, with the earliest references in an ancient script, the Vedas, dated around the 6th century BCE. The practice then spread eastwards into China and found its way into the west through the contacts created through the Silk Roads, the trade routes through which all commerce and culture were trafficked between the ancient worlds.

In general, all meditations propose an inward look into ourselves, both in body and mind. A particular research study from the University of Kent in the UK[11] has shown that the practice of Mindfulness Meditation can alter the perception of time. In this research, an experimental group and a control group were given tasks to perform and their perception of the flow of time was investigated. In the case of the group practising Mindfulness Meditation, the results consistently showed a sense that time passed slower. Mindfulness Meditation is a therapeutic type of meditation used in psychology and psychiatry to treat certain types of disorders. It involves experiencing the present (the *Now*), being aware and fully attentive as to what is happening here and now in a non-judgmental attitude.

Meditation aims at creating a contemplative inner mind state that allows what is believed to be a higher state of peace and alertness of our mind, our body and its connection with the world at large. Meditation tends to mean different things to different people and indeed different types of meditations focus on different aspects of this body-mind-world connection. Most commonly, meditation involves, to some degree or another, these five elements:

Body – Breathing – Mind – Energy - Spirit

As you can see the elements go from the very material – the body – to the most immaterial – the spirit. Each one of these elements is defined and exercised, as we shall see in the next paragraphs. Note that the immaterial aspects of the spirit are not related to any particular creed or religion, it should be taken as related to the human condition rather than any deity. It is said that if these five elements are controlled and regulated in the correct manner then we will be in a meditative state with our bodies and minds focused on a single objective. And that is the essence of meditation: focus, the aim is to focus our entire being into a single objective. This general definition of meditation does not oblige us to carry out the act itself in any particular pose, sequence of movements or using any type of clothing or being in any particular setting, it just gives us pointers as to the elements that need attention in order to achieve the meditative state. In that sense, the definition allows for meditative states to be achieved while performing any type of activity, be it passive (playing chess, looking at the sea, etc.) or active (playing tennis, running, etc.). If we manage to combine these five elements and make them work in conjunction then we are meditating.

As an example of one particular type of meditation based on the practice of Chinese Qi Gong (or "Chi Kung") I will describe the objectives and actions for each one of the five elements:

Body

> Get the body into a relaxed state, without unnecessary tensions or strains. Let the structure of the body be its support and relax the muscles. A relaxed body enables good breathing.

Breathing

Deep breathing that incorporates all of the lung's capacity, extending the thoracic cavity and including the lower abdomen. Concentration on this type of breathing is the key to the next step, the mind.

Mind

The mind needs to be "quiet". In general, our mind is permanently at work, sensing the outside and inside world, the aim here is to quieten the mind concentrating on relaxing the body and breathing correctly. When this is achieved we can tap into our inner energy.

Energy

The inner energy of the body has many different names, in Chinese cultures, it is known as Qi ("chi"), in Indian cultures as Prana and in the West, it has been named as the biochemical energy that flows within our bodies and that makes our muscles, vitality and feeling flow. In meditation, the aim is to be able to generate and channel this energy to where it is most needed in our bodies. This gives rise to the final stage, the spirit.

Spirit

The spirit can have many definitions and they are

all complementary and correct depending on our beliefs. In this case, the spirit, refers to our essence, to the most inner part of the being that we are and to the driving force that makes us exist. The final objective is achieved when the previous four elements are regulated as described, it is then said that the spirit is "raised", that is, you have a clear head, an alert mind, a calm disposition and a general feeling of well being.

The practise of meditation can be achieved in different ways, some are contemplative, static and quiet like the famous image of the Buddha in the cross-legged Lotus position. Meditation can also be achieved by chanting, as do Tibetan monks, this practice helps them control their breathing and generates a rhythmic tune to help the mind achieve focus. Tai Chi Chuan is also a meditative practice, in this case, the five elements described are worked together while adding movement, through pre-established form sequences, in order to achieve the synchrony between the five elements. But as I have said at the beginning of this section, meditation can be achieved in any type of activity, you just need to be aware of paying the correct attention to the five elements and make them work in unison to achieve the feeling of well being that is the sign of a raised spirit. Meditation can be used as an effective method for tapping into our internal clocks, feeling and listening to our bodies and hopefully allowing us to escape, at least momentarily, from the rigours of external time.

6

TIME FOR A STORY

Transcending

IN ORDER TO survive as a species, we have understood the need to transcend the span of time that any one of us is present on this planet. This is most patently apparent in the way we reproduce and hence leave something of our essence and being behind for "all time". This fact is true for any living organism. Plants and animals do it all the time and it is the normal form of transcending, at least as far as the gene pool is concerned.

But beyond the physical need to perpetuate each one of the different species in the physical form, all be it with the improvements that evolution can give us, we as humans have developed another set of skills that are made to perpetuate ourselves, to build on what has been learned in the past and also, in a way, make us ever-lasting, or at least some part of us: our ideas.

One of the most powerful mechanisms that we have invented to do this involves making up stories and telling them to one another. We have done this almost from the very beginning of time, even before we created language we could warn each other of dangers or of where food could be found by gesturing or pointing in some direction. Such gesturing would be a very primitive form of story but very essential to our survival.

From these early beginnings, we have invented different ways in which to create stories, using different themes, protagonists and formats. The forms stories take are very different and depend on the "media" that they are stored in. Originally the only media available to us was our own brains, so stories needed to be efficiently transferred from one brain directly to another, usually through speech. Since our brain specialises in capturing information that has some relation or association to other information already stored, a technique known as "relational information", the best format to safely keep our information at hand would be one that evokes associations between memorized elements. Our ancestors found that if they used techniques for associating words by the way they sound, that is, phonetically similar words or phrases as in rhymes, things became easier to remember. In the same way and taking advantage of the visual bias of our brains, if they could "paint a picture" with the words, that is, describe and evoke an idea in visual terms ("imagery"), it would also be more memorable.

Associations of how some objects behave or seem like other objects, as when we use metaphors in a phrase like "she has a heart of gold" and all the other literary devices that we learn in school, also helped in recalling stories. All these devices were quickly enhanced with rhythm –a tonal or musical analogy of rhyme- to create songs and music. Stories in the form of songs have a particularly "stickiness" that makes them ideal for passing on messages. In songs there are two ways in which the story can be stored in the brain: one is through the words themselves, that is, learning them by repetition and storing them as a word pattern. The second way is storing the tune or music of the song, which will also evoke the words and message along with it. This second method is so powerful that we can even store a complete song with words in a language that we don't even understand or speak and repeat it without much difficulty.

Whichever way, we have the need to pass on what we have learned to the ones that come after us.

Rhyme and Rhythm

Songs and poems have been a traditional form of distraction and of passing-on knowledge from one generation to the next. There are recurring themes for these songs and poems that touch on the essential knowledge that we need to pass on generation after generation: Fear, Loyalty, Companionship, Fate, Grieving, Betrayal, Hope, Honour, Parenthood and Danger, to mention just a few, each type of story addressing an essential need or knowledge that was deemed important enough to be passed on to others. There are also other essential story enhancers such as Comedy, Suspense and Love that, as well as passing on knowledge, have an engaging component that makes them very attractive and more memorable. A well-constructed comical song can be a powerful vehicle for delivering a message.

Nursery rhymes are another example of songs that are used to pass on teachings or experiences. In England and most of Europe, the great plague of the 17th century killed millions of people. It is believed, although some folklorists dispute it, that the famous nursery rhyme below is a description of those terrible days:

Ring-a-ring o' roses,
A pocket full of posies,
A-tishoo! A-tishoo!
We all fall down.

Peter and Iona Opie, leading authorities on nursery rhymes, have written about this rhyme:

"The invariable sneezing and falling down in modern English versions have given would-be origin finders the opportunity to say that the rhyme dates back to the Great Plague. A rosy rash, they allege, was a symptom of the plague, and posies of herbs were carried as protection and to ward off the smell of the disease. Sneezing or coughing was a final fatal symptom, and 'all fall down' was exactly what happened."

PETER AND IONA OPIE

In religion, this form of storytelling is used throughout the ritual ceremonies of most cultures. Indeed in the early days of all religions, literacy was not widespread and was a tool reserved for a very limited number of people, so memorizing the "rules" and rituals was an essential part of belonging to any religious grouping. In the same way most cultures and tribes use song to pass on their way of life and beliefs, this even includes sub-cultures within a society, such as the teenage culture, that not only use song to share their view of life but also use it as a symbol to show their affiliation to a particular trend or movement.

Stories and Histories

Like every other human invention, stories are not made to create "good" or "evil" but their effectiveness depends on how we use them. A story that is told to do "good" can make us get up from the comfort of our chair and go and donate money for people in another continent, who are suffering from some natural disaster or war and that are total strangers to us. On the other hand, a story that is told to do "evil" can make us get up from that same comfortable chair and join a movement that will hunt down and kill other humans who are, in some arbitrary way, not "like us". Stories are powerful.

In general, stories have a relatively common three-part structure: first there is the set up at the beginning were the characters and their environments and relations are presented, that is followed by the declaration of the conflict or conflicts that need to be addressed and the final act presents us with the resolution of the conflicts to end the story. Of course, there are multiple variations of this basic structure but as a general pattern, this is the way we learn to understand narration. Most stories use a chronological method for the narration to flow, that is, they go from the furthermost instant of time and advance through time as the story develops. This is not a requirement in the telling of a story, other non-time-linear methods are also used in which the dis-order of time adds to the surprise and novelty in the makeup of the plot.

The stories we tell each other describe the reality we live in, even when they occur in other worlds, times or even distant galaxies, what always transcends are human conflicts and resolutions for us to understand, judge and empathise, for a story to be of any use to us, it cannot be any other way. But at the same time, stories are so powerful that they can even transform reality itself showing us other ways to approach different subjects and alternatives to resolve conflicts.

Ever since the invention of the written language some 5,000 years ago[1] written stories have become even more powerful and we find that in most societies there is a profound reverence to the written word, the "if it is written it must be true" paradigm has prevailed with its positive and negative consequences. It has been immensely useful in allowing societies to write down laws, agreements, wishes and memories to make them transcend time, but it is also a fact that up until very recently the means to write down and distribute stories for the masses was the privilege of a few, as was the ability to actually read what was written. This has started to change with the spread of the Internet and the newfound ease for anyone to write and publish on any subject and for that content to be accessible to almost anyone in the world who is connected to this ever-growing network.

Stories written down to describe past events in time

become our history, it is no surprise that both words: History and Story in most western languages have the same etymology or root, both coming from the Greek *histor*, meaning a "wise man" or "judge". History is the great teacher of our species, in a way, it is what differentiates us from other animals and what enables us to build on what has already being learned and not make us start from scratch with each generation, this extends our time-frames for handling complex concepts or situations. We can even use this ability whenever we find it difficult to understand current day events or present "stories" by tracing back in time to the events or moments that might have preceded the current circumstances. For example, the great debate that is always present in the US about gun laws and the right to bear arms, a law which gives rise to the horrible events that have brought death and terror to US schools and public places, is easily traced back to its origin in the settler history of that country. The second amendment of the US constitution, which is the pillar on which gun tenancy supports itself, was drafted in the 18th century to enable "the people" to create armed militia in order to protect the newborn states from insurrection and slave rebellions, this was common in a time where there was no regular army in the land. At that time this amendment was deemed a necessary and unquestionable means of self-defence and protection, as there were no other legal structures to protect the population, quite a different context from the modern US legal system. This generates the debate as to whether this amendment is still necessary in the US constitution given the current reality of the country and the world. History should teach us, though it might take some time, that changing circumstances in our society necessarily demand changes in the way we choose to organise ourselves and the laws that we create to implement this organization.

Although history is a great teacher, authors have their own interpretation and subjective view of a situation as they write down their stories, this gives an incredible amount of power to their words and points of views about events.

Mary's Story

February 7, 1587. After a drab dinner, she retired to her room with her attendants. It felt like another cold night in the castle, her room, although spacious and comfortable, was far removed from the main fireplace and the log stove that she had been given was not enough to make her room as warm as she liked.

During dinner, she had heard horses and carriages arrive, but as she was not informed of the comings and goings of the castle or household, she could not know who it was that had arrived or what purpose had brought them to Fotheringhay Castle. Suddenly one of the castle pages knocked on her door and bid her company into one of the drawing rooms on the ground floor.

She put on her double cape since the stairway at this time of the evening was always cold and droughty with the cool evening air drifting through the small arrowslits leading directly to the outside, pointing towards the valley and over the main entrance of the castle. A good vantage point in case the need arose to defend the building.

The large wooden door to the drawing-room was opened by two manservants just before she stepped in. Inside she saw five people, all of them men, and immediately she recognized George Talbot, the Earl of Shrewsbury, her ever-present guardian and keeper, also present was Henry Grey, the Earl of Kent and Lord

Lieutenant of Bedfordshire. At that same instant she felt a sharp pain and tightening of her stomach, this was not to be the routine house call she was accustomed to and which happened from time to time. Those visits were commanded by Queen Elizabeth who sent one of her advisors or close confidants to see how Mary was and whether she was ready to change her unruly ways and finally accept the true faith and the rule of her cousin. The Queen, as family, had still kept the hope of resolving this conflict without having to come to more drastic measures.

"Good evenin' Ma'am", Talbot greeted a stone-faced Mary. "I hope you fare well" he continued. "We come bearing some news from Court" he continued as he glanced around the group of men present and finally rested his eyes on her. Mary remained silent and hardly listened to what was being said, lost in her thoughts as to what the next steps would be. After all, she knew exactly what they had come to tell her, she had known from the moment she set foot in the drawing-room.

Up to this point, everything that I have written is pure fiction. It's the way I imagine the events to have unfolded; it is a story, my story of an event that happened over 500 years ago. I have no real way to know if all the detail, as I recount it, is what actually happened on that particular day, I can only base my account on what I have read about the episode in books, in the many written articles, eyewitness accounts, films enacting the stories and interpretations of others with respect to how it all might have happened. But, just like them, as I wasn't there, it is all a story created by my imagination.

The story is, of course, part of the life of Mary Stuart, best known as Mary, Queen of Scots. Mary was born in

1542 and being just 6 days old she acceded to the throne of Scotland after the death of her father James V. While regents ruled Scotland, she spent most of her childhood in France. When she was 19 years of age and already a widow of King Francis II of France, she returned to Scotland in 1561. In Scotland her life continued to be an eventful one, she married and widowed once again regaining and losing the throne of Scotland until she fled southwards to seek refuge with her cousin Elizabeth I, Queen of England. It was only about 25 years -in 1536- since England had separated from Catholicism as the country's main faith and there were large portions of the population who still professed faith and allegiance to the Pope and wanted the re-establishment of a Catholic King or Queen in the land. Mary was accused of being part of at least a couple of attempts to overthrow Queen Elizabeth I, the last one being the so-called Babington Plot which eventually led to her being charged with treason, sentenced and finally executed.

When she heard the news, it did not come as a surprise but rather a sharp realization of a moment many times imagined in her mind. Knowing that something will happen, however certain it might be, never prepares you completely for the instant when it finally occurs.

The message was delivered clearly enough: she would be executed in the morning, a few hours from now. Knowing that she would be no more on this earth did not fill her with fear, it was somehow a welcomed relief as she had spent too many years imprisoned, sometimes within walls and at others, although not incarcerated, forced to move constantly and not able to fulfil what she had convinced herself was her rightful place and duty: that of being the monarch of her people and to profess her true faith.

Although I have kept to the broad facts, as we know them through the ages, I have taken full liberties in expressing the feelings she might have had and of describing the atmosphere as I imagine it might have developed. But what if I had actually been there? How accurate might the story be if I had written it at the time it happened? If I had been an eyewitness of the events, would it be truer to the facts? Is there only one truthful account that can immortalize an event for ages to come? Looking at how stories are handed down through the generations we need to understand whether the passing of time affects or modifies our accounts of the past, how much of what we call our "history" is, in fact, just made up "stories"?

Studies[2] have shown that even if you have witnessed an event *your* version of the "facts" might be very different from the version of someone else who also was there as witness. According to these studies, amongst the main factors that can affect the accuracy of these eyewitness accounts are: stress or anxiety, the violence of the event and the direct involvement of the eyewitness with the action[3]. This is without accounting for intentional modifications that might be added by an eyewitness who wants to put across his or her version of what should have happened due to some personal view or belief.

Some modifications that the original version might suffer can be accounted for by the oral tradition of recounting events, typically the narrator might enhance a version of the events every time it is told (for entertainment purposes for example) thus creating new versions of the story with each re-telling. In the same way, another narrator who has heard the "original" story might recount it with her own enhancements to someone else, and so on. It is the same effect as the children's game of the "Telephone", which you might know, where a message is relayed secretly from a source (the first child) down a line of several children until the last one in the line reproduces what she was told. In general little of the original message remains and this creates great amusement and laughter for everyone involved. Which are the "telephone" stories that we might consider and recount as truths at this very moment in time? Maybe some of those stories have a profound effect in our lives affecting our beliefs and our values, but if we were able to trace them back to the facts, the original versions might be totally different.

Written testimonies are less prone to the types of modifications described above where an oral message is altered by the compound effect of the different interpretations as it passes down the chain. The only disturbance to the written message from one edition to the next can arise at the moment a copy is made, either by hand or by a machine. Before the invention of the printing press, copies were made manually, each letter, word and phrase copied, by hand, from the source to the new page by a scribe working carefully on each document. As in all manual processes, it was prone to errors and the possibility existed for the copied text to be modified, wittingly or not, by the person doing the copying. An "inspired" copy artist could transform literal copying into a sort of re-interpretation of the content similar to the Telephone game. This transformation-by-handling of the message is further complicated when the copying also involved translation between languages, in this case, interpretation of the written word is necessary in order to convey the correct idea across to the other language and it is a process generally freely entrusted to the hands of the translator. Of course, there are cases where misinterpretation of the source is totally accidental but at other times they are strategically calculated to modify the narration and influence the reader in a specific way. With the advent of printing presses and machines to carry out the copying, the accidental errors have been virtually eliminated but the explicit changing of the messages due to ideological, political or religious purposes, as happens for example with war-propaganda, is still possible and, as it is well understood, most of our history has been interpreted and written down by the winning side and not the losers as we will see by continuing with the story of Mary.

The execution of Mary Stuart or Mary Queen of Scots in 1547 was attended by a large contingent of people, over four hundred according to official records, some of those eyewitnesses wrote down their accounts and we have a chance of reading and comparing those stories in order to have some clues into the nature of stories over time. Does history become more removed from the truth as time ticks over or does it maintain its essence and withstands the passing of time?

We shall concentrate on three eyewitness accounts: the most famous one is by *Robert Wynkfielde* and is found in the Landsdowne Manuscript 51/46 in the British Library[4]. This is the "official" version, which was forwarded from Fotheringhay (where the execution took place) to the Queen's Court. The second account is by *Pierre de Bour-*

deille, a French nobleman, historian and biographer and, finally, the last version corresponds to an *anonymous* account from a catholic eyewitness and sympathiser of the catholic queen.

The first thing we can say is that reading all these accounts we can immediately detect that each one has its own style of writing and narration particular to each one of the writer's abilities and general points of view. It seems that the Wynkfielde story is the one that is the most neutral and descriptive, at least it reads more objective from the point of view of the prose itself.

Within the three accounts we can compare three particular moments of the day of the execution:

The first one is at the moment when the queen's garments are being arranged for the execution, this involved some disrobing, which was done by the executioners, to expose the queen's neckline, these are quotes:

Wynkfielde Account

(She says) that she "never had such grooms to make her unready", and that she "never put off her clothes before such a company".

Bourdeille Account

...saying that she was "not used to disrobing in public, especially before so large an assemblage".

Anonymous Catholic Account

(She says) "Now truly, my lords, I never had two such grooms waiting on me before!"

Note that, at least to our modern eyes, the tone of the three descriptions read very different going from a very factual description in the case of Wynkfielde to an almost comical saucy tone in the anonymous account.

The second moment is what the queen is supposed to have said in order to stop her ladies-in-waiting crying and sobbing and hence persuading the officials to let them remain in the hall and not be forced out for causing a nuisance in the proceedings:

Wynkfielde Account

(She says in French) "Ne crie vous, j'ay prome pour vous" ("do not cry, I have promised that you wouldn't" sic.)

Bourdeille Account

One of them was unable to keep from crying so that the Queen had to impose silence upon her by saying she had promised that nothing of the kind would interfere with the business in hand.

Anonymous Catholic Account

(She says) "for," quoth she, "I have passed my word to these lords that you shall be quiet and not offend them:"

In this case, the three versions relate the same idea except that in the Wynkfielde account we are told that the message was relayed in French to her ladies-in-waiting. In the second account, we are told that the message was directed to one particular person while in the other two it is not specified, but one tends to think that it was more directed to the group as a whole.

Finally, the third comparable snippet narrates what would become her last words at the moment when she is near or kneeling by the execution block, this is what she is reported to have said:

Wynkfielde Account

(She recites a Psalm in Latin) "In Te Domine confido, non confundar in eternam"

Bourdeille Account

"In te, Damine, speravi; nan canfundar in aeternum"

Anonymous Catholic Account

"I believe firmly to be saved by the passion and blood of Jesus Christ, and therein also I believe, according to the faith of the Ancient Catholic Church of Rome, and therefore I shed my blood."

In this particular case, the first two accounts are very similar, with some differences in spelling and two alternate words for "trust" (*confido* and *speravi*). But it seems clear that the anonymous catholic account is biased toward relaying the religious message of the significance of the sacrifice of a true believer, such as Mary is portrayed, and the similitude with the sacrifice of the religion's messiah himself. After all here was one of the last bastions of the English catholic faith being put to her end.

Strangely enough, although the three accounts agree that the execution was not very well performed by the executioners and that it took more than one strike to the neck to complete, the accounts differ as to the number of strikes it took: Wynkfielde claims it was two while Bourdeille reported three strikes.

What can we say about the accounts? First that, in general, the broad facts appear to agree. So we can be fairly certain that what happened indeed did happen. But if we start delving into the details there are some discrepancies as we have seen: two or three axe blows? Did she speak some of her last phrases in Latin, French or English? Was her tone nonchalant, frivolous or stern? Almost five hundred years away from the event the discrepancies are just a curiosity and hardly relevant to the broad facts, except, maybe, to scholars. In fact, if we look today (2017 CE) in the official British Royal Family Website, the execution is just given the following short paragraph[5]:

> *Mary was finally executed at Fotheringhay Castle in Northamptonshire on 8 February 1587, at the age of 44.*

It is interesting to note that at the time of the execution

the greatest storyteller in the English language, William Shakespeare, was 23 years old. He had already been married for five years and had three children. He was still a few years away from writing what is considered to be his earliest work "The Taming of the Shrew" at some point before 1592[6]. Although the play is a comedy, how much of an influence is there on the play's strong-headed main character, Kate, from the life of the contemporaneous, rebellious and unruly Queen Mary?

Details are important and they can, and are, manipulated, sometimes explicitly and some times unintentionally. In the explicit instance, it might involve creating or modifying the details to incriminate or acquit a person. This might be for something as serious as murder or as mundane as somebody breaking a drinking glass and not wanting to take the blame. Sometimes there might be unintended manipulation that has the effect of changing a story, it may just occur due to the personality, education, experience or emotional state of the eyewitness in the event in question. In the case of the execution of Mary Stuart, we can expect the catholic eyewitness account to take a much more affectionate and partisan viewpoint of the proceedings with respect to the official version of the event as told by one of Queen Elizabeth I's close emissaries.

So, in conclusion, it looks like time itself may have little to do in blurring events of the past, even if they are distant. The veil of doubt on the accounts as reported is, for the most part, added by the subjective interpretation of what was seen or experienced by the eyewitnesses. It can be affected by explicit objectives to re-count the story the way we want it to be read or it can be modified unintentionally by more mundane factors such as the writing skills of the witness, his or her emotional state, education, storytelling flair, amongst other factors. Since the invention and use of writing it is important to consider how accurately the originals have been copied and language translated through time.

Found in Translation

Translation and the deciphering of ancient writing have acted like time-keys and enabled us to open up the secrets of our history. Writing methods that allowed us to express ideas and concepts started around 3,100 BCE in Mesopotamia, before that there were only ideograms or numbering systems which were invented to describe the things we observed around us. Apart from Mesopotamia, there were other places and times around the world where the skill of writing also arose, notably in China around 1,200 BCE and in Central America around 300 BCE. Nevertheless in the 4th millennium BCE, the Sumerians in Mesopotamia are generally recognized to be responsible for the first written word, at least as far as the classical western historical period is concerned. Throughout the written recorded history, which now extends through 7 millennia, there have been manuscripts, usually found carved onto stone tablets, that have acted as time-keys and have allowed a glimpse to previous eras acting almost as time portals into the past. In particular, inscriptions written in more than one language have allowed us to translate between known idioms into unknown writing methods. There are many examples of these time-key documents such as the Trilingual cuneiform inscriptions that have allowed us to understand Elamite and Babylonian[7] and the famously influential

Rosetta Stone discovered in 1799 which gave us the key to decipher the mythical Egyptian Hieroglyph script. The stone itself was made in the year 196 BCE and was discovered after almost 2,000 years from that date during the Napoleonic campaigns in Egypt in the 18th century[8].

In total there are four inscriptions similar in nature to the Rosetta Stone that have been found and that span the period between 243 BCE and 196 BCE, all of them correspond to official decrees that specify certain laws and attributions to government officials or describe military exploits of the time. Since all of them were written under the rule of one of the Ptolemy pharaohs they are sometimes called the Ptolemaic scriptures. The Rosetta Stone, the most famous of the series, is not the oldest of them, there is another time-key of lesser fame called the Decree of Canopus that is almost 50 years older. The first one of these Canopus decrees (there are several copies) was discovered in 1866 by an Egyptologist who was also a linguist, Karl Richard Lepsus at Tanis in the northeast part of the Nile Delta.

Before the foundation of Alexandria, Canopus was an important Egyptian port and a main thoroughfare for Greek trade. In the year 238 BCE, in a great assembly of priests held there, a decree was passed that apart from honouring the current Pharaoh Ptolemy III and his family, set out to correct a major error in the way solar time was being measured.

Originally, writing was used as a means of ruling and organizing the population by means of publishing decrees for all to follow. Even so, very few people were literate and the medium was used mostly for official stock counting or legal matters, which were read out aloud by public officials.

Decrees, once formulated, were inscribed in stone tablets that were placed in public areas, squares or public buildings as a sign of order and rule for the whole population.

The Decree of Canopus is written in two languages but using three different types of scripts: Hieroglyphs, Demotic and Ancient Greek. Although less than one per cent of the population[9], could read any of these three scripted languages, they were in official use at the time so any communication needed to be published using all three. The languages in the scripts span over five millennia of usage (from 3,200 BCE to 500 CE approximately) so they are able to give us a brief glimpse of some of the concerns of Egyptians at one particular point in time. Reading the translated version of the decree itself[10] we find that it touches on themes such as:

- **The Military**, recounting the way some statues were recovered and replaced in their original states.
- **Famine**, mentioning the droughts that had occurred the previous year due to the fact that the Nile did not flood as it did most years and hence there was not enough water for the fields.
- **Religion**, the creation of a new cult for a deceased princess.
- **Government**, describing some donations that were made and their destiny.

All of these inscriptions were incredibly important in allowing us to finally decipher the ancient Egyptian Hieroglyphs. In that sense, the Rosetta Stone, the first such time-key found, was fundamental being the one that started to show us this world. But the Decree of Canopus stone, discovered 67 years later, had a larger variety of hieroglyphs than the Rosetta Stone and hence gave the experts more vocabulary to decipher. The work by the linguists involved tracing back from the Ancient Greek, through some of what was already known about Demotic, so that they were able to arrive at deciphering the Hieroglyph signs piece-by-piece, sign-by-sign, in the case of the Rosetta stone this painstaking work took over 20 years. For our purposes, the most interesting part of the Decree of Canopus was something that is sometimes overlooked, and that is that for the very first time in history it was officially recognized that the solar year is not exactly 365 days long, as it had been measured previously, but that there was a slight yearly offset that meant that in a period of four years, another day needed to be added to synchronize precisely with the movements of the stars. In other words, it was the very first time that the leap year was recognized to exist in our calendars. The Egyptians realized this by observing the position of the stars, in particular, the star *Sothis* (Siris). The decree states:

> *"the rise of Sothis advances to another day in every 4 years"*[11]

The new law should have been a popular one since the additional day that was added every four years was added to the New Year festivities that were already in place. At that time the calendar was made up of 12 months, each of 30 days, plus an additional 5 days of New Year festivities giving a grand total of 365 days to every year. The decree goes on to finally summarize:

"...therefore it shall be, that the year of 360 days and the 5 days added to their end, so one day as feast of Benevolent Gods be from this day after every 4 years added to the 5 epagomenae before the new year, whereby all men shall learn, that what was a little defective in the order as regards the seasons and the year, as also the opinions which are contained in the rules of the learned on the heavenly orbits, are now corrected and improved by the Benevolent Gods."

TRANSLATED FROM THE HIEROGLYPHIC VERSION BY SAMUEL BIRCH, 1876

Even though the new calendar was proclaimed with the publication of the decree in 238 BCE the calendar reform failed to be adopted in Egypt at that time and it was in the reign of Augustus in 25 BCE that it was finally imposed in Egypt. Meanwhile, a few years earlier in Rome, in 45 BCE, Julius Caesar did take heed to this new calendar and was so keen on it that it became known as the Julian calendar. The Julian calendar has been one of the longest-serving calendars and it was in use in Europe until the 16th century at which time it was replaced by the calendar we use today in the west, the Gregorian calendar named after Pope Gregory XIII in 1582.

Finally, let us note that as the Gregorian calendar is just a modification of the Julian calendar and as we have seen, the Julian calendar is, in fact, the Egyptian calendar proclaimed by the Decree of Canopus, we have here a direct link and connection, through time, from that day in 238 BCE when the gathering of priests and dignitaries made the decree official and proclaimed the need for the creation of a new corrected calendar, right through to our present-day when a version of that calendar forms part of our every day lives.

7

TIME TO LISTEN

HEARING AND LISTENING are both possible because of the action of time. Our auditory sense is a precise and delicate machine, which decodes vibrations in time and transforms them into useful information, sometimes this information is used for our very survival and at other times it is used merely for pleasure. We hear all the time, 24 hours a day, 7 days a week, but listening is different because it requires our attention, our conscious mind needs to be involved.

Listening can take several forms, listening to nature: birds, water, the wind, the sea; listening to a city: traffic, horns, machines, people walking; listening within your home: in the kitchen, in the bath, when you are having lunch; each one of those moments conjures up familiar sounds that we know and that are essential to the places in which you are present, the absence of those sounds would make the place strange and even eerie or menacing: "why is the house so quiet?", "why is there no traffic noise coming from the street?" Amongst the many sounds we hear throughout our day, there is also music. The music you hear on television, radio, as you go into a shop, when you travel in public transport or a taxi, in the elevator, when you call the doctor and you are put on hold and of course the music we choose to listen to, in our phones, radios, music players and streaming services. Music is ever-present in our lives and as we will discover, listening to music is, in effect, listening to time. Music needs and uses time to form pattern upon pattern of sound, which compel and grab our attention and connect deeply with our minds. Sometimes it is said that music can be defined as the "creative organization of sounds" or as the composer, Edgard Varèse famously said "organized sound"[1], I would go one step further than this definition and say that music is the "creative organization of time" to create the ultimate art form.

Sound

It all starts with sound. Sound is an effect generated by the rapid vibration of matter when a force is applied to it. Most matter exhibits this property, to test it, it is enough to use your hand and strike something that is around you like a table, chair or a cup and you will find that sound will be created as you give that matter energy with the blow. Energy creates sound but that sound we define in terms of time. A sound is defined, physically, as the effect produced by the number of vibrations of matter that occur in a period of time, usually within one second, or as it is usually called, vibrations per second.

But vibrations per second are not enough to define a sound, for vibrations to be perceived as real sounds by our main sound sensing organ, our ears, those vibrations need to happen within a range of 20 to 20,000 times each second, outside this range our ears cannot detect them and so we cannot describe them as sound. The measure of "vibrations per second" occurs so often in our world that we have given it a special name and called it "frequency" and we measure it in Hertz after the German physicist Heinrich Rudolf Hertz, who is best known for the study of vibrations at much greater frequencies, not perceptible by our ears, called electromagnetic waves, that are used for telecommunications such as television or radio.

The last ingredient that is needed for sound to exist is a transmission medium, that is, some matter to vibrate. Sound travels or propagates through matter, in our everyday life, most sound will arrive at our ears after travelling through air, the air molecules vibrating at the same frequency as the object that has made the sound. The vibration is allowed to travel by the fact that each air molecule affects the next molecule and the next and the next, so causing a chain reaction that finally arrives at your ears. If we go beyond our air-filled atmosphere, into space, we will find that the lack of this transporting matter (air) makes space totally silent, with no air, no sound waves can propagate and so we hear nothing. That means that you should not believe those films where you see rockets in outer space and hear them making a "whoosh" sound as they pass the camera! that's is just not possible.

Hearing and Listening

Hearing is one of our most essential survival tools and that is true not just for us humans but also for all mammals and most of the animal kingdom. Some animals cannot detect light, they are blind and usually live in dark environments but, as yet, scientists have not discovered an animal that has not some sort of hearing capability. Unlike our dominant sense, vision, hearing is fast. With vision, that is, the eye and brain working together, we can expect to visualize and recognize something in about 0.25 of a second. This latency is the reason that we can enjoy movies, where a collection of still images displayed at a relatively fast rate gives us the illusion of continuous movement. With hearing we can recognize sounds in about 0.05 of a second that's about 5 times faster than vision and that is the reason that sound, unlike vision, can easily startle us or make us jump from our seats, another trick also used in the movies!

If we think of the brainpower needed by each of the senses, vision uses about 30% to 40% of our cerebral cortex to function compared to only 3% that needs to be devoted to hearing. This reveals two things: firstly that vision is deemed of such importance to us that we have evolved to invest a lot of our brain capacity to make it work and secondly that hearing is such an ancient and low-level feature that it needs little brain attention to work, it is deeply wired into us going straight into the most primitive parts of our brain. Not only is hearing a privileged sense in relation to the brain but also it is a sense that does not shut-down or stop working during certain periods of the day, it works 24/7, that is: all day, every day. Even when we are asleep, hearing is always alert to the surroundings.

Although all five senses affect and complement each other, working together to involve us in experiencing the "Now", hearing has a profound effect in our ability to learn language and speech, which at some levels, is the basis for our mind's thought processes. That does not mean that deaf people are in any way more or less intelligent than the rest of us, they just have to develop other ways to express their internal "voices" and thoughts. It has been shown[2] that it is essential for completely deaf children to learn sign language very early on in their lives (just as a hearing child would learn a speech language) in order to give their brains a structure from which to build and develop their thought processes. In this way, a deaf person's inner voice is, in fact, a narration in sign language, rather than, speech language. There are many examples of extraordinary musicians and composers that are or were deaf, one of the most remarkable ones in the present day is the Scottish percussionist Dame Evelyn Glennie who started to lose her hearing at the age of 2 and was completely deaf by the age of 12. This fact has not hindered her career as a percussionist, quite the contrary, she studied in the best music schools and has won countless awards throughout her career and is an extremely successful artist.

The visible parts of our hearing system are our ears, the receptors of external sound perfectly positioned to help us pinpoint the source of a sound to a fine precision. This ability of being able to identify the source of a sound, a vital necessity in terms of survival, relies entirely on the time relationship between the sound received in one ear and the time we receive that same sound at our other ear. It only takes our brain a fraction of a second to calculate the difference between those two time events and from that information identify the place in space where the sound emanated. Even the strangely shaped grooves of our ears are a key aspect of the way we capture that external sound, experiments have been carried out where changes in the shape of the grooves within our ears can generate extremely interesting results. One particular experiment changed the grooves in such a way that it made the subjects believe that a sound coming from above seemed to come from below.

Furthermore, and only proving once again the power of our brain, after a few days of having the ears "modified" in this way, the subject's brain had made the necessary "correction" and it was once again able to correctly identify the direction of the source of the sound.[3]

Rhythm

Our next stop in the discovery of time as music is rhythm. Rhythm brings us to the subject of patterns and repetition and is another of the essential ingredients of music. Rhythm is a sequence of events that happen in time and that repeat in a certain pattern, rhythm can take many forms from visual, through movement, and of course sound. Looking at our own bodies we find several rhythmic patterns that govern the most important processes of life: our heart, our breathing, our sleep, etc. In effect, rhythmic presence starts at the time we are in the womb, where our whole existence depends on our mother's body. Research has shown that we have sensory perception from at least sixteen weeks into gestation, that is the time when we start to be exposed to our mother's heartbeat and breathing rhythms as well as her voice patterns. This fact is seen by some as the basis for the strong bond between different rhythm patterns and us. Rhythms that appear similar to heartbeats, for example, are always found to be compelling, this has been observed in most cultures around the world. Some studies have determined the most universal features of music throughout our different cultures and they have arrived at the conclusion that "simple, repetitive rhythms play a fundamental role in coordinating group performance in almost all of the world's music"[4].

We can find rhythm beyond our own bodies too, nature

and the universe show us the many ways in which time organises itself in cycles to form patterns and rhythms: the repetition of days and nights, the seasons, the cycles of trees and flowers, the Moon and the stars with their different rhythmic expressions, they all allow us to see the importance of time repetition and how it shapes our lives.

Music

Time, with its expression in sound and rhythm, starts to construct what we call music, and this complex arrangement has been converted into a deep-rooted art form. As we listen to any piece of music, be it classical, pop, opera, rock, gospel or any other style, what we are perceiving is the manipulation of time at many different levels and layers, from the physical aspects of sound itself, to the composition of the musical piece by the mind of the artist, to the instrument or instruments used to perform the piece, the interpretation of the performer and finally to the reaction by us, the listener.

Music is made up of a series of components, each one with its own ability to take time as it's raw material and shape it, making patterns from it, repeat sequences in time and give it a special kind of order to finally convert it into an experience for us to enjoy. But let's start with the basics, it all begins with energy and sound.

Sound by itself is not music as our earlier simple experiment of slapping the table showed us. We need further ways to play with sounds in time in order to convert it into what we call music. An essential factor that we need to consider is how that sound feels to us, is it a pleasant or an unpleasant sensation that occurs within us when we hear the sound? As far as music is concerned, we usually look for pleasing sounds and we have found that there are, indeed, some sounds that please more than others and once found we have given them names and called them "musical notes" or simply "notes". Notes are just pleasing sound vibrations which we have defined, by convention and throughout history, and given them names. In western music, there are two main camps in naming those notes: the traditional Do-Re-Mi-Fa-Sol-La-Si which most of the western world uses and that we call the *Solfège* and the A, B, C, D, E, F and G convention used in English and Dutch speaking cultures. The equivalence between the two naming systems is direct where "Do" is "C", "Re" is "D", and so on. Solmization is the term used for the association of syllables with particular notes and the Solfège is one particular solmization of musical tones into syllables, there are many others and they vary from culture to culture. The western solmization method is attributed to Guido de Arezzo who in the 11th century used the first syllables of the first seven lines of a hymn to St. John the Baptist to represent the first seven notes in the musical scale:

Ut queant laxis
resonare fibris,
Mira gestorum
famuli tuorum,
Solve polluti
labii reatum,
Sancte ***I***ohannes.

Ut-re-Mi-fa-Sol-la-SI

In the 17th century, Giovanni Battista Doni changed

"Ut" for "Do" to arrive at the Solfège that we use today. It is believed that "Do" stands for either Giovanni's surname (Do-ni) or more likely, for "Do-minus", that in Latin means God.[5]

What Guido de Arezzo did in the 11th century was later modernized and recreated nine centuries later in the musical "The Sound of Music" where the actress Julie Andrews sang that famous song that starts with the lines *"Doe (Do) a deer a female deer, ray (Re) a drop of golden sun"* playing with the homophonic qualities of the sounds between the name of the notes and common objects, that is, using solmization to teach the musical notes to the children she has in her charge in the movie. In the same manner, as de Arezzo did, the song was created in such a way so that the name of each note is sung and played in the correct pitch (frequency) for each particular note.

Each one of these notes corresponds to a specific and well-defined frequency (vibrations per second), for example, "Do" –or its equivalent "C"- has as one of its frequencies 261.63 Hertz (Hz), "Re" –or "D"- 293.665 Hz and so on. The Solfège scale gives us seven well-defined notes but those seven notes, alone, do not cover the whole range of possible notes within the audible range. To achieve this we repeat this note pattern throughout the audible scale thus:

...Do-Re-Mi-Fa-Sol-La-Si / Do-Re-Mi-Fa-Sol-La-Si / Do-Re-Mi-Fa-Sol-La-Si / Do-Re-Mi-Fa....

Each "Do" to the next "Do" sequence is called an octave and it turns out that we can fit about 10 octaves within the normal human hearing range, these octaves are numbered from 0 to 9 in order to identify them and distinguish the different possible "Dos" or "Res", etc. in the range. We also find that each note in any octave is exactly double the frequency of it's similarly named note one octave below, so for example "Do-0" has a frequency of 16.35 Hz, "Do-1" 32.70 Hz, "Do-2" 65.41 Hz and so on. Once again time shows us its patterns and order. In fact, the notes are so well ordered that the frequency of each one of them can be described by a mathematical formula:

$$\text{Note Frequency} = 2^{n/12} * 440 \text{ (Hz)}$$

By convention, this formula defines 440Hz as a reference frequency belonging to the note "La-4" or "A-4" which is taken to be the tuning reference note for all instruments and, thus, all other notes are defined with reference to this note. In the formula, "n" is the number of steps you are away from the base note, for example, Do-4 ("C-4") at 261.63 Hz is -9 steps from the tuning reference so it's n=-9.

Although most people can agree as to whether a sound is pleasing or not to the ear, it is very rare for someone to be able to directly identify and name a note with the precision that we have just defined them here. According to research "Absolute Pitch", as this phenomenon is called, is only something that about 1 in 10,000 people are capable of achieving[6]. One famous person doted with this gift was Wolfgang Amadeus Mozart who is said that not only was he able to name precisely any note played, he could also memorize and reproduce whole musical pieces after hearing them just once.

Here is a quote from a biography of the great master written by E. O. Deutsch[7]:

> *"Furthermore, I saw and heard how, when he was made to listen in another room, they would give him notes, now high, now low, not only on the pianoforte but on every other imaginable instrument as well, and he came out with the letter of the name of the note in an instant. Indeed, on hearing a bell toll, or a clock or even a pocket watch strike, he was able at the same moment to name the note of the bell or time piece"*
>
> MOZART: A DOCUMENTARY BIOGRAPHY. E.O. DEUTSCH

So we have achieved naming pleasing pure sounds or notes which we make by vibrating matter (strings, air, vocal cords, etc.) a certain number of times a second. Time has been turned into pleasing sound but we still do not have music and so we need to continue our search.

If we want to start making music we need to continue playing with time, notes will be like bricks to a house, they really start to work when you organize them together. When we put notes together in a sequence, that is, played one after the other in time, we begin making musical phrases, just like spoken phrases. When we find a musical phrase we like or find pleasing we may have a "melody". The melody is usually the most recognizable part of a song, we usually remember or recognize songs by their melodies. Melodies are notes in time, notes are vibrations per second, time unfolding over time in a pleasing sequence.

At first thought, you might think that with seven notes, the number of melodies might be limited and that some day we will run out of melodies that have not been invented. In fact the sequence from Do to Si has 12 notes, the other 5 notes are notes that lie in-between the 7 "natural" notes already mentioned, the in-between notes are called "accidentals" and are denoted as sharp (♯) or flat (♭) versions of the natural notes and are pronounced as "C sharp" or "C flat" and written as "C ♯ " and "C ♭ " respectively. So the complete sequence of 12 notes in our western system is:

1	Do	C
2	Do♯ or Re♭	C♯ or D♭
3	Re	D
4	Re♯ or Mi♭	D♯ or E♭
5	Mi	E
6	Fa	F
7	Fa♯ or Sol♭	F♯ or G♭
8	Sol	G
9	Sol♯ or La♭	G♯ or A♭
10	La	A
11	La♯ or Si♭	A♯ or B♭
12	Si	B

Musical Notes

Observe how each "in-between" note can be named as a "sharp" (ie. Slightly higher in frequency) or "flat" (ie. Slightly lower in frequency) depending on whether it is referenced to the note above of below. Also note that there are two intervals: one between Mi and Fa and the other between Si and Do that do not have sharps or flats between them, there is no mistake here, this is only the case because we chose historically to divide the octave into 12 notes and has remained this way throughout time. This particular definition is what gives pianos their traditional keyboard distribution between the white keys and black keys. The white keys being the natural notes while the black keys being the sharps and flats.

So going back to our original question of whether with only 12 notes at our disposal to compose all the music in the world we might run out of novel or new note patterns, we can use a bit of maths to find that once all the combinations are taken into consideration and using the whole human auditory range, the quantity of possible melodies runs into several million (26.9 million for a seven-note scale). Once we add chords and rhythm the numbers skyrocket to the billions[8].

Harmony

Sound, melody and rhythm all combine along time as a sequence of events to conform music. The last component of music we will describe is the one concerned with simultaneity in time, when events happen at the same time and that is what is called in music, Harmony.

Harmony is the addition of different notes, which are played at the same time, to create a new sound which is still pleasing to the ear but which is perceived as having more "depth". Since more than one note is being played together the sound has the quality of being more complex which makes it more interesting to our minds. Guitar chords are an example of notes that, when played together, form a harmony of sound.

Undoubtedly the whole subject of music is well beyond the scope of this book, the remarkable aspect that I have considered here is the way music and time seem to be intricately fused together. Well beyond the common figure of speech of "keeping time" to the music, music *is* time. Notes are defined by the number of times of a vibration, melody and rhythm use the notes to construct musical pieces sequentially and repetitively in time and finally, the simultaneity of harmony adds depth and complexity to each individual musical time instant. Time playing, unfolding and coming together to create patterns that stimulate our minds and bodies.

Music for the mind

However and wherever music is created it has profound effects on our minds and bodies. There is a lot of investigation into this subject by several fields of study including the medical, neurological and physiological areas as well as the social sciences. Music is seen as a very in-rooted aspect of what makes us human. For a start it is not clear whether other species have a sense for music, some researchers have pointed out to parrots, apes, dolphins and others, as species that have some sense of rhythm recognition but no irrefutable proof has been put forward, even Charles Darwin devoted quite a few pages in his book "Descent of Man" to the subject, describing how on investigating the effects of music on animals, he went several times to London Zoo to play the harmonica to "Jenny", an orang-utan. Suffice it to say that Jenny was not very moved by his performance and no significant observation was described by Darwin as a result of this particular experiment [9].

Most studies tend to point to the fact that the music-related reactions that we see in animals are in fact sequences and responses learned due to some sort of behaviour training or repetition and not something that is innately recognized by the animal. An example of this is the sport called Horse-Dressage that is normally performed to music. Although it may seem that the horse is following the music by the way we see it mark the rhythm and keep in perfect step with it, in fact, the horse is quite unmoved by the music and is only following a learned routine.

The second big debate in this field of music perception relates to whether or not our brain has a specific area dedicated to the interpretation of music or whether it just "piggy-backs" on other sensory processing areas such as speech and language[10]. Not being a scientist expert in this area, I rather like the idea of music "piggy-backing" and in effect inundating other sensory areas. If you think about your own personal experience with music you will agree that when we listen to our favourite recording, we seem to feel a lot of our sensory systems within our brain activate. Apart from activating memory, music has the key to open our emotions, music can make us happy, sad, melancholic, angry, romantic and most of all the other emotions we have accumulated in our lives. Some studies even mention that just like a particular memory is able to re-enact some of the same neural patterns associated with the time when the event in memory took place, music can transmit some of the same neural footprints that the artists, composer and performer, had when the musical piece was created or performed. This can explain the synergy that we experience in a concert, where thousands of people are tuning in to the musical, and hence neural, patterns being performed by the artists. You could even think of this effect as a kind of synchronizer of our minds, a way for our minds to connect in synchrony with others and experience the same feelings and emotions.

This same synchronization effect that music (melody and rhythm) has on our minds has also been studied and is an important aspect of the way we experience music. Our neurons seem to respond and resonate to music and hence tend to exhibit a more orderly behaviour in harmony to what is being heard. The more general term for this effect is called neuroplasticity and describes how our brain is capable of changing throughout our lives as a consequence of sensory input, motor action, reward or awareness[11]. This fact has been used to explain how music helps patients suffering from motor diseases such as Parkinson's or dementia. On hearing music the mind and body seem to "sync-up" and the effects of the condition decreases while the music is being experienced by the sufferer. This is dramatically seen on tests with musicians that are suffering from dementia, although they may walk with difficulty, have difficulty in remembering their children's names or what they had for breakfast, once they start playing their instruments, they can perform unhindered and just as they did before their ailment[12].

An interesting aspect in all the current research is that there is no particular type of music that causes these effects, in general, all music does and the music that works best is the particular music that each individual person likes and has as favourite. If music has this profound universal effect on us and is able to "interfere" with our sensory perception systems, it is no surprise that it can also play havoc with our time perception. When music evokes memories it makes us travel in time. When it engages us fully it suspends the notion of time passing, making it seem like time has no relevance, as when you attend a concert by your favourite artist or group and once the concert ends you believe that it has only just started brief moments before. On the contrary, if you are taken to a concert of music that you don't particularly enjoy (maybe accompanying a loved one), those couple of hours can seem like an eternity!

Too much sound?

On Earth, most things make sounds, our air is filled with sounds and we hear them all the time, unfortunately, a lot of the sounds we hear are artificial, man-made sounds and it has become a serious problem with what is now called, noise pollution. Some studies show that man-made noise pollution has become so intense that even in protected wildlife areas in the US, the level of noise pollution can be 10 times the natural background sound level[13]. Sound does a good job in travelling through matter and the more matter there is, the better and further it travels. So when we go beyond land, in the denser medium of water, sound propagates much faster and for longer distances, this fact has brought severe problems to ocean wildlife with whales beaching for no apparent reason, porpoise found dead with severe internal brain haemorrhages and many other disastrous effects. One of the sources of this underwater noise is sea traffic, consider that over 90% of the worldwide goods we consume travel by sea at some point of their journey, that is around 50,000 ship[14], each one containing an extremely noisy diesel engine as its source of power. Another source of underwater noise pollution is the use of sonar devices for commercial and military activity.

Noise pollution in the oceans is much worse than what we experience on land but since it is inaudible to us not only are we not aware of it but also we do not regard the negative effects it is having on the underwater eco-system. In the underwater world where thousands of animal species live, vision is not much use since even in clear waters light does not travel far before being absorbed, on the other hand, sound travels for great distances without any problems and so for water dwellers, it is the main tool for communication and orientation. On land and using vision we can see mountains that are many kilometres away, we even see stars that are millions of kilometres away (our sun for example)[15], imagine for a second changing this vision-centred paradigm to an audio-centred one where the same capabilities that vision offers us on land are available to us in water, in such a case, if we were in water, near the west coast of the US then we would be able to hear a sound that was emitted in the Indian Ocean, or if we were in the east coast of the US we would hear sounds emanating from the coast of Europe or Africa. This is exactly how sea creatures experience their environment. If we add the interference that man-made noise has brought into their habitat, sea creatures are constantly being bombarded with extreme levels of noise, the equivalent of our land environment being flooded with high-intensity light and hence blinding us with its power. The sound transmission capability of the sea is so powerful that during the Cold War a listening and monitoring system was constructed by the US in order to surveil USSR submarine activity, the system was called SOSUS (Sound Surveillance System) and it is still in use today, amongst it's more civilian uses is the constant monitoring of natural activity such as earthquakes or volcanoes[16]. A highly recommended documentary about our noisy oceans is Discovery Channel's award-winning documentary called "Sonic Sea", where the effects of ocean noise on ocean life[17], such as whales and dolphins[18], is clearly seen at first hand.

II

PART II: TIME FOR LIFE

8

TIME TO BE BORN

Life and Death

FROM THE TIME we are conceived, we become part of the fabric of time. It doesn't matter whether we live for 100 seconds or 100 years, we have become, and are a part of, this mesh that we call time. Every living creature develops on this virtual stage; every living creature has a limited, although unknown, "run" in this race.

I used the phrase "run in this race" in the previous paragraph as a metaphor to describe the act of living for a limited period and to avoid the use of the word "time" to define itself, and this is an interesting observation of the way we take the definition of time for granted. Time is something so embedded in our lives and in our *selves* that it is part of us, nevertheless, this same familiarity has meant that we tend not to take much notice of it and disregard its importance and meaning. Isn't it strange that although we have many types of different professions, careers and specializations into which we mould ourselves, we do not have "Time Engineering" or "Time Studies" or even "Timeology" or "Chronology" as a university major?

In itself, the very definition of time poses several problems even for the most experienced of scientists since they are still trying to fathom the complexities of the concept. Here we will not delve much into the science of time but we will concentrate more on its effects on us, as people, and on the lives we live.

From our point of view, even before we are born we are experiencing time, time in its most delicate and precious state, every initial second of our life has a tremendous effect on our future, cell division and cell ordering at the very onset of gestation will have profound effects throughout the rest of our existence, the perfection of the DNA sequences inherited from our parents, the way they will bind together and reproduce are crucial at this moment of time.

At this stage, every second counts: imagine the precise moment when you are "one second old", at that moment just the passing of another second has doubled your lifespan: each one of those two precious first seconds of life account for a whole 50% of your entire life! This process of second-accumulation will repeat itself throughout your lifetime adding relentless seconds, minutes and hours to your life. On this same scale, we see how those seconds will seem to diminish in importance, for example, by the time you are 30 years old, you will have amassed 946,080,000 seconds, the next second to tick over accounts only for 0.0000001% of your total lifespan, almost insignificant you might think.

In human foetal development every second counts: at 2.5 million seconds (week 4) the spinal cord and brain start to appear, at 3 million seconds (week 5) the heart, lungs, liver, gallbladder, pancreas and spleen start to make their appearance and at 3.6 million seconds (week 6) it's the turn of the eyes, the extremities, blood, kidneys and stomach. All our major organs are already on their way to being developed before we are 4 million seconds old. In our lifetime journey, that amounts to only about 0.2% of our total existence.

If and when we reach the grand old age of 80 years we would have lived for over 2.5 billion seconds (2.5 thousand million) each second of our lives accounting for just an 0.00000004% of our total life.

If we talk about the start of life then it is only fair that we also touch on the other end of the time scale, the point where we are no more, Death. At some stage, once we have a conscience and we start to experience life, we will learn that all living things eventually will cease to exist. This moment of realization may happen when one of our pets dies or when we have to experience the first death in our family or one of our friends. That's when we realise that this –death- will also happen to the ones we have around us, the ones we love and also it will happen to ourselves. As the popular saying goes, *the only sure thing about life is that we will die*.

Unlike life, death treats us all in the same way, in that sense we can think of it as very "democratic" and just. It doesn't matter who we are or what we have done during our lives, we will all end our days of existence at some point. We may have been the best person who ever lived: helping others, being a great discoverer of new places or theories or even cures to terrible diseases. On the other hand, we could have been the worst human being that ever lived: having killed thousands or made people suffer just to enrich ourselves or to take some advantage, it doesn't matter, the end will be the same for all of us.

Although this may sound somewhat fatalist I believe that this is a clear sign that life has to be lived here and now, it is no good going through life worried that it will end, that is a sure way not to make the most of it. My belief is that life is the reason we exist, it is the journey, death is just something that happens at the end. The point is to enjoy the journey, trying to be the best person we can be, having good and loving relationships all around you and choosing to live by your principles and values.

Because death is an irreversible state (nobody has come back from it save some stories associated with myths and religions) we have a general fear of it, of being no more. This fear has been exploited by some religions where it has been used to reassure people of the continuity of their existence beyond death through the belief in a particular afterlife. Ultimately, belief in the continuity of our existence or an afterlife after our bodies are consumed will always require a "leap of faith" since, as I have mentioned, there is no scientific evidence to sustain any of the life-after-life religious claims.

If you are curious as to what it will be like after you die, my personal view is that we all know exactly what it will be like. I believe that when we die, we go back to the same, exact state we were in before we were born, the state that we have all already been, the state of just not-existing, the state of not-being. So how does it feel? Well, it doesn't. Try to remember what it was like before you were born. Well, you can't since your perception and memory systems were not functioning, that is, they did not even exist, nothing could be sensed or remembered, nothing could be imagined, nothing could be felt. But although there is no memory or sensibility you can conclude that it was nothing bad or undesirable. There is no feeling, there is no anguish or fear associated with the state of not being. It just is.

When we are no more, our atoms will disassemble from the human structure that they were and become other structures, the energy that had gathered to become “you” does not cease to exist but dissipates and enters other states or beings, as pure energy. Our consciousness disappears since the conditions that gave rise for it to exist are no more. Our mind is no more and so what we call “us” or “I” is no more, just as it was before we were born.

There is nothing sad about this, it’s the way matter behaves, it’s the way energy behaves, accumulating, giving form and power and then waning, dissipating, travelling and gathering in other spaces to start the cycle once again.

I believe that what we call life is created by the conditions found in our planet, indeed if these same conditions were to be found in other planets then surely life, similar to the one we observe around us, will also arise.

In the same way, our conscious selves, “us”, our minds, exist because of the conditions found in this organic structure we call our bodies. Once the conditions disappear then the mind also disappears leaving the energy and fundamental atoms free to create other materials or living organisms. In this case I am just talking about pure matter, atoms and energy that will take other forms, I am not proposing what could be termed “re-incarnation” where the belief is that aspects of the mind are transferred from the deceased being onto another being, as I stated, I believe that the mind exists only when there is a body structure to support it, once the structure is gone the mind ceases to exist.

For some people, this crude and matter-of-fact account of what we are is not acceptable since it appears that the process has no purpose or importance. That particular way of understanding life seems to me to be a fabrication of our minds in order to manage the fear we have of death. In itself, the fear of death is not a bad thing and in fact, it serves as a protection mechanism and is something that we need to have around to survive and extend our lives! After all, we don't walk in front of a bus because we *fear* that it may injure or kill us.

Survival is one of the skills we develop early in life and it is mostly acquired from our parents and our surroundings together with some basic instincts that we bring into the equation from before we are even born.

But why do we need to survive if we know we will eventually die? We won't delve into this philosophical question here although if we see life as a journey, as we stated earlier, then the question starts to make less sense since it seems that the point to life is to create our own road to travel and to be fulfilled by the journey and not so much by the final destination. In other words, the ultimate experience of time will arise during our journey and not when we reach the final destination.

We will expand some of these topics in the following chapters, for now, let's go back to timely issues.

Ages and Numbers

As we progress through this journey called life, how do we measure the time that has passed? How old are we at any particular time? These questions seem common and easy enough to answer but when we analyse them a bit further, we might be a little surprised. The minute you are born you are zero years old and you are living, although you haven't yet completed, your first year of life, year one. When you celebrate your first birthday, you are celebrating that you have completed and survived one year and from that moment on you start to live your second year. This repeats through life, of course, each year celebrating the completion of a year and the start of a new one. So for example on the day you celebrate your 35th birthday, you have already completed your 35th year of life and are now starting to live your 36th year on Earth.

This may seem somewhat confusing but it is only a consequence of the way we have agreed to count things and the numbering system that we use. Originally and by necessity, we invented a way to count tangible things like sheep, trees, stones etc. the natural way was to invent some conceptual representation for each group of things, for example, "three" means "a group composed of more than two but less than four things". We see that even trying to define a particular number, is no mean feat. It is not easy to make this definition without having to refer to the number itself in a recurring fashion. Think back to the beginning of this chapter and the similarities this problem of definition has on how we tried to define "time" itself without recurring to using the word "time" in the definition in an iterative way. Even when we look at the definition of a number and refer to standard dictionaries such as the Oxford Dictionary we find that it states the following for its definition of "Three":

> "Equivalent to the sum of one and two; one more than two; 3"[1].

Webster's dictionary does it in a similar way "a number that is one more than 2", this dictionary even offers a second definition: "the third in a set or series"[2]. All very confusing!

More than tangible entities numbers are in fact concepts, ways of expressing an occurrence in the real world for which no tangible object can be found. Within this family of what we call numbers, "zero" is even more intriguing and goes far beyond its own definition and needs a bigger conceptual jump in order to understand. It is believed that the initial concept of zero was not so much that of a number but in fact, just a "placeholder" when doing arithmetic calculations. This idea is first encountered in records written by the Sumerians, the first people to develop a counting system, over 4,000 years ago, although their idea was not the full zero concept we understand today, it was going in the right direction. If we jump in time to about 300 BCE we observe that the Babylonians had refined this concept and were now using a symbol to denote this placeholder in their calculations. Interestingly enough, in quite an independent way, as far as we know, in the Americans, the Mayan culture also developed the concept of zero and we see that in around 350 CE it was used in their elaborate calendar systems.

Most scholars agree that the current use of zero originated in India around 450 CE and that whether independently derived or as a consequence of the previous knowledge imparted by the ancient world, it was also linked to the spiritual notion of emptiness or void. From this point, the concept spread to China, the Middle East and the

Arabic world until a Persian mathematician, Mohammed ibn-Musa al-Khowarizmi, suggested that a little circle should be used to denote it.[3] The spread into Europe was somewhat more tortuous since it coincided with the period of the crusades in which everything that came from the east was seen as undesirable and blasphemous. So much so that in 1299, zero was banned in Florence along with all Arabic numerals![4] Two centuries had to pass for zero and all the other numbers to be finally accepted in European academic institutions. Nowadays, of course, zero sits at the very root of the information revolution and digitalization as computing systems are based on the idea of the existence of 0 (and 1 of course!). Zero is such a fascinating subject that there are countless books written about it and there is even a foundation that promotes research on the subject, ZerOrig-India (www.zerorigindia.org).

Just to show some of the complexities of the number-concept that is zero we can think of the following example: It is very easy to visualize a number concept when someone uses it, if we say that there are 3 books we understand immediately what we mean, there are some books and their number is exactly more than 2 and less than 4, visually we could imagine that if we held a book in each hand we would have another book that we could not hold, that is three. In the same way, if we talked about having zero books, then we could imagine holding out our empty hands, having no books to hold. If we took the same concept to something less tangible like temperature, which we also measure using numbers, we can learn to understand what 30° C feels like on your body as opposed to say, 10° C. Indeed we also learn to understand what zero degrees feel like (if you live away from the equator!) but in this case zero has a very different meaning. In this case, it does not mean the absence of something, 0° C does not mean that there is no temperature, in fact, it is a very tangible and real experience! It is only referring to the relative sensations that we feel when experiencing the energy that is present in our surroundings and to the way we have agreed to measure those sensations.

For the purposes of counting time, zero is also essential: it is the starting point of each day as the clocks show 00:00 hours, it is also the start of every minute and every second. There is a big exception when we count years: in the Gregorian calendar (the calendar we use nowadays in the western world) and also in the old Julian calendar there is no year zero, no 0 CE or 0 BCE, in both of these systems year 1 BCE is immediately followed by year 1 CE. But we can find examples of other calendars in which there indeed exists a year zero, notably the Buddhist and Hindu calendars. In the case of the Buddhist calendar, year zero identifies the point in time when the Buddha achieved the state of Nirvana.

Parenting

Going back to the start of a human life, but this time from the point of view of the parent, we can say that it is definitely not easy. Although there are some books or "manuals" nowadays, it's never enough to prepare you for the immense change that parenthood brings to your life. Most of the changes are good; some will give you a new perspective on life while others may challenge some of your basic principles. That feeling when you see the pure, innocent and loving face with which your children look at you searching for answers without a motive other than that primal bond that binds a child and its parents, is something that unless you have had the experience, is very difficult to explain. It has it's roots in the responsibility you feel, all of a sudden, as you realize that the survival of that being is completely and utterly in your hands coupled with the intense feeling that he or she is a part of you, just as real as any part of your own body and hence requires the same care and attention. In that same way, you also realize that even your own life falls into second place when you think of the life of your children, that's the way the primitive survival instinct that we carry within us suddenly switches on and its primary objective is the survival of your offspring even over your own life.

Once you know, as a couple, that you are "expecting" there are no real changes that can be observed. The infamous morning sickness that may be suffered by your partner is quite real and very tiresome, but talking as a man, the changes at this stage are small. I will not pretend to give an account of pregnancy from the female perspective as it would be, and would sound false and contrived, so I will just limit myself to my own, perhaps narrow, male-experience, I apologise for this.

Birth

In the days when my wife and I had the experience of being first-time parents, in the early 1990s, ultrasound scans were performed only after the first trimester of gestation. Until that time the only signs of change were in my wife's morning drowsiness and a general feeling we had of entering into a new and very much expected but unknown stage in our relationship. A new shared experience. Our lives were little affected and all that was about to happen was read, talked about or felt, but nothing could be seen, smelled, heard or touched, not yet. The external senses played no part at this stage, it was more about our innermost world of feeling, imagining and planning. Planning plays a part when you start thinking of the space the new baby will need, the clothes that will have to be bought, the things that might need changing around the house, the small and big changes in our future daily routine.

At times worry also creeps in. It's so easy to think of all the things that can go wrong within those nine months of pregnancy. My rational self, at times, played the awful probabilistic game with itself when it started thinking that of all the millions of processes, chemical reactions, physical changes, biological combinations that must take place during this time, surely the probability of failure is large. But, immediately the same rational side of my brain responded that in most cases, most things go right. That's the beauty of life.

After the first trimester then, it's time for that first ultrasound scan. The first time we get to see visual clues of what is going on, the first time there will be more information as to how all this is really developing. It is a true wonder that our bodies are capable of all this construction, all of it executed on a sub-conscious, "automatic" mode. The woman has no conscious control of what goes on inside her body. The different stages of growth follow one another carried along inexorably by the unfolding of time. Atoms combine, molecules and cells are created, arranged and deployed exactly when and where they are needed in an automatic symphony that creates the living being that is dictated by the primal score sheet in the form of the DNA recipe inherited from our parents.

The ultrasound scan is our first visual contact with this unfolding hidden world. Laying on her back with her mini-bump exposed, my wife and I were ready, or so we thought, for that first encounter. The monitor screen started to show what seemed to us like some random light and dark areas, it was a very basic type of screen. In 1992, when this took place, there were no 3D, HD, full-colour images for this type of exam procedure. What you actually saw on the screen looked more like the image you see on a television when you tune in to a channel that has no signal or that is not working properly, the only difference being that it was darker and the dots moved at a slower speed. At one point among those black, white and grey spots on the screen, we started to see a pattern. Some of the dots seemed to have organized themselves and joined in groups, even more so, some of them seemed to be switching on and off in some sort of recognizable rhythm. Out of all the rest of the screen that seemed like a random mess of noise there were four spot-clusters that seemed to be turning on and off together at a certain coherent rhythm.

Once we spotted this pattern on the screen and without any knowledge or training as to how to interpret what we were observing, speculations set in within our minds: "Maybe it's just a sort of machine-type-scanner-type of rhythm that is generated by the interference of the ultra-sound waves" – I thought bringing in my engineer-me into the stage. I quickly eliminated that possibility when the doctor moved the ultrasound sensor and the light and dark spots stayed in their place with a very distinctive sense of them showing that there was definitely something "real" there. My second guess was, and this time based on my very basic knowledge of biology at the time, that it was the heart. Yes, it must be the heart, the rhythmic pulse fitted into what I had read somewhere – babies have a much faster pulse rate – "It must be the heart and what we are seeing on screen must be the ventricles beating" – I thought clutching at every biological straw I could manage. This went on for some time, apparently, the doctor wanted to take a good detailed look at the heart, making sure there were no abnormalities.

At one point the doctor declared "The heart". "Yessss" – I thought, a fine guess from my part! He carried on exploring this region for some time, from various angles, so much so that I started to get worried that he might have spotted some abnormality or malformation.

It is interesting how all this thinking was going on in both, my wife's and my own mind but in a very internal mode, together but separate since, apart from the noises of the machines around us, there was complete silence, we just held hands. Each one of us intensely trying to collect all the clues possible from what we were experiencing in order to know how to interpret all this information.

Finally, the doctor spoke – "It all looks fine", he started – "I see two hearts".

With just that single phrase everything fell to bits for what seemed like an eternity.

Malformation of the heart, a sick child, a child that might be born dead.

What did we do wrong?
What happened?
Is my wife safe?
What happens now?
What do we do?

"I see two hearts. You have twins and it all looks

perfectly fine" - the doctor spoke once again. More silence, time stopped.

The gentle holding of our hands turned into an intense clutch. An avalanche of feelings: happiness that everything was fine, confusion, fear, happiness and more confusion.

The words "It all looks perfectly fine" repeated again and again in our heads. We looked at each other and smiled a deep loving smile. Then the questions, this time not in our heads but said out loud one after the other: "Are there any complications?", "Is there any abnormality?", "Are they fully separated?", "Is everything OK?", "Is EVERYTHING OK?".

"It all looks perfectly fine" – the doctor repeated.

The four light and dark dotted areas continued their titillation. Our hands continued clutched.

I couldn't say how long this went on, the expression on our faces transmitting all the questions and doubts as well as the emotions of the moment. The doctor then says "I will step out and leave you two alone for a little while". The embrace, the tears. Not only had we created a new life. There were two people hidden inside those four light and dark areas, which in the end turned out to be two pairs of heart ventricles and "It all looked perfectly fine".

Our twins were born six months later, in perfect condition. They are identical twins, that is, created from a single egg-sperm combination that divided spontaneously to form two separate embryos. This happened as a random event, during the first five days of gestation, that is, within the first 432,000 seconds of life. Even up to this moment in time, science does not have an explanation or reason as to why this spontaneous division takes place although when measured across cultures it is found to be evenly distributed and to affect approximately 3 in 1,000 conceptions. A random occurrence in our lives, of which we consider ourselves to be infinitely lucky.

9

TIME IS NOW

IF WE DIVIDE time into three separate and distinct epochs: *Before* - *Now* – *After* and consider *Before* as everything that has already happened, *After* as everything that has not yet happened and finally *Now* as everything that is happening at this instant in time we can come to some very interesting observations and conclusions as to how we perceive and interact with time. To start with we note that all three epochs are linked and interconnected together in the following way,

> *Now* becomes *Before* just as *After* becomes *Now* and as we shall see, *Before* is an essential part of preparing for the coming *After*s. They belong together, to a continuum that cannot be separated.

Before / After

But, when is *Now*? As soon as we even say the word "Now", that time has already become *Before*. This is the way we really experience time every moment of our lives, time permanently advancing and unfolding in a continuum of *After-Now-Before* and as we will see also flowing in the other direction, that is, *Before-Now-After*. We can imagine this flow as something similar to the symbol for "infinity", ∞, with *Now* right in the middle at the intersection of *Before* and *After*.

Now, let us separate our physical or **material** perceptions, that is: what we see, hear, touch, taste and smell, from our non-physical or **immaterial** perceptions that is: what we feel, think, remember and imagine. Combining these two ideas of a continuum of time flow and the way we perceive it in the physical and non-physical sense, we could say that there is a material flow perceived which moves from *After* to *Before*, with the things we actually sense, and an immaterial flow perceived which moves from *Before* to *After*, with the things we imagine, think or remember.

Material: Before ← After
Immaterial: Before → After

It is through the material flow or path that we experience the real world, using our external senses to experience the effects of this flow as we see, touch, smell, hear and taste the world around us. This is a very external-to-our-body path where our surroundings play a vital role. The immaterial flow representing the path from *Before* to *After*, uses past experiences, that is: *Afters,* stored in our memory to evoke thoughts and emotions that enable us to understand the world and play a key role in how we experience our *Now* and even prepare to receive the new *Afters*.

. . .

We use memory, learning, concept association and other techniques to bring back the *Before* to the *Now*, in a very internal-to-our-body path. The external physical body sensorial system does not play a role in this process although we can still "see", "touch", "smell", "hear" and even "taste" through internal *feeling,* this time not using our external senses but our internal ones evoked by the memories of past experiences. These evocations can be just as powerful as the experiences that our external senses provide, a very sad memory can make us just as sad as when the event happened and even bring tears to your eyes, a feeling of despair can be just as strong as the despair felt in the real, original experience.

So, what we have called the physical flow, the one that we can perceive with our external senses, goes from *After* to *Before*, the future that has not yet happened will become sensed as *Now* and then flow into the past to become *Before*. The other flow, the one we have called the immaterial flow, is generated by elements stored in our memory, learned in the past that can bring the *Before* into the *Now*, that is, the past into the present. Our ability to plan for the future comes from using our *Before* and our imagination, which enables us to feel and predict possible *Afters* before they become *Nows*, in other words, our experience helps us to foresee, prepare and even act upon possible future events. Our *Before* is a key feature when it comes to interpreting *Nows* and eventual *Afters*, in this case, it is the use of *Before* in conjunction with our imaginative capacity that allows us to achieve interpretation and prediction.

The Now Singularity

One of the key things to realise is that both paths, the material and immaterial communicate and connect through the *Now* combining and making each moment different in a never-ending, infinite, mix of past-present-future experiences. In this way of viewing time, *Now* becomes an incredibly rare and interesting point: a singularity, a unique point in space-time where things behave in a very special manner. Take our senses: touch, sight, hearing, smell and taste, these senses only work in this *Now*-singularity point, only at this precise infinitesimally small moment, our external senses are truly at work, at all other times they are totally useless. Just imagine how important this singularity point is for evolution to have managed to accomplish the refinement of five parallel ways of sensing it. It truly is a wonder of nature that such an infinitesimally small event in time requires so much investment, but it is that particular point that can make the difference between our survival and our demise.

Although the real *Now* is transient and ephemeral, we can still recreate the feel of how something was sensed and perceived using our internal immaterial *Before* in order to "replay" a *Now* as many times as we desire, sometimes we even store triggers in our *Before* so that the mere act of recalling or sensing them recreate a past *Now*, as an example: when a piece of music evokes a particular aroma or feeling, or when a particular taste evokes a moment in time.

We can even think that since our experience of the world is through this *Now*-singularity, it is this singularity, our own singularity, that is travelling through time, collecting the *After*, processing it and storing the useful stuff in our *Before*. Alternatively, we can think of this Now-singularity as a two-dimensional plane or permeable barrier separating our *Before* from our *After*, everything that comes *After* is filtered through the singularity plane and when it passes, it becomes *Before*. This *Before* is the accumulation of all the experiences that leave a mark as they pass the singularity plane and through our internal processes and are finally stored as memories that can be evoked once again.

Each one of the three epochs has its own tools to be able to work and process the information that flows through it:

EPOCH	TOOLS AVAILABLE
Before	Memory, Imagination, Learning, Analysis, Thinking, Creativity, Intelligence, Intuition, Reflexes, Prediction, Planning
Now	Vision, Hearing, Smell, Taste, Touch
After	All the combined effects of *Before* and *Now*

Before / Now / After Tools

The elements listed for *Before* (above) are not meant to be necessarily all the tools that our mind has at its disposal and includes some elements that are combinations of others, like "intelligence" for example, but it serves to make the point that we have a large set of tools and skills available to us to help manage our *Befores*.

We can see that our *Before* is where most of our skills and abilities reside, our mind provides us with imagination, creativity, memory, learning, analysis, etc. as essential tools for our survival, so much so that these are the elements that distinguish our species from others, gorillas may have strength, cheetahs speed, lions power but humans have an incredible set of, mostly hidden, skills for survival and they all reside in the power of our minds. Our *Now* has the external sensing tools that we are all familiar with and that, although we take for granted most of the time, are the essential tools that allow us to cope with the external world. When it comes to the *After* we note that we have not assigned it any particular set of intrinsic tools, there seems to be nothing particularly developed to cope with this epoch. In fact this is quite the opposite since all the tools and skills we have just described and that reside within the *Before* and *Now* are there exclusively to work together and help us navigate and travel through the *After*, we need all our skills in order to cope with the unknown future so the toolset for the *After* is the combined set of skills present in the *Before* and *Now* all designed and working in conjunction in order to move us forward through the time that has not already passed.

This is Now

We have defined *Now* as the moment in time when our external senses are truly at work, in other words, *Now* is when you truly see something, or when you truly touch something. It is more difficult than we realise to be at *Now*, our mind tends to take us into *Before* and *After* constantly, swiftly and effortlessly remembering, analysing, predicting, combining in its continuous, infinite and tireless mind grind. Most of the time we may need to work hard in order to experience how it feels to be at *Now*, one way to focus on how it feels to be at this singularity is to concentrate purely on what our five senses are experiencing at any particular time. As an exercise sit in your office, apartment, park or anywhere and with your eyes open concentrate on what your five senses are detecting. What do you see?, What smells are you able to identify? What do you hear? –Traffic? children playing, birds, the air-conditioning system?- Can you taste anything? What does your skin feel? –cold?, wind?, heat?- or What can you feel in your hands? Try to keep this multi-sensory experience for a few minutes, don't delve into any sense in particular, just get a sense of all these multiple feelings all at once. The most important thing is not to let your mind take over and wander into *Before* or *After*. If you can achieve and maintain this state for some time you can truly say that you are experiencing *Now*.

This realization that *Now* is an infinitesimally small, transient and fragile state has even driven some philosophers to state that the world we live in is just imaginary. In the real *Now* sense they are mostly right, if you compare the three epochs (*Before-Now-After*) at any particular point in time, *Before* and *After* are phenomenally larger than *Now*. You could correctly state that most of our existence is spent in an imaginary world. On the other hand, if you imagine that your *Now* is, in fact, a point travelling in time, then that point has lasted and will last for as long as you live, accumulating time travel throughout your life. In that sense, you can argue that instantaneously in time, *Now* is infinitesimally small but its accumulated trajectory through time extends for several years.

Our senses are always at work. Usually, our mind receives and processes the information generated by our sensory organs as a background task and most of the time we are not even consciously aware of our surroundings unless something is detected as being out-of-the-ordinary or a sudden change is perceived and our mind quickly informs us of this situation. Although this may seem like a huge waste of available information, it is a key component of our brain, since if we were aware of everything that surrounds us all the time, we wouldn't have time to think about anything else! That is why the previous exercise of trying to bring the senses into the conscious mind is a great exercise in being aware of how the real *Now* feels and of the large quantity of information our minds are really receiving all the time. A further experience of how to focus on *Now* can also be attempted with an exercise that is similar to the previous one but this time you concentrate for some time on only one of the senses and explore all the minute details that you pick up with just that sensory organ. For example, Hearing: try to block out your *Before* and *After* and also the other four senses, what do you hear? How many things can you hear? Which of those things are loud? Which are soft? Are there human sounds? Are there sounds of nature? Machine sounds? As you will realise if you perform this experiment, it will require a lot of concentration and will power to maintain the focus on only one sense since the suppression of *Before* and *After* and also of the other four senses becomes hard work for your mind.

The most "*Now*" experiences we have are the ones that connect us directly to the essence of being alive and that are the most basic of experiences that make us human. All these experiences have one thing in common and that is that all of our external senses are involved in a very active manner. Some examples are Eating, Sex, Hunting, Fighting and Fleeing. In each one of these cases, all our sensory organs play a vital role in creating the particular experience of being immersed in *Now*.

Delving Deeper

Let us explore this even further to see if it sheds some light into our journey-through-time experience. Say, for the purposes of a thought experiment, that we are immersed in a world where there is no *Before*, this would be a reality where we would not have the capacity to store memories, learn or recall earlier events, in this case, everything we experience at *Now* would always be a new experience and so we would have no way to manage any new situations. This is such a strange and fascinating scenario that several books and movies have explored the theme, for example, the film "50 First Dates" a comedy in which the main character finds himself in the situation of meeting, and falling in love, with a girl who suffers from short-term memory amnesia. This results in her forgetting him every night when she goes to sleep and him having to re-befriend her every day making her remember, through different ploys, that she used to like him before the day is over and she forgets him all over again. There is also the Christopher Nolan thriller "Memento", in which the main character can no longer create new memories and is attempting to solve the case of his wife's murder. The film is a great piece in several aspects, one of the things that it explores is the way we learn about people and their intentions, who do we trust and why? For the main character, this was a key element since the people he met and who became aware of his condition started to take advantage of it and hence he had no way of knowing who to trust. To try and remedy this he left written clues to his future-self to pass-on the knowledge he had briefly acquired. The film is also ingeniously shot and edited so that we, the audience, can also experience the desperate attempts of the main character to construct his own *Before* in order to cope with his new *Afters*. Both stories help us to understand what a life without *Before* would be like and in both cases, we realize the importance of the things we take for granted and how our *Before* is essential in order to be able to cope with our *After*.

A second thought experiment we could attempt would be to ask ourselves the opposite question: What if there was no *After*? In this case, life would also be complicated. There is a condition called Aphantasia where the sufferer cannot create images in his mind so that it is not possible to for him or her to imagine, at least in pictures, any sort of future situation. This leads to the impossibility of creating *Afters,* at least in pictorial terms, as most of us can. The condition does not impede the sufferer from the process of creation, though it's a creative process without an "image-ination" that is, it lacks the "image" component and hence makes future scenario prediction more difficult. People who suffer this condition (it is not classified as a disability) often describe that it provokes the emotional impact of making them feel less creative or, at least, slower in conjuring up the past since their imagination works more like a list of verbal descriptions rather than a picture of what happened. On the other hand, they also report[1] that there are benefits to be gained from the condition and that one of them has to do with the fact that they can live more fully the *Now* (the present) since they cannot be distracted by picturing the future. Also, since they know that it will be difficult for them to relive -in memory- a "*Now*" (present) moment, they tend to cherish each experience even more when it is actually happening[2].

We can visualize the way the three epochs evolve as we

develop through our lives. When we are born, we have no *Before* and our tools to deal with *Now* are limited. As we grow up and we build up our *Before*, our capacity for dealing with *Now* increases and we start to develop tools to handle what we have been calling the *After* or the immediate future. The more *Before* (experience) we have the better we can handle *Now* and *After*. As we further develop and get older, the ever-increasing *Before* we build, tends to make us much "wiser" or more able to deal with *Nows* and *Afters*, the downside can be that the *Before* baggage we carry as experience might make us less prone to seeking new, riskier *Afters*, so as we get older and we "settle in our ways" we tend to privilege known experiences, where we have more certainty of their outcome, over new experiences where the outcome can be less easily predicted.

Although I will not delve into the subject, I cannot leave this section that has presented the idea of the three epochs, without mentioning that this model or system is inherently imperfect, in particular, the way that we store and recall our *Befores* is full of personal interpretations which makes everyone's view of reality potentially different from everyone else's. Our minds do not act as an unfiltered recording device storing images and sounds that it picks up from our senses and emotions, it is more like a multi-filtered and multi-indexed storage where our previous experiences, emotions, feelings and judgements, amongst other things, categorize, label and even adapt the information that is held in our *Befores*. We have seen in other chapters how eyewitnesses will recall different descriptions of the same situation even though they were present together at the same time, we have also seen how the perception of time changes under situations of stress, sleep or relaxation, so we can conclude that time cues are not always accurate when we access our *Befores*. There is also the intentional interpretation of circumstances to improve the prospects of an argument, as may be the case when describing a car collision in order to get insurance cover for repair purposes, the recollection of the different parties will be inevitably slanted, to try and favour the position of each one of the claimants. Recollection and storage of *Befores* can also be affected by illness, whether physical or psychological, in these circumstances altered versions of real experiences can be either stored or recalled from memory, in such cases distorted interpretations of circumstances or even alternative descriptions of the reality perceived by most people will be conveyed as truths.

Other Nows

Having defined *Now* as the experience that our senses generate we can ask ourselves how do people who have some sort of sensory impairment experience their *Nows*? How different is their *Now* from the *Now* of people who do not suffer from any impairment? Lets take two examples, first people with no vision (blind) and secondly, people without hearing (deaf), these two senses may be considered in general as the most "important" senses, although having no capacity for tasting would not only produce a rather dull life but also a dangerous one as some flavours alert us of toxic substances that may harm us.

The Blind and Now

Vision is the dominant sense in humans, it takes up the largest area of brain processing in comparison to the other senses. Not only do we react to the information that our eyes detect, vision also enables us to construct a mental model of the world around us which allows us to choose our movements within this world. Sight also enables us to explore this mental model within our minds, to imagine and predict future circumstances as well as to analyse past events by replaying them in our *Befores*.

There is a great difference between the cognition of people who have been born blind and people who have lost their sight later in life. If you are born without sight the image-oriented external-world mind-map cannot be constructed but since our brains are immensely adaptable, the other senses come to our aid, in particular, the sense of hearing and touch become the sources from which we construct the model of our world, memories and our *Befores*. It is not that those senses are specially developed in sight-impaired people, but because they are not in the shadow of sight they become more important to us, so much so that studies show that they take over and use the parts of the brain that would normally be reserved for vision processing. In other words, they get more processing power from our brains. One of the tools used to create a map of the external world is echo-location where either through a click made with the tongue or by tapping objects with a cane, we can hear the echoes generated by the objects around us and so sense our surroundings, much like animals, such as, bats and whales use they sonar capabilities in order to sense their environments[3].

From the experience of blind people we also learn that

some things that we think are only detected through vision have also other sensory components, for example, a sunny day can not only be seen but also felt, the feeling of warmth, the way the Sun will feel on our skin, the different smells we detect in the air as objects become warm and release their scented particles, etc. Much in the same way shadow or darkness can be sensed without sight, the coolness of the air, the way air feels as we breathe it through our noses, the quietness, etc.

In a sightless world, detecting the passing of time is more of a challenge, but our body has an additional tool to help us. Not only do we have the more obvious clues carried by the information that normally surrounds us such as watches, radios, television and other people, we have a mechanism that allows us to synchronise our internal clock, called the Circadian cycle, with the 24-hour Earth cycle. The sensory aspect of this mechanism resides in the retina but is not part of the rods and cones structure that enables us to see. This means that a blind person with a damaged visual system is not necessarily also blind to this stimulus and so, like all of us, is still be able to sense at a biological level, the difference between night-time and day-time[4].

The Deaf and Now

Hearing is a multi-purpose sense, at the most basic level it can allow us to scan the environment and detect sounds that pose dangers to us, such as a predator that might be after us for its dinner or a bus that might run over us. On the other hand, it also enables us to detect sounds that are key to our survival like our mother's voice or a river where we might quench our thirst. On the cognitive level, sound is associated with language, we learn to speak a language by listening to the sounds and understanding their meanings or associations. This language acquisition and development is associated with our thought processes, all of us use a language structure in order to store, think, plan, imagine, etc. we often talk of the "voice in our head" when we refer to our own thinking process.

But language is not the same as speech. Deaf children have difficulty in speaking because they cannot hear and hence cannot copy and repeat what has been heard. Assuming the child is not also visually impaired, sight and touch will come to the rescue enabling the child to be taught and learn a sign-language in much the same way as he or she would learn a speech-language. With this language structure learned, all the thought processes that are usually speech-driven will become sign-driven enabling the child to have the normal learning process in all fields including reading and writing.

In both cases described: sight and hearing impairment, the other senses are used in order to adapt our toolkit for detecting the *Now* and hence enabling our *Before* to be constructed. As I mentioned, these two epochs being the essential, necessary elements for us to develop as beings able to deal with the *After* and travel thought our lifetime.

Time and Now

As most of our lives are spent in the internal processes of *Befores* and *Afters* it is not difficult to imagine how time perception is not an easy task. In our every day lives, in the world outside our bodies, time advances at a regular and predefined pace but inside our minds time can flow as a continuous, variable wave shifting from *Before* to *After*, transiting through *Now* and back again to our *Befores*. Sometimes our mind gets so involved in these processes that it loses track of time "outside" and it may appear that real-time flows slower or faster than it's actual speed. In other chapters, we investigate the ways in which the perception-of-time mechanisms work and we see the effect of different *Nows* on our perception, for example: when we live through a stressful event or when we take different actions and strategies in order to regulate the way our mind connects to the *Now*.

10

TOMORROW-ME

Ever changing

WE CAN ONLY BE certain of a few facts in our journey through life: That time will not stop, that the Sun will always come back over us (understanding that the Sun doesn't really "rise" or "set" anywhere!), that we will die, and a few other unmovable facts like these. It is also true to say that, whether we like it or not and whether we are aware of it or not, every day, hour, minute that passes in our life we are receiving and processing a vast amount of information that makes us understand, or at least re-interpret, the world in a different manner. For example, a simple exercise of walking down a familiar road might enlighten us in many ways, we may observe a building that we had never noticed before or even a new detail in a known building that surprises us. We may notice how many leaves there are in the trees and knowing which season we are in, we may re-enforce our knowledge of how nature changes throughout the year. Another example may involve reading a particular book or watching a documentary on a particular subject you are interested in, both of these activities will leave something in your mind that was not there before. With new knowledge gathered in this way every single moment of our life, we permanently re-evaluate how we see the world and our surroundings and modify the internal model of perception each one of us possesses.

We call this information gathering, "experiences", and each one of these experiences is made up of different types of information: *sensorial*, related to the five senses and *derived*, constructed by the interpretations and models we build upon this information. Each one of these experiences is then related to all the other experiences we have already gathered and together they form a dynamic flow of how we see the world.

Using the fact that everything is in permanent change all the time, we can ask ourselves: Who are we, really? Or, in a more insightful way, we can ask: "When" are we who we are? Or even: When is the time in our lives when we are who we are? From these questions we can start searching for some answers: we may come to an initial conclusion that there is a Yesterday-me, a Today-me (or Now-me) and that there will be a Tomorrow-me. So, which one of these is the real-me?

The first answer that might come to us after a short pause is that, obviously, the "Now-me" is who I really am. But after some thought, we realize that if that "now" happens to be at one of the extremes of our lives, in other words, when we are a baby or when we are "old". Is that who we really are? In one case, without even the ability to talk or exchange ideas and at the other extreme, without all the faculties that we used to have at some time or another during our lives.

A second possible answer to the question of who or

when am I me? Might come along the lines of saying that, in fact, as we are part of a complex interconnection of relationships with our surroundings, we are Always-me, "I am Always-me", and that my changes are a normal evolution of my interactions with those surroundings.

Yet another way of answering the questions is that the Now-me is, in fact, a collection of all the Yesterday-me's passed. This seems reasonable when focusing on the mind, as our knowledge and mind development tends to be a cumulative process, but in our physical aspect, that is: our bodies, this is not quite the case since our biological makeup has periods of incremental capabilities, as when we are in the process of growth, while in our latter stages of life this process is more like a deterioration as we start to lose our physical capabilities.

The Biology of Time

Biologically speaking, our physical body renews itself constantly. Most cells have a limited life span and they die and are replaced by new cells. Here are some examples of cell renewal times in our bodies[1]:

CELL TYPE	RENEWAL CYCLE
Stomach	2 - 9 days
Lung alveoli	8 days
Skin epidermis cells	10 - 30 days
Red blood cells	4 months
Liver hepatocyte cells	0.5 - 1 year
Fat cells	8 years
Cardiomyocytes (heart)	0.5 - 10% a year
Skeleton	10% a year

Cell Renewal Cycles

In most cases, the regeneration process will slow down as we age but as a whole, there is an overall rule that says that most of our body cells are replaced in 7 to 10-year cycles, though this is still under scientific investigation. But although it may be partly true, you could say that some parts of you –though you couldn't really tell which ones!- are brand new or at least newer than the "now-you", taken as a whole. This cell replacement can easily be observed as you watch your nails or hair grow or more dramatically when you notice how your body heals itself after an injury, for example, a cut on your skin.

Some of our tissues and organs are better at regeneration than others. A healthy liver, for example, can accomplish the mean feat of regeneration even if a large part of it has been damaged or cut away as would happen in a traumatic accident.

On the other side of the scale, we find some parts of our body that do not have the regeneration capability, in other words, they cannot repair or renew themselves. Here is that infamous list:

- The Central nervous system
- Our Eye Lens cells
- Oocytes (female gametes)
- Cerebral cortex neurons

Looking at the list above and trying to find a common denominator we are struck by the fact that all these cells that do not re-generate are part of what we could call our "inner-core", that is, they are cells which are the basic and central areas of our very being, the most precious of all, and yet we have not been able to make them renewable throughout our biological evolution. Most of the cells listed above have a close relationship with the brain, they might even be connected directly to it as is the case of the eyes and spinal cord. Although these cells may not renew themselves, we do know that most of them seem to have special treatment as far as the allocation of body resources is concerned and it is always the case that brain cells seem to have the upper hand as far as sharing what is available. This is shown in the extreme scenario of food deprivation, as in starvation, where the brain will consume all the available energy compromising all the other tissues and organs in favour of its own survival. This mechanism becomes a survival necessity since, as it cannot regenerate itself, it will sacrifice other organs in the hope that when there are more favourable conditions, the other organs will, in time, be able to recuperate[2].

So biology tells us that, as far as our physical bodies are concerned, we are permanently being renewed. Only a small percentage of our cells are there for the whole life journey, most of them die and are replaced by new cells throughout our lives, at least at the cell level, we are not who we used to be!

Experience-Me

Biological regeneration is only one aspect of the permanent changes that our Now-me has to endure. The other component of ourselves is what we experience and learn about the world every day and with every interaction. What we process in our minds, store in our memory and what we convert into ourselves through learning and knowledge.

This second source of permanent change makes us understand the world in different ways and change the way we react and perceive future events. Although it is not easy to calculate, the estimates carried out by researchers at the University of California-San Diego[3] say that we are bombarded with the equivalent of 34 Gigabits (GB) of data or information every day, that's the equivalent, they say, to some 105,000 words a day. Our brain does not have to process all of this data, luckily the brain has developed cunning ways of ignoring most of the stuff that does not grab its attention.

Nevertheless and understanding that the brain is not a computer, the amount of data to which we are exposed is large and, invariably, some of it is relevant to us and needs to be absorbed and understood.

This data or information has a great influence on permanently defining or re-defining what our Now-me, the self or our personality, as Psychology calls it, is and becomes. It is not easy to define what "personality" or the "self" are, psychology nowadays tends to agree, although it is still disputed, that personality can be defined by the "big five" general traits:

- **Openness to Experience:** Observed in the appreciation of art, emotion, and adventure and supposedly defining the degree of intellectual curiosity and creativity.

- **Conscientiousness:** Observed in the tendency to be organized and dependable and supposedly defining the degree of flexibility or obsession.
- **Extroversion:** Observed in sociability and assertiveness and supposedly defining the degree of attention-seeking or domineering.
- **Agreeableness:** Observed in the form of compassion and cooperative behaviour and supposedly defining how we react to others.
- **Neuroticism:** Observed in the tendency for depression and anxiety and supposedly defining how emotionally stable we are.

Although it was thought that these traits were fixed an immovable after the age of 25 or 30, it is now clear that they are permanently changing throughout our lives[4].

In one study reported by The New Scientist magazine in May 2003, for example, it was found that:

"...neuroticism decreased with age for women but not for men. Openness also declined slightly with age for both sexes.

They also found that people tended to show a spurt in conscientiousness – which involves the ability to deal with tasks and organisation – in their twenties. Agreeability, which encompasses affection and warmth, improved on average in most people's thirties."[5]

NEW SCIENTIST MAGAZINE, MAY 2003

There are many other models that attempt to describe or typify human personality, however, all of them are mere models and classifications which only help to categorize general trends giving them names in order to perform research. But any model of the real world is just an approximation and often demonstrate the limitations present when describing our surroundings, our perceptions and ourselves, all models are imperfect and should only serve as a reference. Our most important tool for creating models is our language, but language itself is a kind of model and has its own restrictions. Under certain circumstances language does not allow us to entirely describe our perceptions, for example, imagine trying to describe a "colour" without resorting to the comparison with coloured objects, the case may arise when you try to describe the colour "blue" to a blind person, in this situation you cannot use the comparison technique in a phrase such as, "blue is like the colour of the sky" and would be facing a very difficult challenge in order to complete this description. Our spoken language is an incredible tool that we have developed but it is more useful at describing objects, such as mountains and rivers, than it is at describing complex concepts, such as a colour, emotions and feelings. This fundamental imprecision of our description models reminds me of the ancient Chinese text called the "Tao Te King", a book that is, in essence, the description of the Taoist philosophy and that it is believed to have been written in the 6th century BCE but that in it's very first lines states that,

---

"The Tao that can be described, is not the real Tao"

In other words, it is saying, from the very outset, that although this book is entirely about the description of the essence of Taoism, it is impossible to fully and accurately describe something as complex, complete and dynamic with mere words and when it is attempted, it will invariably end in failure.

Without wanting to promote the different methods or models of personality categorization and invariably end in failure, I will share with you a particular method that I have encountered and have used to evaluate and construct teams of people in work environments.

The method is called the "Enneagram of Personality" and has been derived from the teachings of Oscar Ichazo and Claudio Naranjo[6]. It describes nine types of personality (*Ennéa* means *nine* in Greek), their basic characteristics and the relationships between them. Interestingly the model describes a base personality for each one of us and allows it to modify itself and appear like another, related, personality under certain circumstances. In other words, the model recognizes that although we have a base personality, under certain circumstances, like when we are feeling confident or depressed, we can exhibit the traits of another related personality.

Here is a list of the simplified characteristics of the basic personalities described by the Enneagram model:

1. **The Perfectionist:** Ordered, highly structured and self-demanding.
2. **The Generous:** Warm, generous and sentimental.
3. **The Winner:** Practical, ambitious and vain.
4. **The Artist:** Creative, intuitive and temperamental.
5. **The Intellectual:** Reserved, curious and a loner.
6. **The Loyal:** Cautious, dependable, indecisive.
7. **The Optimist:** A dreamer, adventurous and superficial.
8. **The Authoritarian:** Assertive, powerful and impulsive.
9. **The Conciliator:** Adaptable, relaxed and foolish.

Although this is a very abridged version of the characteristics, we can see that each personality has positive traits and also some characteristics that might be less desirable.

These nine basic types are related and their relationships are described by the following diagram:

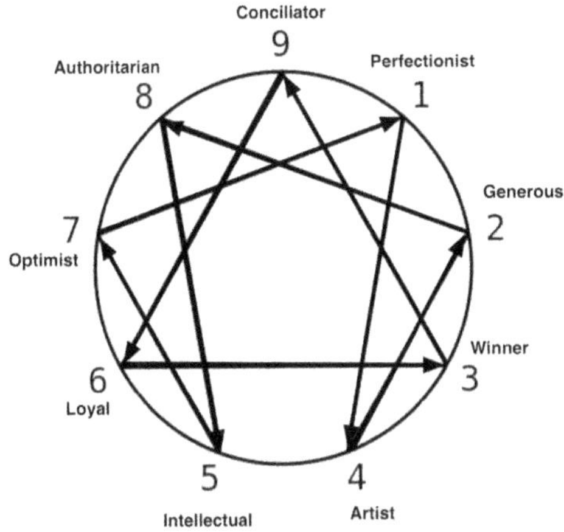

Eneagram Types

Without going into the detailed description of how the Enneagram of personalities works, we note that although each one of us is classified by one of the personality types, each personality-type will also contain all the other traits to some degree and depending on your mental state you might temporarily change your state in the direction the arrows in the diagram indicate. For example in the case of personality type 6 (The Loyal), when the mental state is weak or somehow diminished it will temporarily become a type 9 (Conciliator). On the other hand, if the mental state is overconfident or excited it will become, temporarily, a personality type 3 (Winner). The Enneagram is just one of the many models used to describe our personalities and behaviours, most of these models allow for the fact that personalities will change in time, whether temporarily or permanently during our lives.

. . .

Our minds and bodies are in permanent change and, strictly speaking, we are always different and renewed, in flux and changing, our skin cells, hair, blood cells, our views on the people that surround us and also our beliefs and understanding of the world.

So what really defines us? Maybe a better way to define ourselves is by our relations or interactions with others and with our surroundings, by the way we make our selves a part of the whole.

Me and Others

When we first meet somebody new what are the first things that we find out from them?:

"What do you do?"
"Do you know such-and-such?"
"What do you think of this-and-that?"

All these questions (and the others we conjure up) are related to discovering what relations the new person has with other people, other concepts and other things. From this knowledge, we start to make a picture of the new person's personality and views about the world and from this information, we start to know whether we can or cannot form our own relationship with this person.

Some of the relations we have are not of our choosing, some cannot be broken, some are temporary, some are good for us and others are not so good. The very first relation we have is with our mother, this is not only the first relation we have but also an example of one of the relations that are permanent and although they might change they cannot be broken with time. A mother is always a mother to her son or daughter, the relation does not rely on choice even if it is not a good one, it will always endure, there are no “ex-mothers” or “ex-daughters” in the world. All family or blood relations are the same, they are fixed and do not change their status with time, this fact drives a large part of our primal survival instinct since we are programmed to try and make our genes survive in time, we will always protect our kin. This is why rulers hand their kingdoms to their sons, why kings from different lands marry their offspring and why wars are waged. Everything in order to make a more secure future for themselves and their families, this is also why we try to choose a healthy stable partner to start our own family.

Other relations, the ones we choose for ourselves, do change in time. We can follow a football team or a music band for some time and then move away from it or replace it with another similar or indeed, opposite choice. Sometimes we say, for example, that our taste in music has “evolved” when we change our affinities towards other sounds. The same is true with people, friends or even partners that also change in time. A relationship that was very close at one point in time can drift apart or conversely someone you were acquainted with can become a very close friend at a later stage in your life. There is an old saying in Spanish "*Dime con quién andas y te diré quién eres*” which roughly translated would be something like “Tell me who you go with and I will tell you who you are” which is similar to “You are the company you keep” or “You can judge a man by the company he keeps” which are sometimes used in English. Following this idea it could be argued that the important thing about who you are has more to do with how you fit into the world, the relations you keep, your likes and the actions you take with others rather than just your individual self. We can further investigate the idea of being defined by the relationships we build through life by posing the question: "If I weren't here what effect would that have on the world?" The void that absence creates can be thought of as a measure of the effect your relationships and creations had on the rest of the world.

Some people need more than a lifetime for their effect to be recognized as having been of importance to society and culture. We find that the void that some people leave behind makes them exist beyond their own lifetime and be present and even influential in the future, their Tomorrow-me becomes more alive than their Now-me.

Success can be measured in many ways, some grand and some more mundane. In the case of a painter, it can be measured by how many people relate to their craft, or by counting how many exhibitions they present in or how many paintings they manage to sell. One of the most influential and better-known painters in the history of western culture created over two thousand paintings but allegedly managed to sell only one of them during his lifetime. For most of his life, he lived a miserable life with just his younger brother as his financial support. He was depressive, psychotic and had to spend time in psychiatric hospitals. He is most famous for an episode in which, out of rage, he severed one of his own ears. Vincent Van Gogh finally committed suicide at the age of 37. This is where van Gogh's story would have ended if it weren't for Vincent's brother Theo and his sister-in-law Jo (wife of Theo). It was through their persistence in showing Vincent's art and, most importantly, in the publication of the letters that the brothers exchanged throughout Vincent's lifetime, that Vincent's story and art became known and conquered the imagination and fascination of the art community[7]. Vincent's story serves as an example of how the material we are made from sometimes is not what makes us who we are, it is the stories we leave behind and our creations that have the power of conquering time and make us immortal.

Meet and greet Yesterday-me

Our Today-me has many opportunities to meet its Yesterday-me. It's a matter of finding or creating the conditions for it to happen. If you are one of those people who can never throw anything away, then it helps communicating with Yesterday-me.

This is a story about my own Today-me and Yesterday-me, I had been playing with one of those online music-streaming programs or services that are popular nowadays, the kind of program that lets you listen to virtually any music from any era you might think of. I had been exploring one of its many features, in this case, the feature that lets you create music "Playlists". A playlist is just a series of music tracks that you can select, store and then play back whenever you want. One of my sons had told me about this feature, but to me, it just sounded like a lot of work having to build these playlists. After all, you could simply select an album, an artist or even the mood you were in and the program would automatically build a playlist for you, what could be easier?

At some point though, I started to play around with this feature and began to build some playlists of all the "old" songs that I could remember. In fact, more than "oldies", it was a list of all the songs that have meant something to me at some point in my life, yes, something like a trip down "memory lane". It turned out to be quite fun and I spent several hours entertained in this task. At one point while I was doing this, I remembered that I had a drawer full of old cassette tapes that I had collected when I was a teenager and a young man. The drawer was still full, as I had never wanted to get rid of them even though technology had already moved on two or three generations and we were now talking about listening to our music "in the cloud", that is, uploaded into the invisible Internet and not "on tape", that almost magical magnetic stripe set in a plastic box that allowed us to store the music we liked. In the drawer, along with complete albums from different artists, I had kept seven or eight very special tapes that I (my Yesterday-me) had made. Some of you might remember or even might have spent time doing the same thing as I did with cassette tapes. I am talking about an age where there were no computers (or very few), no Internet and certainly no streaming services, a time when the only recordable media you could have access at home, were cassette tapes. What teenagers used to do in those days was to make "cassette mix tapes" recorded directly from the radio and that's exactly what Yesterday-me had been doing some thirty-seven years ago.

So I went to the drawer and rummaged around a bit to look for those mix tapes, I had the great idea that once I had them all and had listened to them I could re-create those mixes and convert them into twenty-first century playlists in my streaming service. Once I started to think of the details of my plan I came up with two potential problems: first of all, did I have a cassette tape player in my house? And secondly: once I put the cassettes in the machine, would they work? After all, cassette technology was famously fragile and prone to tangling, a typical scene of the time involved a pen or a pencil while you tried to wind some loose tape onto one of the tape spools.

As I took the cassettes with the music mixes from the drawer, all of them with their plastic cases, I realized that Yesterday-me had written down each one of the names of the tracks contained in the cassettes. With great care and with very legible handwriting, each one of those thin cardboard sleeves had all the information that was to be found within the cassette tape and that Today-me needed to create those playlists. Today-me did not need to find a player (which as it turned out, I still did have at home!) nor would Today-me have to take the risk of entangling or tearing the tapes if I had had to put them in the machine and attempt to play them. Yesterday-me had done a good job and was working with Today-me on this project, thirty-seven years apart, but together.

While creating these playlists it was interesting to feel the connection between these two "me"s. I realized that although I could not remember the exact details of how each tape was created, the general sensation was there. The way I had to wait for the precise moment to press the record button as the DJ on the radio cut to his next track, the way I had to rewind the tape and set it ready for the next recording. The way that, sometimes, the method did not work properly so I had to scrap the recording and try again some later time. Yesterday-me, through my memories, was being brought to the present and the thirty-seven-year time gap instantaneously disappeared.

Listening to the playlists themselves brought back other memories that were not apparent at first, like the way that sometimes I would know exactly which track would follow next, this was a product of having listened to the tapes repeatedly throughout my teen years, listening to tapes is a totally sequential experience, there is no "shuffle" or "random" mode so that the play order gets etched into memory just as much as the tracks themselves. Yesterday-me had many surprises and it was a great experience to meet him and work with him after so many years.

Hello Tomorrow-me

Travelling in the other direction of time, forwards, it is very common to communicate with our Tomorrow-me. Think of the everyday situation where you make yourself a cup of tea in the morning and realise that there is no milk in the fridge. At this point with a long day of work or activities ahead, you know that the only way to be sure you don't forget to buy some milk in the evening is to communicate with your "later-me" either by a mental note (running the risk of forgetting!) or a written message to be read later. Nowadays it is also common to either send yourself an email, a text message or program an alarm on your mobile phone as a reminder. Whichever method you choose to communicate with your later-self you are communicating through time. This communication into the future is also present when you take holiday photographs, write diaries or leave yellow sticky notes on the fridge door!

Several movies convey the fascinating stories of people that suffer from some sort of amnesia and that have to communicate to themselves through time in order to maintain some sort of continuous thread in their lives. "Memento", a film by Christopher Nolan, which I briefly mentioned in another chapter, relates the case of a man who suffers from *anterograde amnesia*, a condition where he cannot form new memories and so suffers memory loss every five minutes or so. Eventually, the main character starts taking instant photographs (the film is set before the era of the mobile phone!), tattooing himself and leaving messages to himself in order to make his *Now* communicate with his *After*. Obviously, this is an extreme case but it serves to illustrate how communicating to oneself through the passing of time becomes a relevant and, in this case, a vital resource.

There are other types of mementoes we use for communication through time. Time Capsules have been used to convey artefacts and information from present to future generations. Although not the oldest one discovered in the world, the Time Capsule buried in 1795 just 20 years after the start of the American Revolution by Paul Revere and Samuel Adams, two iconic figures from that period, serves as an example of how we have communicated to our future selves through time. In this case, the capsule was buried, with great pomp and ceremony, on July 4, 1795, in the Massachusetts' State House in Boston. Two hundred and nineteen years later in 2014, it was discovered by repair workers and, after some debate, historians decided to open it to investigate and conserve what was inside. In the Time Capsule box, they found coins, the first volume of the Massachusetts Colony Records, a George Washington Medal, a silver plaque and some newspapers.[8]

This particular capsule has become more of a time-hopper than a Time Capsule, as the experts discovered, the box had already been un-earthed and re-buried in 1855 during the construction of a new part of the building. At that time its contents were placed in a sturdier box and new items representative of that year were added. And so in

2015, after an investigation by historians and experts, the Time Capsule was once again re-buried for future generations to re-discover[9]. As before, more artefacts were placed inside the capsule, a small reflection of the culture at the time of re-opening. Future-us: get ready for the Time Capsule's next hop in about 100 years time!

11

TIME FOR CHOICES

Intersections

IF WE THINK of life as a path that leads us from the moment we are born to the time we die we can also imagine that this path will have many turning points throughout its journey and make many intersections with other paths. Although this may sound very poetical, or even Zen, it is a good analogy to describe the way our life develops, creating in its course each one of our futures. Following through the analogy, it quickly makes us think about how and when those turning points will appear and whether we can control the new direction our path will take after the next turning point. In most every day cases I believe that we can control the new route we take at the turning points but there are cases, of course, where the outcome is beyond our control and we fall prey to the life-paths and choices of others or we are led to adjust to a change of path that is governed by nature or circumstance, such as when we suffer an accident or are involved in one of Earth's natural disasters.

Let's try the following familiar scenario to see if we can work through some aspects of this concept of intersecting paths:

Say you are thinking about buying a car. You have already decided on the brand and model, you have the necessary money and all the logistic details have been thought over and worked out. All that remains is deciding WHEN you will buy it: Today? Tomorrow? During the weekend? Let's assume for the purposes of this exercise that the car will be available for you to take home immediately once purchased, so what is left to be decided is the simple choice of when to purchase it and take it home. What difference will the decision of when to purchase make on your life? On someone else's life? On society? On the world? On the universe?!

Let's now imagine various parallel paths, or worlds if you like, that might develop from this scenario, we could think of various "yous": The "*Now*-you", the one with no car, and the other *yous*: the *you* with the car a little later **today**, the *you* with the car **tomorrow** and the *you* with the car at the **weekend**. These various *yous* that can be pictured in our minds, will carry on with their "lives" according to their new means of transport, in each case interacting with very different people, situations, and indeed, other choices and intersections. Do those other *yous* exist? Which *you* is better? Our own answers to these questions will bring us to a conclusion and will finally help us to decide as to when we actually do buy that car. We can also see that once one of those *yous* becomes the *Now*-you, at that exact same time, all the other *yous* and your *Before*-you cease to exist. The important thing to note here is that the final choice as to when your next-*you* enters into action is, generally, in *your* own hands.

We take turning point decisions every day, many times a day. Do I cross the road here or there? Do I go out of the house at 8:32 or at 8:34? Do I make that phone call now or in an hour's time? Choices and decisions pile one on top of each other all day long. Each one changing our life-path, sometimes with small consequences, and at other times with long-lasting effects.

Small Big Choices

World history is made from the crossing of many different life-paths and by making many small and large choices. At times, small choices have created large changes in the paths of many people and countries, as we shall see in the following story.

There have been many assassinations of world leaders throughout our history, a shortlist of some famous names can include Julius Caesar in the first century BCE, Mahatma Gandhi in 1943 CE, Abraham Lincoln in 1865 CE and J.F. Kennedy in 1963 CE. Each one of those statesmen's lives ended by, up to that moment in time, complete strangers. Brutus and other collaborators were famously involved in the multiple stabbing of Julius Caesar, Mahatma Gandhi was shot three times in the chest by Nathuram Godse, Abraham Lincoln was fired a single bullet in the back of the head by John Wilkes Booth and J.F. Kennedy received two rifle shots by one Lee Harvey Oswald, each one of these men having their own story of how they came to act in such a drastic manner and attain their place in history. One other famous assassination that is part of modern history is the shooting of Franz Ferdinand Carl Ludwig Joseph Maria or Archduke Franz Ferdinand in 1914. This historical event was one of the many circumstances that precipitated the start of World War I, also known as the Great War, which in consequence gave rise to our modern states, World War II, the reliance of the world in oil for it's energy, the rise of the US as a leader of nations, the Cold War and many other events leading up to our present day.

Although the assassination was planned in advance, the way that the events unfolded was full of unforeseen circumstances driven by the instantaneous choices made at the time by all the characters involved. On this particular day, the paths of five people crossed and through the choices made by each one of them helped to set in motion the wheels of change for their personal and our own world. Four potential assassins and one target, that is how the day started, each one of the potential killers could have found his target but only one did and his actions were the result of all the collective choices made on that day.

The basic scenario was the following: The Archduke was going to drive from the army barracks in Sarajevo to the Town Hall through a pre-established route. At the Town Hall, he would give a speech and then return, using the same route, to the barracks. The assassin gang of four would wait along the convoy route, on the street, and find the best opportunity to kill the Archduke. A very simple plan.

As the events unfolded we can count eight (8) personal choices that were made, which finally defined the destiny of Franz Ferdinand and his assassins.

On that fateful day, the convoy carrying the Archduke and his entourage made its way along the main road after leaving the barracks. The first would-be assassin (1) chooses to do nothing as the motorcade passes in front of him, in later statements he declared that he did not get a good view of the target and that was the reason he did not act. As the convoy carried on its journey, the second potential assassin (2) chooses to throw a hand grenade he was carrying, unfortunately for him the grenade only manages to hit the back of the car carrying the Archduke and rolls under the car behind it, exploding and injuring the people travelling inside that vehicle. After this violent mishap the party and motorcade (3) chooses to carry on with the journey and the visit to the Town Hall and speech, this is something that would be quite unthinkable in modern times where if something like this were to happen, all activities would be immediately cancelled until the whole area and even the city itself was cleared of all possible dangers. After the speech was given at the Town Hall the party (4) chooses to change plans and instead of going straight back to the barracks, decide to go to the hospital first and visit the injured victims of the earlier bomb explosion. As a precaution, one of the accompanying guards (5) chooses to ride on the car's running board, next to the Archduke on the roadside rather than on the side that would be next to the pavement and from where the killer's gun would eventually be fired. The subsequent investigation discovered that the drivers were not told of the change of route so the driver followed the original plan and as he turned on the infamous corner were the assassination finally happened, he was told to stop and back-up in order to continue the journey to the hospital, at this point and with little options left, the driver (6) chooses to stop the car and reverse around the corner from were he had just come. Throughout this time the gang of assassins were very disheartened and confused after their attempts had failed to accomplish their original plan and had dispersed around the streets of the city. One of them though was adamant on carrying through the plan and after stopping at a restaurant to have a coffee and re-evaluate his options he (7) chooses to carry on with the plan and so goes back onto the street where the motorcade would pass on the way back to the barracks. He stands in that famous corner of Appel Quay and Franz Joseph Street just as the Archduke's driver is making his reverse manoeuvre. At this point the final decision in this chain of events is executed and a 20 year old Bosnian Serb man called Gavrilo Princip, born in a remote village of farmers in the northwest of the country, becomes one of the most famous assassins in modern history, when he (8) chooses to aim and pull the trigger of his Browning semi-automatic pistol, mortally wounding Franz Ferdinand in the neck, cutting his jugular vein. Eight (8) life choices made in the space of 60 (sixty) minutes during the morning of 28th June 1914.

If different choices had been made at any of the eight (8) key decision points in the sequence of events, other paths and consequences could have been created. If we account only for the eight (8) choices described in our story and use a little logic and mathematics we could say that as many as 10 other sequences of events could have arisen, some of them having the same outcome, the Archduke's death, but others (maybe 60% of them), leaving the Archduke alive and possibly giving rise to a slightly different history of the modern world.

No-Choice

Although choice gives us control of our lives, there are times when choice is not an option. Contrary to the order, sequence and predictability that we know when we talk about time, there is randomness. How does time and random events relate or combine? Time, being such a predictable and seemingly ordered component of the universe and the randomness of some events being the absolute opposite, unpredictable. These thoughts come to mind when we read of investigations such as the one carried out by the John Hopkins Medical Institute in the US where they found that 66% of cancers are created by errors in the process of cell division and that these occur "spontaneously", that is, as random events[1]. Cell division is the natural process of duplication and growth that a cell exhibits in its normal, ordinary existence. In fact, it is one of the mechanisms involved in the creation of every living creature. The study showed that at this level, in this mundane, but highly specialized process of cell division, unforeseen errors occur that eventually are responsible for the creation of a catastrophic biological malfunction such as cancer.

In these circumstances, free choice is not possible and we have no option but to accept the consequences of the randomness inherent in our universe.

But, is there such a thing as "random" or is this the way we describe processes we don't understand or have not sufficient information to predict? It might be a matter of perception, for some, any particular event might be considered random but for others, with more knowledge or understanding, it might be a predictable, certain matter. For example, for a culture that has no comprehension of astronomy, an eclipse may seem like a random fortuitous occurrence while if there is knowledge of how our solar system works, these events can be predicted with absolute precision. Some think that if, and when, we are able to harness and control all the information in the universe, there will be no more random events since we will be able to predict everything based on knowledge. For the moment we can make a list of some of the most random events we know:

- The radioactive decay of atoms: the movement of atomic particles is still something we cannot predict. Quantum Theory proposes that in fact, it is not even measurable since the mere act of measurement will change the result!
- Variations in atmospheric pressure: This is understood to be predictable, but the number of variables and the incredibly large interaction between them is impossible to calculate with our current technology. Think of the poor predictability that we still have on television, radio or newspaper weather forecasts!
- Raindrops falling on a slab of pavement: The classical schoolroom example of watching a particular slab of pavement and trying to guess where the next raindrop will fall.

From the point of view of time, "random" is just one of the possible ways that events can be ordered and that are perceived by our *Nows*. Just a reminder that we have been discussing *Now* as the singularity point where our physical senses perceive our surroundings (Refer to the chapter entitled "Time is Now" for more on this). There are also other possible ways to order events apart from random such as, sequential, periodic, inverse, unitary or in groups, amongst others. All the different types of orders we perceive are neither similar nor opposite in nature but are a consequence of the existence of time itself or to put it another way, they are manifestations of time. The fact that time unfolds or passes, gives the possibility to have "events" of any ordered nature. Without time running its course, the concept of "event" would not exist, and as a complementary consequence, we can say that without the existence of events we would not notice the passing of time.

Big Choice

Over five thousands days, or fourteen years, that's how long I had been there. The first day I arrived had not been the most memorable of days, as I arrived no one was expecting me, there was no office space assigned to me, no chair, no computer, nothing. Looking back on that day I shouldn't have been surprised, after all when they finally called me over for my job interview, some weeks before that first day, they had made me wait for over two hours before I was given the chance to speak with the Human Resources Manager. That first-day experience was the same that I was going to witness along the years with all the other people I saw start their own first day in the company. Despite this, I was dying to start.

I had been waiting for the opportunity to start on a job like this for over two years. Two years where I had to do other types of jobs, not exactly to my liking, but necessary to sustain a family of four. This was the job I wanted and not being expected or welcomed on the first day was not going to change my feeling of excitement. Working in the media industry is thrilling and challenging. I guess you could say the same for several other jobs or industries, but to me media had always been my passion, so finally returning to it was a great and welcomed relief after two transition years in the financial sector. I had started my career in media but because of several changes in circumstance and choices I made during that period of my life, including moving from one country to another, I had moved away from it for a couple of years and I longed to be back.

Fourteen years can go by very fast and I guess that it is a sign that the time was well spent and enjoyed. I remember when I first started work after leaving university I had great trouble getting used to being confined to one place, sitting in an office all day, nine to five, it was hard for me to accept that work was going to take up most of my awake time, after all, up until then everything I had done, I now realized, had been for my own selfish benefit, learning, studying, investigating, passing exams, getting relatively good grades, all focused on my personal need to know more and to fulfil the challenges posed by myself, my teachers and other classmates. I had enjoyed the last years of school and all of university and realized that a lot of the joy was because I was learning new things. So after leaving this stage of my life behind and entering this new one called "work", I made myself the promise that I would leave any job and find another whenever I felt that I had stopped learning new things. It may seem like a grand promise but when you are young, have no commitments and think that you are truly following your passion, you can give yourself certain licences. Looking back I believe I have more or less kept that promise made by *yesterday-me* all those years ago.

Fourteen years doing the same job may seem like a very long time, particularly in this age of dynamic work environments. But reviewing the details, it now seems that I managed to construct a place to learn and investigate based on the new Internet technology that was just flourishing at the end of the 20th century. Fourteen years of education is more or less what is spent in our school system, this job seemed to have given me a lot of new schooling. And it certainly did, I learned about many things throughout those years until, slowly but surely, I drifted into managerial positions that started to distance me from what I had originally pursued as my passion and had trained to become and it placed me in the realms of budgets, resource management and other administration chores. This is quite normal and tends to happen a lot in most work environments, the more experience, seniority and responsibility you acquire the less you get to do what you really like. But I learned to be in charge of things, to be a boss, a reasonably good boss I hope. Being a boss is one of those things that you slowly become without much prior formal training. You come to realize you have become a boss when you cannot "pass the buck" to anyone else up-the-line, for example when you are in a meeting and an issue arises and suddenly all eyes turn to you in order to make a decision, that is the moment when you realize that you have to make the best decision with the information that you have and that verbalizing what you are really thinking -"I haven't the slightest idea what to do"- is not the right thing to say.

Luckily, I have always been involved in innovation-related subjects where you get a chance to delve into unknown areas, this forces you to learn constantly, so I learned. Since the company I worked for those fourteen years did not have a very innovative spirit as a whole, my team and I were left to our own devices and once we showed that we could sustain ourselves financially not many questions were asked. I quickly learned that if the area you lead in a company is doing well and is generating income for the company it is much easier to get budgets and new ideas approved for the next period. Team building, teamwork and innovation are all good adrenalin-generating stuff, so time flew by until year twelve arrived. Although back then, I was not counting and did not realize what was going on, year twelve arrived with the feeling of being stuck in a rut, of doing the same thing year-in, year-out. The feeling of fighting bureaucracy all day, the feeling of doing someone else's reports and presentations, of doing someone else's work and not really being able to put my ideas into practice. The feeling of not advancing, but above all others, the feeling of not learning anything new any more.

At the beginning you cannot put names to these feelings, they do not come and show themselves with their names and presentation cards. All you can sense is that there is a feeling, with no name, but a feeling that comes directly from within yourself. The feeling is uncomfortable, unhappy and sad, grumpy, the feeling of having to force yourself instead of just letting yourself flow, a feeling that stems from your gut. A powerful, permanent feeling of unhappiness, that starts very gently and continues gathering strength as time passes. In my case, the feeling matured for about a year to eighteen months. It wouldn't go away, I forced myself to find new things to do and learn. I started teaching at university, for example, something that I had vaguely thought about doing at some point in my life and somehow it seemed like the right thing to do at that particular point in time. I took up a new sport and other several things that, as I look back at that *yesterday-me* I realize that he was trying to cure this feeling from within, this "gut" feeling.

So, fourteen years after that long-awaited first day, and having had the chance to negotiate my exit from the company with a comfortable financial package, it was time to make the choice and leave. The last day after fourteen years is exactly the moment when all the theory and planning becomes a reality and enters the *Now*. The theory of what it will be like not going to the place where, every day for fourteen years you sat, listened, spoke, were listened to, where obeyed, recognized, etc. Where every day when you arrived to work you were greeted by the receptionists saying "Fantastically" when you asked him "How are you today?" Yes, he was a very exceptional man, clearly, in-between jobs since he was well-read and very educated, far above his position in the company. When you got to know him, it turned out that he was an out of work teacher with many other life-projects in his mind. I believe he is doing very well nowadays in a more challenging job, "Fantastically" well you might say. All these small every-day details are the things that are really missed, the small moments during the day where you interact with the people you appreciate. The last day is also the day when doubts make their appearance or at least seem more real than ever. "Did I make the right choice?", "Did I do this just because of a passing feeling?", "What will I do now?". Most people do not believe me when I tell this story and say that I really, really, had no new work position to go to after I left that job, that I was just driven by an internal deep feeling to make this decision. Those who do believe me, on the other hand, think that I was crazy and irresponsible to leave an excellent job for "no reason" and for choosing unemployment with three kids in school, two of them about to enter university. In actual fact *today-me*, as he writes this words, although perfectly happy and content with the way things turned out, is not sure that he would, rationally, take the same decision as *yesterday-me*, but what has remained in my memory is the feeling from within that made that particular choice necessary and the knowledge that the same feeling is not present in *today-me's* gut. For *yesterday-me* the feeling was real, it was there and something had to be done about it. The irrational feeling that *yesterday-me* had, pushed him to make the choice that changed the course of his path. At that moment it was a necessity, it had to be done.

Obsessions and Addictions

There are some choices we make that lie in a realm beyond reasoned option and that by their repetitive nature become obsessions, compulsions or addictions. In these cases, although the choice is ours, we feel somewhat compelled to take the option though we might know that the choice we will be making is not totally beneficial to us. Let's first define some of the terms we are using:

- Obsessions are thoughts that a person cannot stop having.
- Compulsions are behaviours that a person cannot stop performing.

Both of these conditions force on us certain conducts and make us dedicate a lot of our time to the objective and focus of a particular behaviour. In general these aspects of our personalities are not harmful, in effect, they are vital and required for our normal development as humans, they are present in emotions such as love, fear and the caring of our young, without the obsession present in love it would be difficult for us to form strong bonds and create the conditions to build a family, without an obsession for the well being of our children we might have not survived as a species, without a compulsion for finding food and shelter our lives would be less comfortable and more dangerous.

Obsessions and compulsions make us spend a lot of our time on the things we believe are important or gratifying, sometimes at the risk of our own safety and comfort and often putting at risk the well being of those around us. This is part of the risk of life but the real danger comes when these behaviours turn into addictions, where our ability to control the behaviour patterns of obsessions and compulsions is lost. According to Adam Alter in his book "Irresistible"[2], obsessions and compulsions are based on the fact that, once we have acquired them, if we do not pursue them they generate within us an intense unpleasant feeling, we might say that these obsessions and compulsions make us take certain choices in order to alleviate this internal feeling of unpleasantness. Addictions, on the other hand, work more directly on us in that they offer an immediate reward, gratification or positive response, the cycle of need-choice-reward is thus almost instantaneous. In other words, we pursue obsessions and compulsions in order not to feel bad, but we succumb to addictions in order to feel good immediately, a more powerful trap. The reward mechanism in addictions is so immediate and direct that it violates all our control mechanisms and makes us behave and make choices in an irrational manner in order to achieve those rewards even if great risks are predicted. The classic example of addictions is the intake of chemical enhancers, that is, drugs. But we live in an age where the so-called social addictions are also a threat to our behaviour and where the objects of social addiction are widely available and usually free. These addictions are taking over some of the time we used to dedicate to other things, some of the activities that are causing addictive behaviour include the over-use of the following massively accessible elements: mobile telephones, gaming, Internet surfing, social networking and online messaging.

Now, don't get me wrong, in no way am I advocating

the evils of technology, we live in a privileged world where the advancement of technology has made the access to information, communication and knowledge available to almost everyone in a way that had never happened in the history of this planet, but because this is something so new and we have had no previous experience with this "drug", each one of us needs to learn the use of these new resources in a responsible and safe manner. We need to manage the use of these technologies in a way that they do not take over our lives and our face-to-face interactions. Electronic contact between humans has a major intrinsic flaw, it cannot transmit feelings and the elements of *Nowness* that we exchange with our physical senses when we interact in the presence of others. Most of the statistical evidence published shows that our time is increasingly spent in front of screens, both at work and during leisure times, it is important that we do not lose our ability to chose direct contact as the way in which we carry out the basic interactions that are such an essential part of what makes us human.

12

TIME TO BELIEVE

WRITING ABOUT TIME, with its eternal flow and its inescapable effects, invariably takes us to pose some deep and essential questions regarding our existence and the purpose of the time we spend in our journey of life.

Some of these questions are very simple and are repeated in all of our different cultures and have been present throughout our human existence:

- How did we get here?
- Why are we here?
- What is the purpose of existence?

As we all know, although the questions appear "simple" the answers are rather complex.

Knowledge and Belief

In this chapter I will try to tackle these questions, the answers will be sometimes based on what is known and sometimes on what is believed, knowledge and belief tend to be confused and misused when we start to answer these questions, that is not always our fault, as we will see, the boundary between the two concepts is sometimes blurred making it difficult to separate them.

Knowledge and Belief form a complementary universe where we, as a self-conscious species, have devised answers to the fundamental questions that have always concerned us. During our evolution in time, this universe formed by knowledge and belief has tended to change its composition, knowledge has increased, as we learn about the basic rules that govern our existence, forcing the space taken by belief to decrease accordingly.

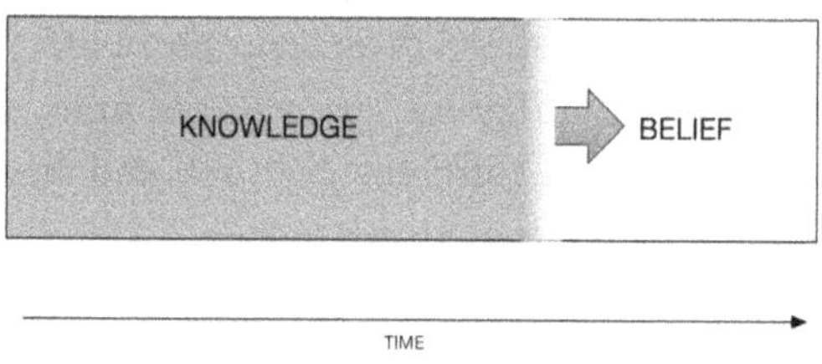

Knowledge and belief space in Time

Let's go back in time to our pre-history, say 200,000 years ago when we were hunter-gatherers, at that time the knowledge we possessed was limited and served us well for the needs of that stage in our development. Knowing the foods that were good for us, knowing where edible animals could be found, knowing which animals were a threat to us, were our means of survival. Although we are imagining life

200 millennia ago, some of the events we experience today in our everyday life were present even then, there were sunrises and sunsets, the Sun, stars, the seasons, rain, storms, wind, fires, death, fighting, bearing children, disease, just to name a few, were already part of our existence. Not having much knowledge to understand some of these apparent "random" events, and even at that early age in our development experiencing the need to have answers to the basic questions, people started to use their skills in story-telling to develop theories and narratives that explained some of the things that they observed but that had no apparent cause. People started to associate the good and bad things that happened as the result of some behaviour related to themselves, their families or to their enemies. For example, "there is thunder because we have stolen some food from a neighbour" or "the great storm ended because we helped somebody fend off a dangerous animal". Some of the people in the tribe or group may have thought that they had more knowledge or understanding of the environment and surroundings and that their theories or models that explained unusual happenings were better than others, some people might have had better communication and persuasion skills and so the other people in the tribe started to listen to them and follow their sayings or teachings and so they became leaders of the group.

Sometimes things simply could not be explained using any acquired knowledge or past experience, for example, the death of a seemingly normal and healthy child or the effects of a particularly severe storm or even an observed eclipse that suddenly turned day into night. On some of these occasions, super-natural explanations were devised where some unknown and superior force was deemed to have created these situations that were inflicted onto humans.

Faiths and Religions

From these circumstances people started to develop different beliefs to explain the things they did not understand, making up plausible stories which gave them a form of understanding and which decreased the uncertainty of not knowing. Uncertainty and randomness have always been a threat to our species and we have always tried to avoid them since we see them as an attempt against our survival.

With time the stories that were posed to explain the uncertain, became the accepted explanation for the events of unknown origin, making all who believed in them deposit all their faith in their veracity. The nature of these faiths depended on the original storyline used to explain the uncertainty and the way those groups of people related to each other and their environment. Some beliefs were punishment-driven "if we don't do this we will be punished", others more effort-driven "the more we work the more we will be rewarded". Some beliefs started to be associated with objects, the particular faith professing that the veneration of an entity, real or imagined, would provide rewards to its followers. The most common object of veneration has been our closest star, the Sun. In effect, this is the most natural and understandable object-oriented faith that we can imagine, since, without any doubt, the Sun is the most essential object that enables our existence.

Object veneration becomes object-adoration, which in turn can transform the revered element into an all-powerful, external creator and carer or God figure. Again depending on the particular belief, there have been single-God faiths or religions where the power resides in one supernatural being, for example, Christianity or multi-God faiths where different aspects of the universe like the stars, water, Earth and the seasons, are governed or cared for by different Gods. These characters have godly relationships and feuds between them, which sometimes affect humans in the form of wars or natural catastrophes. There are several examples of this in Mediterranean and Scandinavian mythologies.

In the knowledge space, that is, the space where we develop ideas based on the things we know, rational thought processes and proof are involved. With knowledge, we can create rational chains of thought, where we can go from knowledge about something we know onto something else we understand until finally, we arrive at a new or more complex knowledge and understanding. On the other hand, belief allows for this rational chain of thought to be broken and allows for the so-called "leaps-of-faith" that will take a person from a state of knowledge onto a state of belief, which permits no proof or rational consequence between one thought chain element and the next. As an example, Christianity is based on the belief that Jesus came back to life after three days of being considered dead. That is the main leap of faith Christianity proposes and asks its followers to believe in. It is a leap-of-faith because there are no instances in the whole of our rational documented history where this has happened to anyone. Not one. So you either believe it or you don't believe it.

Belief is defined by the dictionary as the "acceptance that something exists or is true, especially one without proof"[1]. It is something in which you deposit your complete trust, or faith, in order to accept it.

When a belief becomes a systematic pursuit of interests, usually governed by a set of rules, which are followed in an unquestioned manner, it becomes a religion. Religions have many positive attributes, for example, they give a common set of values and morals for people to work under, and so help its followers define the rules of their community or society. In most cases, it proposes and sometimes enforces, laws of behaviour within societies. If you share a religion you can feel close to someone you do not know, even if that person comes from another town or even country. The beliefs shared in a religion give common values and ways of looking at the world.

Unfortunately together with the creation of religions came people or groups of people that saw "power" behind this idea. The logic goes something like this:

"If I can control, or even invent, a religion that is based on a shared belief, if I manage to make people use the leap-of-faith to explain the source of this religion or belief then I can also make them believe in things that will benefit me or my group of interest".

And so, throughout our history, religion has come to be associated intimately with power, power of some over others. Examples of this are abundant throughout our history, the greatest wars and bloodshed have been waged and spilt in the name of religion. Even to our present day, we are still killing each other in great numbers, every single day, all in the name of religion.

And although we fight over our beliefs, when we look closely, most religions share a common ground, there are basic premises that need to be fulfilled for most of us to accept a religion.

First, there must be a way to be able to explain any kind of observable phenomenon even if it is not explainable scientifically, a supernatural entity is thus often chosen as the all-powerful overlord or master of any and all of the events and actions that we observe in the universe. Secondly, there must be a story of how this supernatural being or power came into contact with the Earth and earthlings. This story itself has usually supernatural events that gave rise to this special being, or his emissary, being in contact with our world. Thirdly the supernatural power or his messengers must start to tell the story that will create the set of beliefs for people to follow, these beliefs often include some rules or regulations for mortals to follow. Finally, the being or emissary must leave, disappear or die and leave behind his teachings and disciples to spread the word and gain the faith of the people.

The story is always full of details and descriptions of the being or emissary in various situations where his/her (it is usually a he!) mantle is tested and his disciples witness some miraculous action, which is then re-told to enrich and give more substance to the story.

Having described the most important ingredients of a religion, it is not my intention to diminish their importance, trivialize their power of persuasion or their power to move masses and accomplish great things. The mighty Roman Empire was completely overrun by Christianity in a relatively short time, Christians went from being the root of all evil to being the only allowed religion in the Roman Empire in just under 400 years and they still dominate the world having just over 31% of the world population following their religion. The second largest religion, in terms of world population, is Islam with just over 24% of the population then comes Hinduism with just over 15% and Buddhists with almost 7% of the world population. The statistics also show that just 16% of the population of the world declares itself to have no religious affiliation[2] which demonstrates the power and need for this aspect of our social bondage in all cultures.

But the power of religion is waning, the more we know, that is, the more we travel into the realm of knowledge, the more we leave beliefs behind. The more we know the less need we have of making up stories to explain the unknown. Slowly but relentlessly time has given us the tools to explain an ever-increasing area of knowledge. We know exactly why and when the Sun will rise and set, we can predict the apparition of celestial comets, we can predict weather conditions, although we cannot predict when earthquakes will happen we know why they occur, we understand the process of life, and so the list can continue describing the things we know or are in the process of understanding. Nevertheless, there is still a large majority of people who believe in religions and there will always be because although we know the mechanics of why things come to be, we still seek the purpose of why we exist and why we are here.

Existence

Sometimes it is necessary to take a different perspective in order to try to understand a particularly difficult problem and with the knowledge acquired, return to the original viewpoint and see if we have gained some useful insights. For example, we can combine different sources of information such as classical western science and eastern philosophy and let the mind explore the concept of our existence. I invite you to follow me in this change of perspective.

Let's start by imagining a tree, a tree doesn't know about distance, it is always rooted, literally, to the same spot on the ground throughout its life. A tree only "knows" about time, it observes how time changes its surroundings, day-by-day, night-by-night. Seasons pass, years, centuries and in some cases millennia. Trees experience no movement, no trips or journeys, just the experience of time passing around them. But although the tree is rooted to the planet and it is not moving at all with respect to it, it is still travelling through space, as we all are, at a staggering speed of 30 km/s with respect to our sun. To put it in terms of a more common observation, that's over one hundred times the speed of a commercial aeroplane.

So, What is a tree? At the mechanical/physical level, it is a system that takes energy from the Sun, gas from the atmosphere and nutrients from the ground to, well..., to **be** a tree. Let us go back on some aspects of this paragraph, "takes energy from the Sun", in other words, it captures energy from a star that is 150 million kilometres away, energy that takes more than 8 minutes to travel that distance and reach Earth. Next, "nutrients from the ground", in other words, it takes nourishment from the planet itself, through minerals and water.

But, knowing how a tree works does not answer the important question, Why do trees exist? What is the purpose of the tree as a species? Trying to answer this question might shed some light to that "other" question of, Why do **we** exist? So let's try to come up with an answer, at least for trees!

When we view the tree from our own point of view as humans, we can immediately identify the benefits of having trees around and we can quickly see those benefits as the reasons for the tree's existence, they produce oxygen and food, they give shade, they provide building material, amongst other things. It's easy to make this list since they are all things that we value and that if somehow they did not exist, we would miss. We immediately see the purpose of the tree's existence, at least from our point of view.

But if we turned the questions around and were able to ask the tree, Why do you exist? and, Why do humans exist? What would it say?

For the first question the tree might have the same self-centred arguments we give when asked this question about ourselves, Why do you exist? To survive and to procreate, both things being related. For the second question: Why do humans exist? It might again start with a tree-centred view, it might say that humans are one of the several means through which they -the trees- reproduce and survive, people eat the tree's fruit and in the process disseminate the tree's seeds, which in turn create other trees. The tree can immediately define the purpose and need for the existence of humans. But we could also imagine that these species had a wider sense of natural awareness and might reply to the same question with something more akin to:

We use the energy from the Sun and Earth to create material that helps to keep the balance and growth of life on our planet. We rely on other species for our procreation and other species rely on us for food and shelter.

This change of perspective can give us interesting insights into the relationships between all living things, we can come to see that all living things rely on other living things in order to be able to survive. We are all each other's means of survival, reproduction, protection, food and shelter. I believe that this is the way of looking at the reason for our existence or the existence of any living thing. I propose that we need to take this wider perspective, the perspective of the indivisible all-encompassing "system of life" and not the perspective of one particular species. So in this respect answering the question "Why do you exist?" in isolation and from the point of view of just one species makes no sense. The question cannot be answered until we see the relationship between all the elements that make up the system of life. Humans could not exist if there were no other living things on this planet. Furthermore, the system of life also incorporates the non-living since we could not exist without some basic material elements that provide the conditions for life, such as, water, soil, minerals and air, amongst many other things. It's all part of the fabric of life and each piece has a purpose and I believe the purpose is the relationship of one piece with all others.

So, we are all in it together. Individually all species exist to survive and reproduce in order to keep their place in the shared fabric of life. Each species has developed convoluted mechanisms to do both, survival and reproduction. Let's go back to trees for a moment and think that since they cannot move, survival and reproduction depends on the relationship to external circumstances and other life forms. Nevertheless, within the limited degrees of freedom that being rooted to one spot give you, trees have optimized themselves in order to maximize their chances of survival. To capture that distant energy that enables their life, they have developed hundreds of renewable, multi-surface, interconnected, redundant, energy capture devices we call "leaves". To protect themselves against predators, they secrete fluids and scents to keep those predators away. To protect themselves from the rigours of the weather they are slender, flexible and yet robust. Paradoxically the all-so-delicate and essential task of reproduction depends mostly on external factors, such as the wind or birds, which help the cross-pollination of the male and female organs of different trees to start the reproduction process. After pollination, wind and animals are again relied upon to carry the seed to an appropriate location for growth. When wind is the carrier, the seeds are usually designed to be good long-distance flyers so that once they are airborne they can spread over a wide range. In the case of animals being used for the dispersion of the tree's future offspring, the seed is packed within an attractive, edible and nutritious package, the fruit, so that once eaten by an animal it will be excreted at an appropriate distance away and again have a good chance or survival in order to start the cycle of life once again.

If we are all part of this fabric of life, Are we all essential and necessary? The answer is probably, No. Dinosaurs are extinct and life goes on. The same is true for the Do-Do bird and many other species that have become extinct throughout time. When extinctions happen the fabric of life finds a new equilibrium point to continue, as long as the conditions for life exist the fabric of life can continue. So, Can humans become extinct? The answer is a definite, Yes. We already know that life was created before humans came into existence, and so it follows that there could be a time after humans.

Why are we here?

We could say that humans exist to participate in this fabric of life. We have a role to play, a role that is totally inter-dependent on the other participants and a role where we cannot participate alone. A role in which we are not essential in any particular way and that, in time, we may even be replaced by some other species.

This answer to the question seems to give rise to another fundamental question,

Why is there a fabric of life at all?

I believe the fabric of life has arisen simply because the conditions for its existence are appropriate on this planet, not because of a grand design or designer but simply as a consequence of the mix of conditions that are found on Earth. This can be thought of analogous to the reason why water flows into the sea from the mountain top, not because of a design or a pre-determined destiny, but simply because the physical and chemical circumstances that water encounters such as the terrain, the Earth's gravitational force and temperature, together create the right conditions on this particular planet for liquid water to flow from a high point, be channelled through valleys and creeks and finally flow into the mass of water we call the sea. So why does water flow into the sea? "Because the conditions are favourable and hence it can". Then following the same logic to answer the question Why is there a fabric of life? We can argue that life exists simply because the appropriate circumstances and conditions are present on this planet and as a consequence, life exists, in other words, life exists because it can or to put it another way, we are here because we can be.

. . .

In fact, and some religious readers might cringe at this paragraph, there doesn't really need to be a purpose for us being here, the physical, chemical and biological mechanisms arose, produced the correct conditions and life was only a consequence, minimal life at first but through a process of natural selection and evolution, it gave rise to ever more complex forms of living organisms creating a fabric of interconnected species that enables and permits the existence of the fabric of life itself. The whole system has evolved adaptive qualities, which means that when one piece ceases to exist, another one takes its place as more pieces are constantly being created.

Life and Replicators

The driving force of this system or framework is life itself, life takes many forms but one of the essential aspect of how we define life is the capacity of organisms to reproduce and thus create more organisms with their own characteristics, generating whole populations. If life is the engine that drives the whole system then what fuels the need to exist?

Why do organisms have an urge to survive and reproduce?

The evolutionary answer to this question is similar to the answer that was given earlier in the case of the reason for existence: "Because they can". Once again we have to go back to the beginning of time to understand this, and for me, one the best explanation of what could have happened in those early beginnings is given by the work of Richard

Dawkins in his book "The Selfish Gene" which I will try to describe briefly in the following paragraphs.

After we got past the **physical** creation of matter in the universe, at the point of the Big Bang, what was left was an incredible amount of energy and matter made up of atoms, which freely started to interact with each other giving rise to the next stage of evolution, the **chemical** stage. In this phase some stable chemical structures began to form, stability is the primal requirement of evolution, the way atoms combine to form molecules must create stable structures otherwise evolution is not possible.

Due to their particular properties, some atoms were more attracted to other atoms and that enabled them to combine and form stable structures, which we now call molecules. With time some molecules, the most stable ones, started to be dominant and establish themselves in the universe. What happened next is the great-leap-forwards in terms of evolution, the occurrence of molecules that could replicate themselves, what Dawkins calls the "replicators".

At first thought, replication might sound like a miraculous occurrence and only possible via the intervention of an external being, which would take us back to the arguments in favour of religion. But given the combination of molecules and a very long time period, we can explain the occurrence of replication in a rather simple manner as was done by Dawkins. Here is a brief summary of the process, I hope my description will do it justice.

Once we have stable molecules formed by the affinity of certain atoms with others, we can imagine how replicators work by applying the principles of electromagnetic and nuclear forces between and within the atoms. Such forces are able to attract or repel other molecules in such a way as to form exact copies of themselves. Imagine a molecule consisting of atoms A and B arranged in a string:

Original molecule:
A–A–B–A–A–B–B

The attraction forces just described will attract similar atoms towards it to form another combination of the same form, something like a mirror image of itself:

Original molecule (positive):
A–A–B–A–A–B–B
A–A–B–A–A–B–B
:Attracted atoms that form a replicated molecule (positive copy)

This could also work in the same way but by opposite attraction with each atom attracting its polarity opposite version to form a negative copy of itself:

Original molecule (positive)
A–A–B–A–A–B–B
B–B–A–B–B–A–A
:Attracted atoms that form a replicated molecule (negative copy)

In either case, the molecule would have a replicating capacity with the ability to create copies, positive or negative, of itself. It is thus easy to imagine how, given enough time, a molecule with such a "superpower" would come to dominate over all other molecules. If it could duplicate itself, it would skip the random process of molecule creation that all other molecules were following. The key for this to happen is the immense expanses of time and energy that such a process would need in order to be triggered and to develop. Such a process would not give rise to life in a human lifetime, but given enough time of random molecule creation, it is possible to imagine such an event happening.

Once replicators are in place and given more time, the replicator structures would evolve in such a way that the more stable mutations, or mutations that could replicate faster, became dominant. Given enough time, more complex structures would be formed giving rise to mega-molecule structures that could start to be called life forms. Within ourselves, our DNA molecule is a replicator of the negative-positive kind, this is our own replicator, our gene that enables our structure to replicate and evolve and that has accompanied humans from the beginning of our existence as a species.

This theory is also the basis for the explanation of our own drive to survive and reproduce, a drive that is simply the product of an evolutionary selected mechanism that has privileged organisms capable of reproduction and that through millions of years of survival has enabled the dominance of these organisms over all others. Humans are simply programmed to reproduce because they can and because, for millions of years, it has proven to be a successful means to survive and maintain our species populous within the fabric of life.

Life and evolution are strange processes that are not intuitively understood at first since they can only function given long periods of time and our reference point as humans has a very narrow time frame. Evolution is a mutation-trial-error system that is not deterministic or designed. The key to understanding how it works is that given enough instances of replication and time, mutations will occur, and if those mutations have benefits in the replication process, then they will become dominant in time.

I believe that when we think about these aspects of our existence, confusion starts to creep in when we start our analysis from the point of view of a highly evolved molecular structure such as ourselves, humans. We analyse our capabilities, the way our eyes work, our limbs or the power of our hearing, and we think that the only way to be able to create such precision and versatility is to have had a supernatural power design such systems with specifications, material and testing such as we would do for a human-designed machine. This is a very self-centred approach to finding an explanation and is encased in our own, limited, time frame. Evolution has been able to create the finely tuned instruments within our bodies through a long process of incremental change and millions of years of trials, successes and many, many errors.

If our replicator molecule had the capability of asking itself: "What is the purpose of my existence?" what would it answer? Probably "To replicate!" But it could also answer in a more generous way by saying something like "In order to enable others to evolve and become molecules like me."

Religion can help us answer our fundamental questions but more often than not the answers are always species-centred and involve some sort of argument that implies that the questioner is part, somehow, of the chosen species, "the chosen ones" which dominate over the other species.

Evolution can explain the mechanics of how we got to be the way we are and how by a slow and laborious process of trial and error it was possible to create complex life forms such as humans, birds, fish or trees. It can also show us that we are all part of a system of interconnected life and material that can only exist by relying on each other's contribution to the fabric of life.

Whether you think that the creation of the universe was due to the designs of a superior being or that we evolved from a primal concoction of chemicals and energy or even that we -humans- arrived on Earth from another planet or galaxy, whoever you are and whatever your reality, you carry it with you as your personal belief. Based on your own particular experience, the knowledge you have accumulated throughout your life, the relationship you have with your surroundings and all the concepts you have created to help you understand your environment, have led you to form your own conclusion of how you got here and the reason for your existence. I believe that your conclusion is your purpose and your reason to live. All of our collective conclusions are correct, none of them are better or "truer" than any other, after all, every theory of how we came into being invariably requires a "leap-of-faith" at some point in their argument. Religions clearly demand such a leap for us to believe in the super natural existence of beings or powers with capabilities beyond our own. On the other hand, science also demands a leap-of-faith and belief in the theories put forward by scientists that make models with the best and most current knowledge available, but that have no indisputable evidence that those theories are true. We don't really know whether the Big Bang occurred and that it is an accurate explanation of how it all started or that the mechanics of replication are indeed how primal life started, we cannot design experimental evidence to prove these theories, they are all unproven and thus, you could say, they belong in the realm of belief.

All beliefs are valid and help us to come to terms with living in this immense expanse of time where we occupy only an infinitesimal period of existence. Even if you think that you do not have "a belief" or "a faith" you still believe in something, not believing is also a belief.

13

TIME FOR MORE TIME

Time is getting crowded

IT SEEMS that for most of our recent history we have been fascinated by our own attempts at trying to do more things in the least possible time. We have been having a sort of rebellion against the nature of time, trying to stretch the margins of what is possible to be achieved within its boundaries.

Our modern way of life revolves around the ways in which we do the same things we have always done but in a shorter time. That may not seem like a bad thing if you take it as a general rule, but what is worrying is that when we achieve doing these things faster or more efficiently, instead of using the time to relax or do things to improve our lives or the lives of the ones we love, we tend to fill the new time-gaps created with even more things to do. In effect, we are creating time for ourselves only to fill it once again with more things to achieve, in a continuous never-ending spiral that overcrowds our existence.

We could even say that in the last centuries we have

been engaged in an extremely violent and bloody confrontation against time. It seems that since we cannot understand its basic nature and we cannot control or manipulate it, we have embarked upon the task of declaring war against it, intending to defeat it. This conquering war has been waged with three weapons with which we have revolutionized the way we live within the constraints of time and they are: transportation, communication and computing.

Let's first look at how the speed of our own displacement or transport has changed throughout the ages. On average a human being can walk at about 4 km per hour (km/hr), so covering a distance of 20 km would take, on average, about 5 hours on foot. The same distance would take approximately 1 hour and 20 minutes on a trotting horse, if we used a fast car it would take about 12 minutes, while on a fast train just 6 minutes. Just doing this simple comparison we can see how we have gone from an activity that took us 5 hours, to the same activity taking us 6 minutes, that is a 50-fold difference in time, saving us a total of 4 hours and 54 minutes if we use the train instead of going on foot. Putting this into context, say you were looking for a job and happened to find work 20 km from the place where you lived, in the first scenario it would not be possible for you to walk to your work and back home every day, so you might have had to move nearer if you wanted to take that job, or just look for work somewhere else to earn a living. On the other hand, all the other transportation alternatives listed above would seem more feasible while also saving you a lot of time that you can use for other purposes.

The second weapon in this struggle against time has been the advancement of communications. The earliest methods of communication relied on extending our senses through longer distances as when we used smoke or light signals between two points or sounds such as drumming or chanting. In both cases, the methods had limitations in terms of the distance covered and relied on good natural conditions, such as a clear day or favourable wind directions. Other systems that were more reliable in all weather conditions and covered greater distances involved carrying messages using the same transportation methods described earlier, such as, horses or vehicles. In these cases, and depending on the specific transport method chosen, the communication would have taken anything from hours to minutes to arrive to its destination. Early examples of this were services such as the Pony Express mail delivery service in the US in the middle of the 19th century or the postal services of today that use trains, planes and ships to achieve their delivery of letters and packages. From these beginnings, we move on to the use of electricity as our main mode of communication, the telegraph, the telephone and lately, the Internet. In the early days these electrically powered technologies were fixed between two points because there were two fundamental constraints to resolve, first, the source of the electricity to power the devices and secondly how the communication devices were inter-connected. This second constraint was usually solved by the use of cables. The first great example of this form of cable communication was the proliferation of the electric telegraph. Starting in the first half of the 19th century we saw thousands of telegraph poles erected to hold thousands of kilometres of telegraph cable around the world, cables everywhere, on land and also through the oceans so that continents could be connected, as happened in 1866 when Europe and America were connected by the first transatlantic submarine cable.

In terms of the evolution in the speed at which communication actually happens, we can compare one of the first electrical signalling systems, the Morse code, with current electronic transmission technology. The Morse Code, invented by Samuel Morse in the 1840s, allowed an operator to transmit text at an average speed of about 5 words per minute, today communication through a Wi-Fi network working at a speed of 100 Mbps (Mega or Million bits per second) can transfer text at a rate of about 7,000 words per minute, if we compare the speed of these two forms of communication, we can say that if we were to transmit a book like the one you are reading, with about 60,000 words, it would take 200 hours using Morse Code and just less than 1 minute over a Wi-Fi connection, saving 199 hours and 59 minutes of your time to do other things!

The third weapon at our disposal in this war against time has been the immense electronic computational capability that we have created and constructed. Based on Boolean mathematics, where there are only two states of knowledge, True or False, and the construction of ever-smaller devices that can store the results of millions upon millions of Boolean calculations, we are able to achieve things that were deemed in the realms of science fiction just a century ago. Some common examples of these computational machines are personal computers, automated banking systems, train schedulers, traffic guidance systems, medical instrumentation, cashiers, automobile control systems, all mobile technology, gaming consoles and many, many other products and services. Computing power has become so commonplace that it would be almost impossible to imagine a world without most of the things that we take for granted and that make our life a lot easier, more informed and safer today than ever before. We have become so sophisticated in the design and manufacture of computing devices that we can place huge amounts of this computing power into very small devices, devices so small that you can carry in your pocket, such as mobile phones, watches or gaming equipment. This industry has grown so fast and given us such power that any one of the smartphones or smartwatches that we own in the first decade of the 21st century has over 500 times as much computing power than the whole of the first Apollo Mission's Guidance Computer that controlled the first journey and landing on the Moon in the 1960s[1].

The advances in these three elements, Transportation, Communication and Computing, are extremely powerful when taken in isolation, but when combined, the effects are even more stunning and have provided us with such concepts as mobile and wearable technology, which include all forms of communication –written, spoken, visual- and computation –calculators, countless applications- that can be taken with us as we travel freely between different locations.

The power of ubiquitous information, that is, information wherever we are, has revolutionized the way we interact with each other and since cultures are based on human relationships, it has started to have effects on the way our societies develop. Technology has also revolutionized the way we use time and given us the permanent possibility, wherever we happen to be, to connect, read, watch, calculate, write, listen, talk, with any source of information or person in the world, whenever we want.

All these technologies have enabled us to do things in a way that takes less time to achieve, freeing time to do more things. As we all know this process is going on right now with new technology being invented to "help" us in this way. So where is this evolution taking us? What is the ultimate goal we want to achieve? When will we deem that we have won this battle against time?

Technological Evolution

Not too long ago, technological evolution advanced at a pace much slower than today and this meant that our relatively slow biological clocks and adaptation processes had time to learn and absorb the use of the new technology. For example, it took over 60 years for the telephone to reach 80% of the US households, giving plenty of time for people to learn to use the technology and to get used to calling their relatives! As the pace of technological evolution and development started to increase in the last decades, the time for humans to learn the way to use the new technologies has had to speed up but has not been able to accomplish the task at the rates that have been imposed by technology. Another example, it took just over 15 years for over 80% of the US population to use the mobile or cell phone[2], this has forced us to adapt to huge changes within a few generations, something that we were required to do in longer time frames until not so long ago. This means that there is technology around today that for anyone over 15 years old did not exist at the time they were born. As a simple example, you might find that your grandfather was born when fixed phones were starting to be common, your father with the first colour television sets, yourself with the start of personal computers, your first child with Internet, your second child with HD television and your third child with mobile phones! Technology is evolving much faster than humans, that is to say, technology is evolving much faster than biology. Although we think of ourselves as being capable of achieving anything, our biological bodies and minds need certain times, and the right conditions, in order to develop and absorb the changes in its environment and surroundings. We need to understand those human-times and not compete against the technology we have created. In a speed race, natural biology cannot defeat artificial technology.

We have to choose not to race, choose to respect the timings of our own bodies. As we saw in another chapter when the body is left to its own devices its natural response is to slow down, in fact, without external references, it can settle down into an almost 48-hour cycle, that is half the speed we are used to operating. So on one side, our biology feels more comfortable at a slower speed, while our technology is driving us into an ever faster mode. We need to apply our intelligence in order to respect our biology taking full advantage of our technology but without having one overwhelm the other.

Multitasking

We experience time as an inexorably linear or sequential series of forward-moving events so we should not be surprised to find that our brains, and hence minds, have also been wired in the same manner, linearly doing one task after another. I am talking, of course, about our conscious mind, our non-conscious mind can accomplish several tasks in parallel such as maintaining our hearts ticking, our breathing in check, processing the food we eat and managing the information that arrives from our external and internal senses, eyes, ears, skin and other organs. When we talk about our brains or minds, notice that we tend to use both words as synonyms, for the purposes of our discussion here I will take the approach of using the word "brain" when I refer to the material stuff that's within our skull, the various tissues, nerves and cells, and I will use the word "mind" when I talk about the immaterial things that our brain can accomplish such as thought, imagination, emotions and feelings.

As our conscious mind works in a linear fashion, that's the preferred way, that's the way we are built because it makes sense when we are immersed in our perceived linear time-space. Nevertheless, we can switch between these linear tasks very fast, we are able to focus our attention on something at the "blink of an eye" in fact even faster since the average blink takes 100 - 400 ms[3] while task switching in our minds has been measured at under 100 ms[4], the actual speed depending on the complexity and familiarity with the task involved. But still, we cannot do two things simultaneously, we can only have one attention point at any one time. If we put it in computer jargon we might say that our consciousness has only one Central Processing Unit or CPU.

In this war to defeat time that we identified earlier, where we have been trying, by all means, to do more and more things during a particular period, we are constantly stressing our linear minds in the effort to process more data, we even take this to the point where we can misunderstand the real capacity of our minds. At the beginning of the twenty-first century there was much talk about how young people could "multi-task", meaning that they were able to do more than one thing simultaneously, we even studied how the new generations, that had been born with modern technology, the so-called "Millennial" generation, were apparently able to do this multitasking while the older generations, the "Baby Boomers" as they are labelled, could not, or at least had more difficulty, achieving this feat. Some people gave credit to the theory that in the span of only one generation our minds had suddenly acquired this "super-power", that somehow it had just appeared by the mere presence of the new technological gadgets. But after the dust finally settled on this hype, evidence finally came from biology and the neuro-sciences demonstrating the facts in favour of linearity and explaining the impossibility of our brain from performing tasks simultaneously. The hyped-masses were quietened.

Nevertheless, we can still talk about multitasking if we apply a slightly different definition. Multitasking can be described as the ability to quickly switch between different tasks giving the impression that multiple things are been executed simultaneously, when in fact all things are been worked upon sequentially, in a linear fashion. This process has a penalty attached to it in that every time we task-switch there is a change in the context of what we are doing and what we are about to do which takes time and effort. A change from task-A to task-B requires leaving task-A on standby and taking up task-B and then remembering the points where we left both tasks if we are to go on and move onto a task-C. Every time we switch, there is a penalty in time and effort in order to pause one task and start another. This switching can be done at various speeds, and someone with some skill and practice can achieve this at a very fast rate. Unfortunately, many studies have indicated that constant and repeated multitasking is not the most efficient way to carry out tasks and that it might even have some negative effects[5] as we shall see in the following paragraphs.

. . .

Let's explore multitasking from the point of view of some common activities. Say you are reading a book, a novel, sitting down in your favourite spot and suddenly the doorbell rings. You hear the doorbell and begin to decide what to do. There are several ways you can respond going from doing "nothing", to getting up as fast as you can to see who is at the door. Let's assume you eventually get up to answer the door, consider that the mere act of hearing the doorbell and thinking of what needs to be done has already taken your attention away from reading, it has taken time and effort, now you close the book, stand up, walk to the door and attend the door caller. After that is done you go back to the book, sit down, open the book and re-engage with it. I say re-engage because it will take a little time to find the position where you left it and remember the context and the events that were happening at the time you paused reading.

All this took time, you were reading, engrossed in a story with characters, tensions and emotions, you had to put all that on hold, attend to the new task of opening the door and then return and re-create the initial situation you had originally left behind. You could say that between the original reading and the second reading scenario, you had to accomplish the following five tasks:

1. Leave reading
2. Prepare to open the door
3. Attend to the door
4. Leave opening the door
5. Prepare to read again

And if we look carefully at the list, we see that the first three tasks form the basic triplet that always needs to be repeated whenever we want to switch from one task to another: Leave A / Prepare for B / Do B.

In the situation above, I have shown how we switch between two very analogue tasks, reading a book and opening a door, both tasks require considerable time and physical effort to be achieved successfully. When we perform tasks that have a large "digital" component associated with them, such as checking email, playing a computer game or sending a text message, there is less physical effort involved but the same sequence of concepts applies, there is doing, switching, doing, switching, doing, etc. Each "switching" phase containing the three basic components just described, leave doing A, prepare to do B, do B, they are always there. Furthermore, the convergence of functionality that we now find in single electronic devices such as mobile phones and computers, where we can do many things within one single device, has meant that the physical effort required in switching has almost been eliminated. The more things we do within a single device, such as a mobile phone, the smaller the switching times and the more things we appear to be doing in parallel or simultaneously but, as we have seen, we are not, we are just faking simultaneity with fast switching from one task to another.

There are several drawbacks to multitasking and some of them have already been documented in various research papers[6] and articles[7]. In the first place multitasking is not our preferred way of using our minds, we have seen that our mind has been wired for our linear existence in our linear time span, it gets tiresome to be continuously switching, especially at fast speeds, and our stress levels rise. Secondly, to accomplish understanding or learning of any sort we need to place full attention and remain in that state of attention for some time, permanent switching between tasks does not allow time for the mind to fully focus and make the necessary neural connections to make them permanent and learn, the result of this is that things start to become superficial and without deep understanding. When I mention here the concept of learning, I don't just mean the formal school-type of learning, we learn constantly, our mind is a constant categorizing and learning machine working on small concepts like finding the best route to work and also big ones such as whether you should buy a house or not! An example of the way our minds work, and something that we can relate to learning, can be shown when we think of the experience you might have had learning to ride a bicycle, to drive a car or to play an instrument. It is impossible, or at least very difficult, to achieve any of these complex tasks if there is any sort of task switching going on. Full attention, repetition and time are needed in order to master any of these abilities. It is difficult to imagine learning to drive a car while at the same time watching television or learning to play the guitar as you talk on the phone with your friends.

Our mind is in a permanent learning process, which can be disrupted by the overuse of multitasking. Confusion and exhaustion have been recorded as side effects of continuous multitasking. Also, general fatigue can arise from doing strictly mind-centric work, our evolution has prepared us to have a fully active body and mind, so having a very passive body and an over-worked mind has negative effects on our balance and wellbeing. Lastly, on this list, are studies that have shown that people with a high multitasking lifestyle, in time, tend to get worst at multitasking!

This is mainly due to the already mentioned repetitive, accumulative exhaustion effect[8]. So a high level of multitasking, in the long run, is detrimental to multitasking itself.

The question is then: Why do we do it? And the answer comes from biology, task switching releases several types of endorphins and chemicals that have a stimulating and rewarding effect on our bodies. Firstly, at switch time, chemicals are released to enhance our senses and to prepare the body for what is about to happen, after all, throughout our history task switching might have been followed by a very quick escape, taking some evasive action or a fight response related to our survival. Additionally, accomplishing these multiple mini-tasks, which we do all day, makes our bodies release reward chemicals to signify success at having achieved a goal. So, like most of our behaviour, it's a biochemical rush that drives us into this pattern of activity, with the difference that with the great technological development of the past few years, we have never had the chance of generating so many opportunities for this type of chemical reward system to function repeatedly over such long periods of time, so much so, that it may even become an addiction in some cases.

There are also social drawbacks to multitasking, how many times have we been in a meeting, presentation or family dinner and we see that some of the people attending are "multitasking"? That is, chatting on their mobile devices, answering emails or surfing the web, as we have seen, what they are actually doing is this process of task switching where for periods of time they do not have their attention on where they are but rather they are focused on wherever their digital device is enabling them to be, in other words, their attention, remember there is only **one** attention, is switching from where they physically are to where their devices allow them to be.

Giving Time some Time

Understanding the principles just described such as the linearity of time, the concept that there is only one attention, that your conscious mind can only focus on one thing at a time and that when we multitask we are in fact switching from one task to the next, might help us in the search for the ways we should give our minds and bodies a rest. It might be impossible and even undesirable to completely avoid the modern way of life, not many people can leave everything behind and go and farm up a hill, contemplating and connecting with nature, indeed you might not even want to do such a thing anyway! But it is important to understand the way we are constructed and the limitations posed by our biological and psychological structure and from that knowledge take care of it in the best way we can. Just as we have learned that it is a good idea to brush our teeth every day to keep them healthy, we must recognize that our bodies and minds also need some form of regular cleansing to maintain the balance and harmony of all their complex systems and structures. Whether it is a sport for the body, meditation for the mind, swimming, jogging, walking, the practice of Yoga or Taichi, or any other activity, we need to accommodate within our lives regular spaces to cleanse the mind and body.

Time and Others

As I write these words, it is the first day of my 54th year here on Earth. That means that yesterday was my 53rd birthday.

Mathematics, just as time, is rigorous and when combined they are implacable.

So what's the score so far?

In the grand scheme of things, I could say that it has not been bad, all systems check and life has had no great upheavals. On the internal side, deep within, some things do stir. The most recurring being a series of questions that seem to have no possibility of finding a definite answer, questions relating to how good I have been at constructing and caring for my human relations.

Questions that start with "Am I a good..." and may follow with whichever of the following words: father, husband, son, uncle, brother, nephew, friend, colleague, boss?

These questions always seem to appear at some point in our lives, but how can we answer them?

One way to approach this might be to make up lists of what you think it means to be a good father, mother, husband, wife, son, etc. and see how many you can check, a little bit like some women and men magazines tend to do when they write articles such as:

"Are you a good husband?, Answer these questions and find out!"

I tend to think that this is not the right approach, it is too mechanical and too simplistic, I don't believe that there are recipes to help us be what we are. As we discover with age and experience, there are pointers and ways of approaching life, but no recipes.

As we have seen in other chapters, one of the possible

answers to the question of the purpose of our existence is that we exist to be a part of what I have called the fabric of life. We play a role in the interconnected lives of all other beings on this planet and in particular in the lives of others within our species, our society, our friends and our families. So, we will approach the question of "Am I a good...?" from the perspective of looking at the amount of time we spend in the company of others, this might tell us something about our dedication towards our relationships and our role within our family and society.

There was an interesting study published in 2017 by the US Bureau of Labor Statistics on how US citizens spend their hours with others[9].

The study analyses the amount of time spent with other people during the day, the day, in this case, is taken to be a waking 8-hour day discounting night-time and it groups the people we spend time with into these 6 categories:

1. Friends
2. Parents-Siblings-Family
3. Co-workers
4. Children
5. Partners
6. Alone

Although this study was made using data from US families, the trends are probably very similar in most countries that share a western culture, there might be shifts in the times when certain things happen, for example, the time when children leave the parental home or the time when partners appear in our lives, but in general if we live in the western world, we can relate quite directly with the data that appears in the report.

The information recollected is very detailed but for the purposes of this discussion, we will aggregate the data and group the age range of the subjects into decades: 0-10, 10-20, 20-30, etc. in this way we will see several interesting trends.

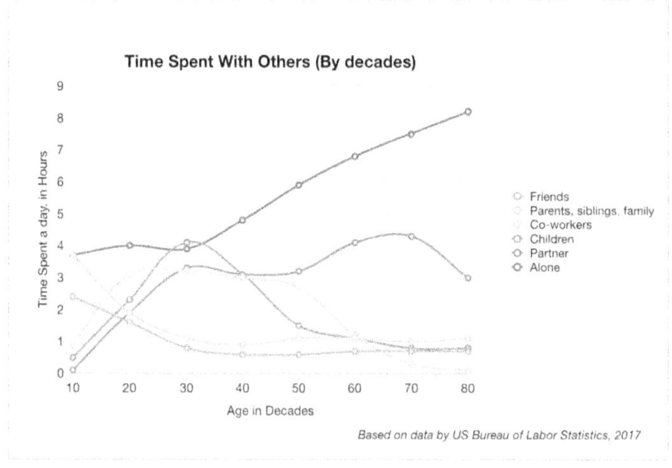

Based on data from the US Bureau of Labor Statistics on how Americans spend their hours with others.

First, and most prominent, is that the time we spend "Alone" increases dramatically from the fourth decade of our lives starting at about 4 hours a day to occupy the whole day by the time we are 80 years old.

The data also shows that our second decade of life is the one that has the greatest amount of overall change, with Family and Friends in decline from around 3 to 1 hours of shared time a day and an increase in time spent with Partners, Children and Co-workers, each one of these categories accounting for around 3 hours of time spent a day. The third decade, from 30 to 40 years of age, seems to be the busiest decade with regards to time spent with others, most groups maintaining their level of timeshare, with the Children category being the most demanding group and Friends the least.

The fourth and fifth decades are marked by stability of time spent with Co-workers and Partners, with about 3 hours each, and in the fourth decade, we see the start of the sharp increase in the time spent Alone and the decline in the time spent with Children. In the sixth decade, as the time spent at work declines, the time with Partners increases to over 4 hours a day and then into the seventh decade most times stabilize once again except for the time spent Alone which continues to increase.

So does this approach help us in some way to answer the questions we posed at the beginning of this chapter?

Am I a good: father, husband, son, uncle, brother, nephew, friend, colleague, boss?

Well, maybe a little. Without delving into the particulars of any relationship and, of course, generalizing from the numbers, we could conclude from the data and description just given that there are two very distinct types of time periods in our lives, periods which are marked by changes in the amount of time that we spend with other people and periods that seem to show more stability in the mix of people with which we share time. The periods of change seems to happen in our second decade and then towards the fifth and sixth decades of our lives while the rest of the time relative stability is observed, at least in the way we choose or need to spend time with others. Dividing the periods in this manner we might propose that in those periods where the time spent is being re-shuffled, that is where the changes occur, we might be more likely to ask ourselves questions or have increased doubts as to whether we are behaving in a desirable manner. On the other hand in the periods less prone to change, it is likely that stability gives us a sense of security and contentment that makes it less likely to be subjected to questioning. And so our late teenage years and our twenties tend to be periods of doubt when we are getting accustomed to being fully working adults, we start having emotional relationships with peers, and maybe start to settle down to begin to form a family. Further on in life, by the time we are in our 50s, there is often an association with some sort of "middle-age" crisis in which the changes make us question, once again, the purpose of our lives, this is often combined with the period our children start leaving home, our working years are passing their mid-point and we begin to think of our lives "after-work".

From the point of view of time then, it seems almost natural that there are periods of doubt and questioning which are related to the changes we experience in our immediate relationship circles. Changes always trigger our inquisitive side in order to find possible solutions. So trying to answer the question I have been posing might just lead us to the answer that we need to concentrate more on making sure that we spend the appropriate amount of time with the "relevant others" that we care about at the different periods of our lives, and to be aware and accept that there are natural changes in our relationships that will change during our lifetime. That would be a starting point but it needs to be complemented with the right attitude and actions that make the most of those times spent with others, making sure that they are of a quality that will be more than just superficial in order to build strong and enduring relationships.

Just to delve deeper into the time we spend with others, there is an interesting article by the German economist, Max Roser called "Working Hours" posted on the web site ourworldindata.org[10], it analyses the change in the time we spend at work from the 19th to 21st century, the article shows how in the last 150 years, in most developed countries, we have decreased that amount of time by an average of 30 hours a week. That means, for example, that in the UK, working periods have gone from an average of 56.9 hours a week in 1870 to just 38.9 hours a week in the year 2000. In the case of Belgium, the change has been even more dramatic going from 72.2 hours a week in 1870 to a mere 36.5 hour a week in the year 2000. So, what have we done with these "free" hours at our disposal? Well, if we look at more data we can pose the hypotheses that most of those hours a week that have been freed, have gone into leisure activities such as watching television, streaming content, surfing the Internet, social media and other screen-based entertainment since data shows that we tend to spend an ever-increasing amount of time in front of a digital device of some sort! It may be a generalization but it highlights the personal challenge that we have in deciding on how to use our free time wisely. Do we practise relationships with machines or with others through machines, as in the case of team online games, or do we nourish our face-to-face, multi-sensory, body-language-rich relationships with others?

. . .

Filling our lives and our time with as many tasks as we can is not only stressful, it also deprives us of having the most precious commodity available, time, and more specifically, time with others. In recent years loneliness has become such a great problem that not only have governments financed studies on the subject but also, during 2018, the UK government appointed a "Minister for Loneliness", when in January of that year, Tracey Crouch became the world's first state politician to attempt to tackle this great problem of our modern world.

The purpose of our life is to inter-relate to other people and to nature, after all, we are part of the fabric of life. It is up to ourselves to create and nourish those relationships and prevent that, towards the end of our life's journey, being "alone" does not turn into being "lonely".

14

(BIOLOGICAL) TIME VS. (TECHNOLOGICAL) TIME

Biological learning

ALL OF OUR most extraordinary and also our most terrible achievements throughout history have been made possible using an ability that separates us from all other species and that is our unlimited learning capacity. Not only do we learn during our entire lives, we then pass on what has been learned onto other, later, generations in a cumulative and ever-growing learning spiral. Learning is an experience based on time since any type of learning requires time for cognition, memory, imitation, repetition, understanding and application, but above all else, it requires dedication or more specifically dedication of our time.

As humans, we are born armed with a wonderful biological machine we call "our body" which, apart from the mostly mechanical external parts, has within it a brain and a mind. The greatest thing about this machine is its ability to learn, without this ability, we would not be able to survive. Unlike other species, a human baby is not able to subsist unaided once it is born, it relies entirely on more developed humans for all its essential needs except for breathing, nourishing from its mother's milk and the excretion of unwanted matter (urination and defecation). But from the second we leave our mother's body and are in contact with the external environment, the process of learning starts. Some essential mechanisms are built into our body-system as fundamental reflexes, most notably as I have mentioned, breathing, but also all internal organ processes that allow our body to function, heartbeat, blood circulation, chemical processing, etc. As for the rest of our survival mechanisms, including the ability to know what is edible and what may harm us, they are learned in time.

Most psychologists agree that the first five years of our development and learning will shape most of our future lives, that period of time corresponds to the first 43,200 hours of our lives or just about 6% of our total life span and in every single one of those hours we are in a constant learning process, non-stop, 24 hours a day, 7 days a week. Within the first month of life –the first 720 hours- the external senses such as hearing and taste start to be tuned up to the new environment. By the third month -2,160 hours- muscle control is taking shape and it goes on until the sixth month -4,320 hours- when grasping is almost perfected. Sitting up comes roughly around month number nine -6,480 hours- and standing is perfected by the first year of life -8,640 hours-. By the second year -17,280 hours- we manage a vocabulary of some 200 words and by year three -25,920 hours- we have learned enough language to make up sentences and start to articulate more complex concepts, build simple structures with wooden blocks and use crayons to produce simple drawings. By year five -43,200 hours- we already know over 2,000 concepts and words and have started to write using the, now mature, motor skills acquired.

Even though the difference in cognition and abilities between a new-born and a five-year-old child are enormous and make the difference between surviving or perishing in this world, the five-year-old is in no way ready to become an active and useful member of our modern society. We need to add the years of formal education which will take us to the time the young person leaves high school, say at 18 years of age, at which point we might consider her in a state where she is ready to become a full member of the community. By 18, she would have accumulated just over 150,000 hours of learning. Furthermore, if we assume a college or university education, we need to add even more hours of training and learning and we might say that by the age she is leaving university, say as a 24-year-old person, she would have accumulated over 200,000 hours of learning.

There is an often mentioned "rule" that states that if you want to acquire expertise in any activity, you have to practise it for at least 10,000 hours. In general, this is cited in relation to any sort of activity such as work experience, sports mastery or musical ability. For example, if you wanted to consider yourself an accomplished guitar player, then following this rule would imply you have to spend 10,000 hours of practice to reach a high level of performance.

But what are 10,000 hours in practical terms? Let's say you take your practice as a full-time job and spend 8 hours a day, 5 days a week and 48 weeks a year practising, we are accounting for a 4 week holiday, then you would sum up your 10,000 hours after 5 years and 11 weeks which roughly coincides, more or less with the time most people with higher education have spent at high school and university. On the other hand if you were a little more relaxed about your endeavour and, say, dedicated 2 hours a day, twice a week for those 48 weeks of the year, this is the sort of time you might spend if you have a hobby such as playing an amateur sport, then your 10,000 hours of practice would be reached after 52 years!

It is also sometimes said that you would need approximately 10 years of dedication to achieve those 10,000 hours of practice, well let's look at the numbers: to accomplish this you could choose one of these two plans I propose for you:

1. The Standard Plan, Requiring a practice of 2 hours and 45 minutes every single day of those 10 years.

Alternatively, for the more relaxed of you I offer:

2. The Light Plan, Requiring you to practice for 3 hours and 21 minutes for just six days a week throughout those 10 years. The plan is "Light" because you get one free day a week!

As we see from the numbers we conclude that not only do we need a lot of practice to achieve the 10,000-hour mark but also a large dose of discipline, stamina, the right material conditions and above all else, a lot of will power. A dose of aptitude is also needed so that some progress is seen, otherwise, 10 years will seem like an awfully long time.

The 10,000-hour rule is often associated with the journalist and writer Malcolm Gladwell, he mentioned and developed the idea in his book *Outliers*, but the concept itself originated some time earlier and was introduced by the Swedish psychologist Anders Ericsson in a paper he wrote in 1993 called "The Role of Deliberate Practice in the Acquisition of Expert Performance". In Ericsson's paper, the concept is presented for the first time and is substantiated by the research described within the document. The paper states that the practice time dedicated is not just any time, it needs to be "deliberate practice" meaning a time spent where the elements related to the ability are "explored and stretched in order to deepen the learning experience" (sic), in other words, the time spent needs to be a time of quality immersion and dedication to the task at hand.

In recent years the 10,000-hour theory has been challenged and nowadays it is recognized that not only practise makes perfect but as we are not carbon copies of each other, there are some differences in our bodies and minds that when well exploited and trained, can give some people advantages over others, for example, a tennis player that has a slightly longer reach, may develop a more powerful serve that might give her an advantage over an opponent. In fact in a study by Princeton University[1] that defies the 10,000 hour theory, it was found that the positive effect of practise on performance varied according to the area of interest, for example in music, deliberate practice accounts for a 21% difference in performance, in games it is 26% while in sports the difference that deliberate practice will make on performance is just 18%[2].

Technological Learning

If we now take a look at the way machines or technology "learns", we observe that this subject has advanced greatly in the past few years. Technology, in the form of computing machines, work by following a set of pre-established instructions, "a program", that describes step by step what the machine has to do. There are simple instructions such as "add this number to that number", "store this number" or "do this 100 times and stop". There are also more interesting instructions, which condition what the machine will do depending on different circumstances, these are the instructions that begin to give a program and technology, in general, a little bit of what we could start to call "intelligence". Instructions such as, "if this happens then do that" give the program control as to what it will do upon certain changing conditions or circumstances, so for example, a real instruction might read:

> IF *the temperature is more than* 32ºC THEN
> *switch on the air conditioning*

You can quickly imagine how a set of these types of rules written in sequence can start to give a program a great deal of flexibility to approach the changing conditions that it might encounter.

A list of this type of conditional statements and instructions can be built into an "algorithm" and in general, many algorithms make up a program. So for example in an airplane-control-program there might be hundreds of algorithms that take care of all the different systems within an aircraft, the algorithm that maintains the temperature in the cabin within a certain range, the algorithm that ensures that there are no sudden changes in the altitude of the plane, the algorithm that calculates and informs the current autonomous flying times with the current fuel capacity, and so on.

These types of programs and algorithms have been with us from the beginning of the information technology era. They all share the same way of being created and designed, that is, human engineers and programmers write them all. Each line of the so-called "code" or lines of machine instructions, has been designed and written by a human or a team of humans that have had to think of all the possible combination of variables that may arise and the way that the program should react to each one of them. This involves a lot of design of different scenarios, testing and running the programs in real, but controlled, conditions before releasing the programs into the real world. Imagine the responsibility those engineers have when designing the algorithms for life-sustaining hospital equipment, traffic control systems, aeroplane systems and other critical equipment. The responsibility sometimes does not involve human life directly but the efficiency of factory processes, the way a market-exchange works or even the correct match between two people in a dating website, all these examples rely on pre-programmed algorithms.

These human-designed programs are giving way to what is generally being called Artificial Intelligence (AI) systems that have the capability of learning by themselves. There are several ways in which this "learning" by machines can be achieved, for example, using neuronal networks, parallel processing and machine instruction programs like LISP, SMALLTALK and others that are designed for this purpose. The most basic type of programming that is used for AI starts in much the same way as the original instruction-by-instruction programs I described earlier, the main difference is that once the program is up-and-running in the real world, it will start to add its own lines of code as it "learns" what works best for certain conditions it encounters. So starting with a set of pre-programmed instructions, these programs have the capability of building further code lines as they test and learn what works best under real circumstances.

The next step up in the ladder of artificial intelligence systems has been given the name of "machine learning" or "ML" for short, this method takes advantage of the large quantity of data that has been available in recent years due to the computerization of all aspects of our life. Data is generated by every action we take on any computer-driven system, when we visit a web site, the pages we read, when we open an App on our mobile phones, the digital payment transactions we make, when we shop, when we fill our car with fuel, to name just a few. Machine learning involves a suitably programmed computer sifting through thousands or millions of bits of data related to some particular task and looking for patterns that generate a desired outcome to be achieved. For example, a machine could churn through medical records and "learn" which medicines were most effective in treating certain conditions, this learning might take into account all the detailed description of thousands of medical cases throughout the world giving the machine a very detailed empirical study of the particular causes and effects patterns involved. From this knowledge it would then be able to construct itself its own machine-rules to be used when confronted with new patient data and be able to diagnose, predict and prescribe the best pharmaceutical combination or treatment that, based on its learned patterns, would best control or eliminate the disease.

Many algorithms already use this technique and you may have encountered them many times, if you are a user of one of the large online stores or services you may have noticed the recommendations that such a site might give you to tempt you into buying some item or another. The typical "Because you bought *this* then you might like *that*" or "Others who have bought *this* have also bought *that*". Sites like Amazon or Netflix use these types of recommendation algorithms constantly, they work by basically sifting through the data generated by the users, when they search, buy or look at items online, and then by using pattern recognition algorithms on that data they attempt to infer what that user might be interested in and find other related items to create personalized recommendations.

Following on from these ideas, what has been remarkable in recent years, and what I believe will mark a turning point in artificial intelligence, is the latest programming techniques sometimes called "Deep Learning" where the starting point is not a pre-determined series of human-programmed instructions, but rather, a very limited and basic rule-set that describes a problem. These basic rules are coded in the computer's algorithms and from this "vague" starting point, these programs work out by themselves, and without a set of additional rules or data, how to behave and perform the given tasks in the most effective way. This technique was demonstrated and published in *Nature*[3] in October 2017, where a program called AlphaGo Zero, was able to learn by itself and play the Chinese game of "GO"[4].

Go is a very popular and ancient Chinese game, invented over 2,500 years ago, with a status and complexity similar to the game of Chess, which was itself invented some 1,500 years ago. The program AlphaGo Zero started with the basic Go rules and used a reward system, which awarded a point for a win and took away a point for a loss. The program was instructed to maximize its rewards by winning as many games as possible and was then set to play thousands of games against itself or to be more precise, with a copy of itself. The results were outstanding, after just one day, the program was playing at an advanced professional level, after two days it had surpassed the level of a grandmaster.

Most interestingly, the researches were able to observe the different strategies that the program used as it progressed in its learning phase. After about three hours the program set itself the objective of capturing as many stones as possible, this is a phase that most Go human beginners also go through. The scientists also observed how the program "discovered" typical play-patterns that are known to well trained human players and also how the program invented new ways of playing the game that, to the human observers, seemed quite "alien".

In order to measure the expertise achieved by the AlphaGo Zero program, an existing standard rating to qualify Go players was used, the rating system is called the "Elo rating" Normally a grandmaster will have a rating of around 3,500 to 3,600 points. After 40 days of training, AlphaGo Zero had an Elo rating of more than 5,000 points putting the machine well above the threshold of being beaten by any human.

In just 40 days, such a machine put itself out of reach of any human at this task, a human being takes years in achieving the same skill.

What will we be able to achieve when such algorithms are put to work on other tasks? How will this shortening of learning times affect the future of humankind? How will humans improve their learning speeds? Or indeed, CAN humans improve their learning speeds? A quick exploration of this last question can be achieved by doing a simple experiment, try to listen to a lecture or speech at an increased speed (hopefully with some clever software that does not change the pitch of the voice!), if you do that, you will find that an increase of 25% to 50% in the speed of the speech that is being heard is quite tolerable to the untrained ear and can be processed by the brain with almost no difficulty. As you approach the 100% increase mark, that is, doubling the speed, it is still understandable but requires a lot more concentration and maybe some training. You can try it yourselves in the lectures and talks site TED.com, for example with this talk: "Teaching Kids Real Maths With Computers" by Conrad Wolfram[5]. The web site offers the possibility of listening to this talk at normal speed or you can choose to increase the speed all the way to twice the original. Although you can now listen to a 15 minute talk in half the time "saving" you 7.5 minutes, we inevitably go back to the discussion we had in another chapter where I looked into all the ways that we have been trying to cram more things into the same amount of time, we saw how this created a whole set of problems like stress and exhaustion as our brains and bodies try to cope with the onslaught of information. So, at least in this simple experiment, trying to increase the speed at which we can transfer information from a recording to a human mind will have an increased cost in concentration and stress for that person.

There are also techniques to increase our reading speeds, in this case, you can read about several different claims that go from achieving increases in reading speed of about 30% to incredible increases of 300%. As an example, normal reading speed is considered to be around 300 words per minute but Anne Jones, a World Champion Speed Reader read "Harry Potter – Deathly Hallows" at a staggering speed of 4,251 words per minute taking just 47 minutes to complete the book! Just to prove that there was comprehension of what was read, she then offered the media a book review as proof! You can see a video of her achievement here: https://thefastlearners.com/worlds-fastest-readers/.

If you want to test what your reading speed is you can use this website to test yourself: http://www.myreadspeed.com.

Although there may be techniques that help us to increase the amount of information that we can input and process in our minds, as far as we know these techniques cannot compete with the potential learning speeds of the machines we are creating. Let's remind ourselves, as we saw earlier in this chapter, that a human being just coming out of school at 18 years of age would have assimilated over 150,000 hours of learning, considering a full 24 hour, 7 days a week process. What would a Deep Learning computer be able to achieve in that same time period?

. . .

"Time" for our machines, has a different meaning than it does for us and we will have to learn to harness this difference in the best way we can in order to complement our biological abilities and limitations. The realization that machines are starting to have these capabilities has divided some observer's opinions into an optimistic and a pessimistic camp. On the pessimist side, there is a bleak future in which machines will have learned so much and have become so efficient, that they will finally take over our lives and rule us into slavery, you may have seen several films about these sort of topics! The other camp, the optimists, take on a different view in that these new machine capabilities will be put into the service of humankind, and the world in general, in order to improve our lives helping us to do the chores that are too dangerous or monotonous to be done by humans, optimizing the consumption of food, manufacturing better medicines, improving our education, health and other human needs. Whichever camp you subscribe to, it is likely that at some point in the not so distant future, there will be machines that challenge even our decision-making capabilities. These machines will be able to manage more information than we could ever access, simply by using their capacity for storing, processing and sharing large amounts of data and information. Based on these capabilities, they will be able to make data-driven predictions and decisions which have the potential of being much more accurate and precise than their human counterparts. Authors talk about a point in the future where machine intelligence will be comparable to human intelligence, they have even called this point "The Singularity" and predict that it will bring unpredictable consequences to humankind. All of this may indeed happen and the results are indeed unpredictable but on any future scenario: Is organic and non-organic intelligence really comparable? Can a machine that has no organic body and its associated feelings, communicate with the rest of the world in the same way as we do? My guess is that this will be very difficult to achieve, after all, part of what makes us human are our imperfections and the un-rationality that we display at times, but then, maybe with time and dedication, even these human features can be programmed and learned by skilled machines.

Predictions

Predicting a future time is an extremely risky business and as we saw in other chapters, taking a look forward in time over more than a few lifespans is generally beyond human capability. Technology is changing at an ever-increasing pace, making our understanding of the world, the universe and even our relationships change with it, albeit at a much slower rhythm. Nevertheless, I will finish this book tackling a final question,

What will time allow us to achieve in the future?

Based on the current tendencies, here are my personal predictions in the following areas:

Health

Diagnosis and treatment will be personalized and individual. Genetic defects will be cured or "edited-out" by simple procedures. Diagnosis will be permanent, we will monitor our body constantly and in a non-intrusive way in order to detect any infection or problem even before symptoms appear. There will be no more one-medicine-for-all, medicines will be manufactured specifically for each one of us taking into consideration and tailored to our DNA.

Education

Education will be individual and imparted mostly by robots and systems tailored to each person. Education will be seen as a lifelong activity and you will be constantly learning what is required to fulfil your life. There will be regular instances of group work that will be carried out in person with others to maintain our face-to-face social skills enhancing our group collaboration activities.

Transport

Whether public or private, national or international, transport will be seen as a service and it will be of such quality and safety that there will not be a need to own the means of transport individually. Air and underground travel will be the norm since surfaces will be protected to privilege human needs such as housing and recreation.

Religion

There will be a shift to religions that are centred on the natural over the supernatural. Devotion to nature and the protection of the planet will be the norm.

Technology

Biology will be the science that will show the most significant advances in technology. Scientists and engineers will be able to design *machinery* that is totally organic in nature and indistinguishable from biological natural organisms. The big debate will be centred around the question of whether this organic technology will be given the faculty of replication or reproduction just like natural organic systems.

Communications

Communication will be ubiquitous and permanent from the moment we are born. There will be devices available that can be implanted subcutaneously so that the wearer can communicate, verbally and in images, without the need to use an external device.

Work

The 19th-century concept of work will disappear, that is, having to attend a fixed place of work, for a fixed amount of hours, every day, will no longer be the norm. Each person will have tasks and responsibilities within society that can be carried out in any suitable place, either at home or from specially constructed common "work" spaces. The total time

> needed to achieve the tasks will be much less than at present since most tasks will be carried out by automated systems or robots. The majority of human tasks will be of a supervisory nature, controlling and modifying robotic or automatic systems. In a thousand years time, probably even less, when our descendants look back on the 20th or 21st century and the work practices we use today, it will probably be thought of as a form of slavery, having to work from 9am to 5pm or 9 am to 7 pm, mostly in one place, indoors and in front of a screen. They might even give it a name like the machinistic-era or the manualistic-era.

Time to Conclude

This book has taken the form of a journey of discovery but only some things seem clearer now than they were at the start of the voyage. Don't get me wrong, much has been learnt as the journey proceeded discovering many of the scientific aspects of time, time's possible origin, how we perceive its passing and the way it is intrinsically embedded in our existence. All these aspects took me into the realms of thinking about the reasons for the presence of the human species in this world and to the question of the purpose of life itself. A journey of discovery indeed, full of real questions and plagued with many speculative and incomplete answers.

Nevertheless, the book concludes having reviewed a lot of knowledge but maybe gained fewer certainties than might have been desired. One of the things that seems clear is that as time passes, our cultures seem to understand more of the world and the universe around us, but this knowledge is probably insignificant when compared to the total volume of knowledge that we ignore. Knowing more does not necessarily lead us to understand more, for example, although we know that there is a delicate balance between all living species on the planet, humanity still has a self-centred view of existence in which, just like in the era when we thought the Earth was at the centre of the universe, we hold the majority view that humans are the centre of existence and that every thing else revolves around our needs. We must break through this pre-Copernican-like model of existence and replace it with one that establishes our species as peers of other life forms and not as master.

This journey has also shown me that we are not conditioned to be aware of things in timeframes different to our own, we are optimized to the way we perceive time during our lifetime and find it difficult to "see" beyond one or two human generation cycles. As an example, we are not much aware of the slow changes in nature such as the slow processes in the lifetime of plants and trees, the slow changes in the temperature of the seas or the changes in the geological landscape, these are some of the reasons that something as relevant as the climate changes we have been experiencing over the last decades has not been given the importance that it deserves. For the same reason things that happen too fast for our timeframes go unnoticed, such as the movement of electrons and photons, giving us the impression of living in a world of instantaneity when in fact actions like turning on an electrical appliance or switching on a light bulb take a known and finite amount of time to mobilise the sub-atomic particles and electromagnetic waves necessary for the phenomenon to happen. Associated with this lack time perception outside our frame of reference, is the fact that our natural sensing equipment, our five external senses, are limited and optimized for the purpose of our own survival and reproduction in our time frame but they are not an all-encompassing detection system, in other words, we cannot directly sense all that is present in the universe. Instruments that can detect phenomena that are beyond our sense's capabilities have been built to try and remedy these limitations, nevertheless they cannot fully replace the direct sensing and feeling of some forms of energy outside the narrow spectrum of our sense's detection capabilities, we lack the breadth of hearing and vision of some sea creatures, the highly developed sense of smell of other mammals, and are blind to many other phenomena that may still remain undiscovered and that are, as yet, beyond our recognition let alone our understanding.

To convert knowledge into understanding, we need languages to describe our universe, build models and communicate them to others in order to enhance and improve on the knowledge acquired. In this respect we need to be aware that all languages and models suffer from the limitation of not being able to truly describe our world, they are just the best approximations we can manage with our limited understanding of the complexities we encounter when we try to encapsulate the intricacies of the fabric of life. Being aware of these limitations will allow us to avoid the pitfalls and dogmas of believing that we have fully understood, when in fact we have only scratched the surface of knowledge.

In any case, improving the understanding of our universe is one of the things that time can allow humankind to do, only time has the power to allow for this slow and complex process to take place, but it is up to humankind to take that opportunity and through investigation, thought, learning, communication and debate, improve the global base of knowledge that will help us to construct the answers to the questions of our eternally inquisitive minds. Maybe one of the last few certainties that I have after writing this book is the realization of how little we really know and that what we think we know is a fragile mix of interpretations of the current knowledge that has been turned into theories or "stories" that try to describe what we observe. Some of this knowledge will stand the test of time but most will suffer the inevitable demise that time will infuse upon them.

Writing the last paragraphs of this book, I realize that although the original intention was to write a book about time, it has turned out to be something quite different. This book is not about the fact that time advances only in one direction or that it does not stop its course or that it is present in all the things we do. This book is about life. Life and how we choose to live it. It's about the realization that, although our life span is short when we compare it with the grand cosmos, if we choose not to take it for granted and we fill it with the things that we believe are important, this short life will be rich and may even transcend our own limited existence.

If we look for a purpose for our own lives, then maybe, just as it happened to me writing this book, the full realization of that purpose will be revealed at the end of our journey, when we look back in time and take stock of all the contributions we have made, big or small, to the fabric of life.

I conclude the book but the conclusions are in the hands of the reader.

It's Time for Life.

THE END

TIME FOR A BIBLIOGRAPHY

FOOTNOTES BY CHAPTER

Chapter 1 - What is Time?

1. http://mentalfloss.com/article/29879/6-oldest-trees-world
2. https://themysteriousworld.com/top-10-shortest-living-animals-in-the-world/
3. https://www.scientificamerican.com/article/experts-time-division-days-hours-minutes/
4. http://www.history.com/news/ask-history/who-invented-the-metric-system
5. http://www.smithsonianmag.com/science-nature/these-tiny-spiders-are-fastest-known-earth-180958682/
6. http://imagine.gsfc.nasa.gov/features/cosmic/nearest_galaxy_info.html
7. https://www.newscientist.com/article/dn7253-

worlds-fastest-transistor-operates-at-blinding-speed/

8. http://internacional.elpais.com/internacional/2015/09/17/actualidad/1442457512_019994.html
9. http://www.emol.com/noticias/nacional/2010/03/09/401838/listado-oficial-de-fallecidos-entregado-por-el-gobierno-de-chile.html
10. https://youtu.be/nZ9Du7VfdSg
11. https://www.nasa.gov/topics/earth/features/japanquake/earth20110314.html
12. http://news.nationalgeographic.com/news/2010/03/100302-chile-earthquake-earth-axis-shortened-day/

Chapter 2 - Time in the Beginning

1. "https://www.cell.com/current-biology/fulltext/S0960-9822(15)00432-7"
2. "http://uk.businessinsider.com/how-dog-breeds-looked-100-years-ago-2016-3"
3. Book: Are We Getting Smarter? – James Flynn
4. "https://www.cambridge-news.co.uk/news/cambridge-news/stephen-hawking-equation-gravestone-westminster-14788881"

Chapter 3 - Frozen in Time

1. "http://www.goodreads.com/quotes/7445-all-

photographs-are-memento-mori-to-take-a-photograph-is"

2. "https://qz.com/647315/mesmerizing-infographics-stitched-together-from-millions-of-snapshots/"
3. "http://photogrvphy.com/interview-with-fine-art-photographer-pelle-cass/"
4. "https://fqwimages.com/"
5. "http://www.bobbyneeladams.com/agemaps"
6. "https://www.nytimes.com/2014/10/09/science/ancient-indonesian-find-may-rival-oldest-known-cave-art.html"
7. "https://en.wikipedia.org/wiki/Netherlandish_Proverbs"
8. "Ways of Seeing, BBC TV Series 1972 and Book"
9. "https://mtvesuvius-oliviasolia.weebly.com/pliny-the-younger.html"
10. "https://www.forbes.com/sites/drsarahbond/2016/08/24/august-24-79-an-hour-by-hour-account-of-vesuvius-eruption-on-the-1937th-anniversary/#363d793e5137"
11. "https://www.theatlantic.com/technology/archive/2015/10/how-the-people-of-pompeii-really-died/408454/"
12. "https://news.nationalgeographic.com/news/2010/11/101102/pompeii-mount-vesuvius-science-died-instantly-heat-bodies/"
13. "http://news.nationalgeographic.com/2016/09/worlds-oldest-fossils-stromatolites-discovered-climate-change/"
14. "http://www.livescience.com/6885-fossils-earliest-animal-life-possibly-discovered.html"

15. "https://www.livescience.com/46773-mammoth-calf-mummy-deaths.html"
16. "http://www.ancient-origins.net/ancient-places-americas/7000-year-old-chinchorro-mummies-andes-001947"
17. "https://blogs.wsj.com/japanrealtime/2014/08/11/worlds-fastest-camera-captures-chemical-reactions-in-single-shot/"
18. "https://youtu.be/-fSqFWcb4rE"
19. "https://en.wikipedia.org/wiki/Chronological_dating"
20. "http://www.physlink.com/Education/AskExperts/ae598.cfm"

Chapter 4 - Time to Travel

1. "https://youtu.be/Z-iPp6ynohw"
2. "http://newsroom.ucla.edu/stories/marco-iacoboni-mirror-neurons"
3. "http://www.bbc.co.uk/nature/history_of_the_earth"
4. "https://www.timeanddate.com/time/time-zones-history.html"
5. "http://www.telegraph.co.uk/travel/advice/How-to-celebrate-New-Years-Eve-twice/"

Chapter 5 - Time to Escape

1. "http://www.cabinetmagazine.org/issues/30/foer.php"
2. "http://millar.bio.ed.ac.uk/andrewM/CBT%

20tutorial/OTHERRHYTHMSULTRA.html"

3. "http://www.psychologytoday.com/articles/199905/the-stirring-sound-stress"
4. "https://www.bbc.com/news/magazine-16964783https://www.bbc.com/news/magazine-16964783"
5. "https://www.medicalnewstoday.com/articles/284378.php"
6. "https://www.researchgate.net/publication/259961610_Time_for_actions_in_lucid_dreams_Effects_of_task_modality_length_and_complexity"
7. "https://www.theatlantic.com/science/archive/2016/04/deciphering-hypnagogia/478941/"
8. "http://journals.plos.org/plosone/article?id=10.1371/journal.pone.0001295"
9. "http://nymag.com/speed/2016/12/how-your-brain-controls-the-speed-of-time.html"
10. "https://www.wired.com/2016/02/new-clues-to-the-mystery-of-how-our-brains-keep-time/"
11. "http://www.kent.ac.uk/news/stories/time-perception-mindfulness-kramer-psychology/2013"

Chapter 6 - Time for a Story

- "http://www.britishmuseum.org/explore/themes/writing/historic_writing.aspx"
- "https://www.simplypsychology.org/eyewitness-testimony.html"
- "https://www.ukessays.com/essays/

psychology/factors-that-affect-the-accuracy-of-eyewitness-testimonies-psychology-essay.php"

- "http://searcharchives.bl.uk/primo_library/libweb/action/display.do?tabs=detailsTab&ct=display&doc=IAMS041-002064313&displayMode=full&vid=IAMS_VU2"
- "https://www.royal.uk/mary-queen-scots-r1542-1567"
- "https://www.rsc.org.uk/shakespeares-plays/timeline"
- "http://www.livius.org/articles/place/tuspa-van/inscription-xv/?"
- "https://discoveringegypt.com/egyptian-video-documentaries/mystery-of-the-rosetta-stone/"
- "http://www.britishmuseum.org/explore/themes/writing/literacy.aspx"
- "http://www.reshafim.org.il/ad/egypt/texts/canopus_decree.htm"
- "http://www.reshafim.org.il/ad/egypt/texts/canopus_decree.htm"

Chapter 7 - Time to Listen

1. "http://music.arts.uci.edu/dobrian/CMC2009/Liberation.pdf"
2. "https://www.britishdeafnews.co.uk/conrad-at-100/"
3. "https://www.nytimes.com/2018/03/06/science/ears-shape-hearing.html"
4. "Statistical universals reveal the structures and functions of human music", Patrick E. Savagea,

Steven Brown, Emi Sakai, and Thomas E. Currie

5. “http://digital.vpr.net/post/timeline-004-guido-arezzo-and-solfege-system”
6. “https://www.psychologytoday.com/articles/200607/the-mysteries-perfect-pitch”
7. “Deutsch, E. O. *Mozart: A documentary biography*. 3rd edition, 1990, London: Simon and Schuster”
8. “https://plus.maths.org/content/how-many-melodies-are-there”
9. “https://www.insidescience.org/news/can-animals-keep-beat”
10. “https://www.nytimes.com/2016/02/09/science/new-ways-into-the-brains-music-room.html”
11. “http://www.the-scientist.com/?articles.view/articleNo/48611/title/Exploring-the-Mechanisms-of-Music-Therapy/“
12. “https://www.newscientist.com/article/2096525-mystery-of-101-year-old-master-pianist-who-has-dementia/“
13. “https://www.theguardian.com/environment/2017/may/04/noise-pollution-is-drowning-out-nature-even-in-protected-areas-study”
14. “http://www.ics-shipping.org/shipping-facts/shipping-and-world-trade”
15. “https://www.livescience.com/33895-human-eye.html”
16. “https://www.pmel.noaa.gov/acoustics/“
17. “https://www.nature.com/articles/d41586-017-00882-6”

18. "http://www.wired.co.uk/article/blue-planet-noise-pollution-fish-oceans"

Chapter 8 - Time to be Born

1. "https://en.oxforddictionaries.com/definition/three"
2. "https://www.merriam-webster.com/dictionary/three"
3. "https://www.livescience.com/27853-who-invented-zero.html"
4. "http://www.bbc.com/future/story/20161206-we-couldnt-live-without-zero-but-we-once-had-to"

Chapter 9 - Time is Now

1. "http://aphant.asia/forum/index"
2. "http://www.bbc.com/future/story/20160524-this-man-had-no-idea-his-mind-is-blind-until-last-week"
3. "https://www.livescience.com/23709-blind-people-picture-reality.html"
4. "https://www.newscientist.com/article/mg19626354-100-blind-people-see-sunrise-and-sunset/"

Chapter 10 - Tomorrow-me

1. "http://book.bionumbers.org/how-quickly-do-different-cells-in-the-body-replace-themselves/"
2. "https://io9.gizmodo.com/5941883/how-your-body-fights-to-keep-you-alive-when-youre-starving"
3. "http://www.tech21century.com/the-human-brain-is-loaded-daily-with-34-gb-of-information/"
4. "http://www.huffingtonpost.com/2012/03/05/personality-change-over-time-study_n_1321720.html"
5. "https://www.newscientist.com/article/dn3713-personality-changes-throughout-life/"
6. "My Book"
7. "https://www.vangoghmuseum.nl/en/125-questions/questions-and-answers/question-88-of-125?v=1"
8. "https://www.smithsonianmag.com/smart-news/what-was-found-inside-oldest-american-time-capsule-180953820/"
9. "https://www.theguardian.com/us-news/2015/jun/17/boston-time-capsule-1795-massachusetts"

Chapter 11 - Time for Choices

1. "http://hub.jhu.edu/2017/03/23/cancer-mutations-caused-by-random-dna-mistakes/"
2. "Adam Alter, Irresistible: The Rise of Addictive Technology and the Business of Keeping Us Hooked, Penguin Books"

Chapter 12 - Time to Believe

1. “https://en.oxforddictionaries.com/definition/belief”
2. “http://www.pewresearch.org/fact-tank/2017/04/05/christians-remain-worlds-largest-religious-group-but-they-are-declining-in-europe/“

Chapter 13 - Time for more Time

1. “https://www.businessinsider.com/infographic-how-computing-power-has-changed-over-time-2017-11”
2. “https://hbr.org/2013/11/the-pace-of-technology-adoption-is-speeding-up”
3. “http://bionumbers.hms.harvard.edu/bionumber.aspx?id=100706&ver=0”
4. “http://news.mit.edu/2014/in-the-blink-of-an-eye-0116”
5. “https://www.psychologytoday.com/blog/brain-wise/201209/the-true-cost-multi-tasking”
6. “https://www.pnas.org/content/106/37/15583”
7. “http://time.com/4737286/multitasking-mental-health-stress-texting/“
8. “http://www.apa.org/research/action/multitask.aspx”
9. “https://qz.com/1010901/the-data-prove-that-you-just-get-more-alone-from-the-age-of-40-onward/“

10. "https://ourworldindata.org/working-hours"

Chapter 14 - Time vs Time

1. "http://journals.sagepub.com/doi/abs/10.1177/0956797614535810"
2. "http://www.businessinsider.com/new-study-destroys-malcolm-gladwells-10000-rule-2014-7"
3. "http://www.nature.com/nature/journal/v550/n7676/full/nature24270.html"
4. "https://www.economist.com/news/science-and-technology/21730391-learning-play-go-only-start-latest-ai-can-work-things-out-without"
5. "https://www.ted.com/talks/conrad_wolfram_teaching_kids_real_math_with_computers"

RECOMMENDED BOOKS

Ordered Alphabetically by Author Surname

- Adam Alter, *Irresistible: The Rise of Addictive Technology and the Business of Keeping Us Hooked, Penguin Books*
- Stephen Banks, *The British Executions: 1500-1964*
- John Berger, *Ways of Seeing* (*BBC TV Series, 1972 and Book*)
- Tim Butcher, *The Trigger: Hunting the Assassin who brought the World to War*

- Charles Darwin, *On The Origin of the Species*
- Richard Dawkins, *The Selfish Gene*
- Roger Ekirch, *At Day's Close: Night in Times Past*
- Lisa Feldman Barrett, *How Emotions are Made: The Secret Life of the Brain*
- James R. Flynn, *Are we getting smarter? Rising IQ in the Twenty-First Century*
- Jonathan Gottschall, *The Storytelling Animal*
- Stephen Hawking, *A Brief History of Time*
- Seth Horowitz, *The Universal Sense: How Hearing Shapes the Mind*
- Arianna Huffington, *The Sleep Revolution*
- Keeper of the manuscripts in the British Museum, *Original Letters, Illustrative of English History*, Henry Ellis, F.R.S. Sec. S.A., Published 1827
- Ray Kurzweil, *The Singularity*
- Maxwell-Scott, Mary Monica, (Hon.), *The tragedy of Fotheringhay, founded on the journal of D. Bourgoing, physician to Mary Queen of Scots, and on unpublished MS. Documents,* 1852-1920; Bourgoing, Dominique, Published 1895
- Carlo Rovelli, *Seven Brief Lessons on Physics*

WEBSITES AND LINKS

Timeline of written language history:

- http://www.ancientscripts.com/ws_timeline.html

- http://www.ancient.eu/timeline/writing/

Time Spent:

- https://www.ncbi.nlm.nih.gov/pmc/articles/PMC4852646/
- https://www.theatlas.com/charts/HJFYm4uQ-
- https://flowingdata.com/2016/12/06/how-people-like-you-spend-their-time/
- http://www.businessinsider.com/how-humans-spend-their-time-2014-12

Visualizing Data:

- https://ourworldindata.org/

Zero

- https://yaleglobal.yale.edu/history-zero
- https://www.livescience.com/27853-who-invented-zero.html

Time for a Story:

- http://www.sath.org.uk/edscot/www.educationscotland.gov.uk/scotlandshistory/renaissancereformation/execution/index.html

Eyewitness Accounts:

- http://www.bbc.com/news/world-europe-34813570

- https://www.scientificamerican.com/article/do-the-eyes-have-it/
- http://www.eyewitnesstohistory.com/

Hearing:

- https://www.designingmusicnow.com/2016/10/17/interview-dr-seth-horowitz-auditory-neuroscientist/
- http://thebrieflab.com/the-neuroscience-behind-inattention/
- http://www.washingtonindependentreviewofbooks.com/index.php/bookreview/the-universal-sense-how-hearing-shapes-the-mind
- https://www.nytimes.com/2012/11/11/opinion/sunday/why-listening-is-so-much-more-than-hearing.html
- https://www.newscientist.com/article/mg21528832-400-is-hearing-more-important-than-seeing/
- http://biologicalexceptions.blogspot.com/2011/09/why-does-your-telephone-have-two-holes.html

Various Topics:

- http://www.medicaldaily.com/neural-pathways-watching-tv-human-brain-reading-book-389744
- http://www.timelineindex.com/content/select/817/1101,817

- https://www.scientificamerican.com/article/how-has-human-brain-evolved/
- https://www.smithsonianmag.com/science-nature/are-you-smarter-than-your-grandfather-probably-not-150402883/
- https://www.telegraph.co.uk/news/science/science-news/11200900/The-Flynn-effect-are-we-really-getting-smarter.html
- https://www.scientificamerican.com/article/how-we-know-humans-getting-smarter-flynn-excerpt/
- https://www.livescience.com/37095-humans-smarter-or-dumber.html
- https://www.economist.com/news/science-and-technology/21741136-small-hours-provided-evolutionary-advantage-early-morning-births-are

NOTES

1. What is Time?

1. http://mentalfloss.com/article/29879/6-oldest-trees-world
2. https://themysteriousworld.com/top-10-shortest-living-animals-in-the-world/
3. https://www.scientificamerican.com/article/experts-time-division-days-hours-minutes/
4. http://www.history.com/news/ask-history/who-invented-the-metric-system
5. http://www.smithsonianmag.com/science-nature/these-tiny-spiders-are-fastest-known-earth-180958682/
6. http://imagine.gsfc.nasa.gov/features/cosmic/nearest_galaxy_info.html
7. https://www.newscientist.com/article/dn7253-worlds-fastest-transistor-operates-at-blinding-speed/
8. http://internacional.elpais.com/internacional/2015/09/17/actualidad/1442457512_019994.html
9. http://www.emol.com/noticias/nacional/2010/03/09/401838/listado-oficial-de-fallecidos-entregado-por-el-gobierno-de-chile.html
10. https://youtu.be/nZ9Du7VfdSg
11. https://www.nasa.gov/topics/earth/features/japanquake/earth-20110314.html
12. http://news.nationalgeographic.com/news/2010/03/100302-chile-earthquake-earth-axis-shortened-day/
13. http://mpe.dimacs.rutgers.edu/2013/05/04/why-do-earthquakes-change-the-speed-of-rotation-of-the-earth/
14. http://www.slate.com/blogs/bad_astronomy/2010/02/27/magnitude_8_8_earthquake_off_chile_coast.html

2. Time in the Beginning

1. https://www.cell.com/current-biology/fulltext/S0960-9822(15)00432-7?_returnURL=http%3A%2F%2Flinkinghub.elsevier.com%2Fretrieve%2Fpii%2FS0960982215004327%3Fshowall%3Dtrue
2. http://uk.businessinsider.com/how-dog-breeds-looked-100-years-ago-2016-3
3. Book: Are We Getting Smarter? – James Flynn
4. https://www.cambridge-news.co.uk/news/cambridge-news/stephen-

hawking-equation-gravestone-westminster-14788881

3. Frozen in Time

1. http://www.goodreads.com/quotes/7445-all-photographs-are-memento-mori-to-take-a-photograph-is
2. https://qz.com/647315/mesmerizing-infographics-stitched-together-from-millions-of-snapshots/
3. http://photogrvphy.com/interview-with-fine-art-photographer-pelle-cass/
4. https://fqwimages.com/
5. http://www.bobbyneeladams.com/agemaps
6. https://www.nytimes.com/2014/10/09/science/ancient-indonesian-find-may-rival-oldest-known-cave-art.html?_r=0
7. https://en.wikipedia.org/wiki/Netherlandish_Proverbs
8. Ways of Seeing, BBC TV Series 1972 and Book
9. https://mtvesuvius-oliviasolia.weebly.com/pliny-the-younger.html
10. https://www.forbes.com/sites/drsarahbond/2016/08/24/august-24-79-an-hour-by-hour-account-of-vesuvius-eruption-on-the-1937th-anniversary/#363d793e5137
11. https://www.theatlantic.com/technology/archive/2015/10/how-the-people-of-pompeii-really-died/408454/
12. https://news.nationalgeographic.com/news/2010/11/101102/pompeii-mount-vesuvius-science-died-instantly-heat-bodies/
13. http://news.nationalgeographic.com/2016/09/worlds-oldest-fossils-stromatolites-discovered-climate-change/
14. http://www.livescience.com/6885-fossils-earliest-animal-life-possibly-discovered.html
15. https://www.livescience.com/46773-mammoth-calf-mummy-deaths.html
16. http://www.ancient-origins.net/ancient-places-americas/7000-year-old-chinchorro-mummies-andes-001947
17. https://blogs.wsj.com/japanrealtime/2014/08/11/worlds-fastest-camera-captures-chemical-reactions-in-single-shot/
18. https://youtu.be/-fSqFWcb4rE
19. https://en.wikipedia.org/wiki/Chronological_dating
20. http://www.physlink.com/Education/AskExperts/ae598.cfm

4. Time to Travel

1. https://youtu.be/Z-iPp6ynohw
2. http://newsroom.ucla.edu/stories/marco-iacoboni-mirror-neurons
3. http://www.bbc.co.uk/nature/history_of_the_earth

4. https://www.timeanddate.com/time/time-zones-history.html
5. http://www.telegraph.co.uk/travel/advice/How-to-celebrate-New-Years-Eve-twice/

5. Time to Escape

1. http://www.cabinetmagazine.org/issues/30/foer.php
2. http://millar.bio.ed.ac.uk/andrewM/CBT%20tutorial/OTHERRHYTHMSULTRA.html
3. http://www.psychologytoday.com/articles/199905/the-stirring-sound-stress
4. https://www.bbc.com/news/magazine-16964783https://www.bbc.-com/news/magazine-16964783
5. https://www.medicalnewstoday.com/articles/284378.php
6. https://www.researchgate.net/publication/259961610_Time_for_actions_in_lucid_dreams_Effects_of_task_modality_length_and_complexity
7. https://www.theatlantic.com/science/archive/2016/04/deciphering-hypnagogia/478941/
8. http://journals.plos.org/plosone/article?id=10.1371/journal.pone.0001295
9. http://nymag.com/speed/2016/12/how-your-brain-controls-the-speed-of-time.html
10. https://www.wired.com/2016/02/new-clues-to-the-mystery-of-how-our-brains-keep-time/
11. http://www.kent.ac.uk/news/stories/time-perception-mindfulness-kramer-psychology/2013

6. Time for a Story

1. http://www.britishmuseum.org/explore/themes/writing/historic_writing.aspx
2. https://www.simplypsychology.org/eyewitness-testimony.html
3. https://www.ukessays.com/essays/psychology/factors-that-affect-the-accuracy-of-eyewitness-testimonies-psychology-essay.php
4. http://searcharchives.bl.uk/primo_library/libweb/action/display.do?tabs=detailsTab&ct=display&doc=IAMS041-002064313&displayMode=full&vid=IAMS_VU2
5. https://www.royal.uk/mary-queen-scots-r1542-1567
6. https://www.rsc.org.uk/shakespeares-plays/timeline
7. http://www.livius.org/articles/place/tuspa-van/inscription-xv/?
8. https://discoveringegypt.com/egyptian-video-documentaries/mystery-of-the-rosetta-stone/

9. http://www.britishmuseum.org/explore/themes/writing/literacy.aspx
10. http://www.reshafim.org.il/ad/egypt/texts/canopus_decree.htm
11. http://www.reshafim.org.il/ad/egypt/texts/canopus_decree.htm

7. Time to Listen

1. http://music.arts.uci.edu/dobrian/CMC2009/Liberation.pdf
2. https://www.britishdeafnews.co.uk/conrad-at-100/
3. https://www.nytimes.com/2018/03/06/science/ears-shape-hearing.html
4. "Statistical universals reveal the structures and functions of human music"

   Patrick E. Savagea, Steven Brown, Emi Sakai, and Thomas E. Currie
5. http://digital.vpr.net/post/timeline-004-guido-arezzo-and-solfege-system
6. https://www.psychologytoday.com/articles/200607/the-mysteries-perfect-pitch
7. Deutsch, E. O. *Mozart: A documentary biography*. 3rd edition, 1990, London: Simon and Schuster
8. https://plus.maths.org/content/how-many-melodies-are-there
9. https://www.insidescience.org/news/can-animals-keep-beat
10. https://www.nytimes.com/2016/02/09/science/new-ways-into-the-brains-music-room.html
11. http://www.the-scientist.com/?articles.view/articleNo/48611/title/Exploring-the-Mechanisms-of-Music-Therapy/
12. https://www.newscientist.com/article/2096525-mystery-of-101-year-old-master-pianist-who-has-dementia/
13. https://www.theguardian.com/environment/2017/may/04/noise-pollution-is-drowning-out-nature-even-in-protected-areas-study
14. http://www.ics-shipping.org/shipping-facts/shipping-and-world-trade
15. https://www.livescience.com/33895-human-eye.html
16. https://www.pmel.noaa.gov/acoustics/
17. https://www.nature.com/articles/d41586-017-00882-6
18. http://www.wired.co.uk/article/blue-planet-noise-pollution-fish-oceans

8. Time to be Born

1. https://en.oxforddictionaries.com/definition/three
2. https://www.merriam-webster.com/dictionary/three
3. https://www.livescience.com/27853-who-invented-zero.html

4. http://www.bbc.com/future/story/20161206-we-couldnt-live-without-zero-but-we-once-had-to

9. Time is Now

1. http://aphant.asia/forum/index
2. http://www.bbc.com/future/story/20160524-this-man-had-no-idea-his-mind-is-blind-until-last-week
3. https://www.livescience.com/23709-blind-people-picture-reality.html
4. https://www.newscientist.com/article/mg19626354-100-blind-people-see-sunrise-and-sunset/

10. Tomorrow-me

1. http://book.bionumbers.org/how-quickly-do-different-cells-in-the-body-replace-themselves/
2. https://io9.gizmodo.com/5941883/how-your-body-fights-to-keep-you-alive-when-youre-starving
3. http://www.tech21century.com/the-human-brain-is-loaded-daily-with-34-gb-of-information/
4. http://www.huffingtonpost.com/2012/03/05/personality-change-over-time-study_n_1321720.html
5. https://www.newscientist.com/article/dn3713-personality-changes-throughout-life/
6. https://www.amazon.com/Ennea-type-Structures-Self-Analysis-Consciousness-Classics/dp/0895560631/ref=sr_1_1?ie=UTF8&qid=1501504577&sr=8-1&keywords=claudio+naranjo
7. https://www.vangoghmuseum.nl/en/125-questions/questions-and-answers/question-88-of-125?v=1
8. https://www.smithsonianmag.com/smart-news/what-was-found-inside-oldest-american-time-capsule-180953820/
9. https://www.theguardian.com/us-news/2015/jun/17/boston-time-capsule-1795-massachusetts

11. Time for Choices

1. http://hub.jhu.edu/2017/03/23/cancer-mutations-caused-by-random-dna-mistakes/
2. Adam Alter, *Irresistible: The Rise of Addictive Technology and the Business of Keeping Us Hooked, Penguin Books*

12. Time to Believe

1. https://en.oxforddictionaries.com/definition/belief
2. http://www.pewresearch.org/fact-tank/2017/04/05/christians-remain-worlds-largest-religious-group-but-they-are-declining-in-europe/

13. Time for More Time

1. https://www.businessinsider.com/infographic-how-computing-power-has-changed-over-time-2017-11
2. https://hbr.org/2013/11/the-pace-of-technology-adoption-is-speeding-up
3. http://bionumbers.hms.harvard.edu/bionumber.aspx?id=100706&ver=0
4. http://news.mit.edu/2014/in-the-blink-of-an-eye-0116
5. https://www.psychologytoday.com/blog/brain-wise/201209/the-true-cost-multi-tasking
6. https://www.pnas.org/content/106/37/15583
7. http://time.com/4737286/multitasking-mental-health-stress-texting/
8. http://www.apa.org/research/action/multitask.aspx
9. https://qz.com/1010901/the-data-prove-that-you-just-get-more-alone-from-the-age-of-40-onward/
10. https://ourworldindata.org/working-hours

14. (Biological) Time vs. (Technological) Time

1. http://journals.sagepub.com/doi/abs/10.1177/0956797614535810
2. http://www.businessinsider.com/new-study-destroys-malcolm-gladwells-10000-rule-2014-7
3. http://www.nature.com/nature/journal/v550/n7676/full/nature24270.html
4. https://www.economist.com/news/science-and-technology/21730391-learning-play-go-only-start-latest-ai-can-work-things-out-without
5. https://www.ted.com/talks/conrad_wolfram_teaching_kids_real_math_with_computers

ABOUT THE AUTHOR

Gonzalo Gili is a full-time reader and a part-time writer. He has dedicated most of his working life to the media industry and all of his personal life to the task of learning to be a human being.

He was born in Santiago, Chile but lived in London for 17 years where he trained as an electronics engineer at Queen Mary College and then specialized in Communications Engineering at Imperial College, University of London. His media career started at the BBC where he worked for 5 years. He now lives in Chile where, for 14 years, he was Head of the Online Department of Canal 13 de Televisión, a large national television network, he is now the CEO and Partner of a Digital Communications agency. He teaches at university post-graduate level on matters related to digital media, he is also a Qigong and Tai Chi Chuan Instructor.

Gonzalo lives with his wife and three sons in Santiago where they share their love for travelling, food, drink, music, books, cinema and the occasional TV series.

www.ingramcontent.com/pod-product-compliance
Lightning Source LLC
Chambersburg PA
CBHW071346290326
41933CB00041B/2685

* 9 7 8 9 5 6 4 0 1 3 3 5 0 *